The
INTERNET
Book

Everything You Need to Know
About Computer Networking
and How the Internet Works

FOURTH EDITION

DOUGLAS E. COMER

The
INTERNET
Book

Everything You Need to Know
About Computer Networking
and How the Internet Works

FOURTH EDITION

DOUGLAS E. COMER

*Cisco Systems
San Jose, CA*

and

*Department of Computer Sciences
Purdue University*

PEARSON
Prentice
Hall

Upper Saddle River, NJ 07458

Library of Congress Cataloging-in-Publication Data

Comer, Douglas.
  The Internet book : everything you need to know about computer networking and how the internet works / Douglas
E. Comer. -- 4th ed.
     p.   cm.
  Includes bibliographical references and index.
  ISBN 0-13-233553-0
  1. Internet.   2. Computer networks.   3. World Wide Web.   I. Title.
  TK5105.875.I57C65 2006
  004.67'8--dc22

                                        2006024111

Vice President and Editorial Director, ECS: *Marcia J. Horton*
Executive Editor: *Tracy Dunkelberger*
Editorial Assistant: *Christianna Lee*
Associtate Editor: *Carole Snyder*
Executive Managing Editor: *Vince O'Brien*
Managing Editor: *Camille Trentacoste*
Production Editor: *Craig Little*
Director of Creative Services: *Paul Belfanti*
Creative Director: *Juan Lopez*
Art Director: *Jonathan Boylan*
Manufacturing Manager, ESM: *Alexis Heydt-Long*
Manufacturing Buyer: *Lisa McDowell*
Executive Marketing Manager: *Robin O'Brien*
Marketing Assistant: *Mack Patterson*

© 2007 Pearson Education, Inc.
Pearson Prentice Hall
Pearson Education, Inc.
Upper Saddle River, NJ 07458

Pearson Prentice Hall® is a trademark of Pearson Education, Inc.

UNIX is a registered trademark of The Open Group in the U.S. and other countries.
Java is a registered trademark of Sun Microsystems, Inc.
RealVideo, RealAudio, and RealPlayer are trademarks of RealNetworks, Inc.
Flash is a trademark of Macromedia, Inc.

The author and publisher of this book have used their best efforts in preparing this book. These efforts include the
development, research, and testing of the theories and programs to determine their effectiveness. The author and
publisher make no warranty of any kind, expressed or implied, with regard to these programs or the documentation
contained in this book. The author and publisher shall not be liable in any event for incidental or consequential
damages in connection with, or arising out of, the furnishing, performance, or use of these programs.

Printed in the United States of America

10 9 8 7 6 5 4 3 2 1

ISBN: 0-13-233553-0

Pearson Education Ltd., *London*
Pearson Education Australia Pty. Ltd., *Sydney*
Pearson Education Singapore, Pte. Ltd.
Pearson Education North Asia Ltd., *Hong Kong*
Pearson Education Canada, Inc., *Toronto*
Pearson Educación de Mexico, S.A. de C.V.
Pearson Education—Japan, *Tokyo*
Pearson Education Malaysia, Pte. Ltd.
Pearson Education, Inc., *Upper Saddle River, New Jersey*

To Everyone Who
Is Curious

About The Author

Douglas Comer is a Distinguished Professor of Computer Science at Purdue University and Vice President of Research at Cisco Systems, Incorporated. He has taught undergraduate and graduate courses on computer networks and Internets, operating systems, computer architecture, and computer software. One of the researchers who contributed to the Internet as it was being formed in the late 1970s and 1980s, he has served as a member of the Internet Architecture Board, the group responsible for guiding the Internet's development. Comer is an internationally recognized expert on computer networking, the TCP/IP protocols, and the Internet, who presents lectures to a wide range of audiences. In addition to research articles, he has written a series of textbooks that describe the technical details of the Internet. Comer's books have been translated into 16 languages, and are used in industry as well as computer science, engineering, and business departments around the world. He is a Fellow of The Association for Computing Machinery (the major professional society in computer science) and editor of the scientific journal, *Software — Practice and Experience.*

Professor Comer had dial-up Internet access from his home in the late 1970s, has enjoyed a direct connection with twenty-four hour per day service since 1981, and uses the Internet daily. He wrote this book as a response to everyone who has asked him for an explanation of the Internet that is both technically correct and easily understood by anyone. An Internet enthusiast, Comer displays *INTRNET* on the license plate of his car.

Additional information can be found at:

www.cs.purdue.edu/people/comer

and information about Comer's books can be found at:

www.comerbooks.com

Contents

PART I   Introduction To Networking

PART II   A Brief History Of The Internet

Chapter 10   The Global Internet   81

Chapter 11   A Global Information Infrastructure   89

PART III   How The Internet Works

Chapter 22   Bulletin Board Service (Newsgroups)   187

Chapter 23   Browsing The World Wide Web   197

Chapter 24 World Wide Web Documents (HTML) 221

Chapter 25   Advanced Web Technologies (Forms, Frames, Plu-   239
gins, Java, JavaScript, Flash)

Chapter 26   Group And Personal Web Pages (Wikis And Blogs)   261

Chapter 27   Automated Web Search (Search Engines)   267

Chapter 28   Text, Audio, And Video Communication (IM, VoIP)   281

Chapter 29   Faxes, File Transfer, And File Sharing (FTP)   **295**

Chapter 30   Remote Login And Remote Desktops (TELNET)   **303**

Chapter 31   Facilities For Secure Communication

311

Chapter 32   Secure Access From A Distance (VPNs)

323

Preface

The Internet Book explains how computers communicate, what the Internet is, how the Internet works, and what services the Internet offers. It is designed for readers who do not have a strong technical background — early chapters clearly explain the terminology and concepts needed to understand all the services. When you finish reading, you will understand the technology behind the Internet, will appreciate how the Internet can be used, and discover why people find it so exciting. In addition, you will understand the origins of the Internet and see how rapidly it has grown.

Instead of using mathematics, algorithms, or computer programs, the book uses analogies from everyday life to explain technology. For example, to explain why digital communication is superior to analog, the text uses an analogy of sending signals through fog with a flashlight. To explain how audio can be played back for the user at a steady rate when packets arrive in clumps, the text uses the analogy of many gallons of milk arriving at a supermarket in one shipment, but being sold one gallon at a time.

In addition to explaining the services users encounter such as email, file download, instant messaging, and web browsing, the text covers key networking concepts such as packet switching, Local Area Networks, protocol software, and domain names. More important, the text builds on fundamentals — it describes basic Internet communication facilities first, and then shows how the basic facilities are used to provide a variety of services. Finally, the book includes an extensive glossary of technical terms with easy-to-understand definitions; readers are encouraged to consult the glossary as they read.

The fourth edition retains the same general structure as the previous edition, but adds three new chapters (19, 26, and 32), and updates material throughout. Chapter 19 explains NAT, a technology many Internet subscribers now have in their home. Chapter 26 explains blogs and wikis, two new Internet applications. Chapter 32, the third new chapter, explains Virtual Private Networking, a technology that allows an employee to access a corporate network safely from an arbitrary remote location.

As with the previous edition, the book is divided into four main parts. The first part begins with fundamental concepts such as digital and analog communication. It also introduces packet switching and explains the Local Area Network technologies that are used in most businesses.

The second part of the book gives a short history of the Internet research project and the development of the Internet. Although most of the history can be skipped, readers should pay attention to the phenomenal growth rate, which demonstrates that the technology was designed incredibly well — no other communication technology has remained as unchanged through such rapid growth.

The third part of the book explains how the Internet works, including a description of the two fundmental protocols used by all services: the Internet Protocol (IP) and the Transmission Control Protocol (TCP). Although they omit technical details, the chapters in this part allow students to understand the essential role of each protocol and gain perspective on the overall design.

The fourth part of the book examines services available on the Internet. In addition to covering browsers, web documents, and search engines used with the World Wide Web, chapters discuss email, bulletin boards, file transfer, remote desktops, wikis, blogs, and audio and video communication. In each case, the text explains how the service operates and how it uses facilities in the underlying system. The fourth part concludes with a discussion of network security, Virtual Private Networks, and electronic commerce.

The Internet Book makes an excellent reference text for a college-level course on the Internet. Although presented in a nontechnical manner, the material is scientifically accurate. More important, in the twenty-first century, an educated person will need to know more than how to use a browser or set up a web page — they should have some understanding of what goes on behind the scenes. They can acquire such knowledge from this text.

Instructors are encouraged to combine classroom lectures with laboratory sessions in which students see and use the technology first-hand. In all courses, early labs should focus on exploring a variety of services, including sending email, using a browser, using a search engine, downloading files, listening to audio, and using an IP telephone, if one is available. I encourage all students, even those who have no interest in computers, to build a trivial web page by hand. In addition to helping them see the relationship between tags in an HTML document and the resulting display, it shows students how a server transfers files on a computer disk to a browser. Seeing the relationship in labs helps one better understand as they read about the underlying process.

Lab projects later in the semester depend on the type of course. Business-oriented courses often focus students on using the Internet or constructing a case study — labs require students to search the Internet for information and then write a paper that analyzes the information. Other courses use labs to focus on tools such as programs used to create a web page. Some courses combine both by having students search for information and then create a web page that contains links to the information. In any case, we have found that students enter Internet courses with genuine enthusiasm and motivation; a professor's task is merely to provide perspective and remind students throughout the semester why the Internet is so exciting.

The author thanks many people who have contributed to editions of this book. John Lin, Keith Rovell, Rob Slade, and Christoph Schuba read early versions and made suggestions. Dwight Barnette, George Polyzo, Donald Knudson, Dale Musser, and Dennis Ray sent the publisher reviews of a previous edition. Scott Comer provided perspective. As always, my wife, Christine, carefully edited the manuscript, solved many problems, and improved the wording.

Douglas E. Comer

August, 2006

This book was typeset by the author and sent across the Internet in digital form to a publishing company where it was converted to photographic form for printing.

Other Books By Douglas Comer

Essentials Of Computer Architecture, 2005, ISBN 0-13-149179-2.

An introduction to computer organization that emphasizes concepts and consequences for programmers instead of low-level electrical engineering details.

Computer Networks And Internets (with a CD-ROM by Ralph Droms), 4th edition: 2004, ISBN 0-13-143351-2.

A broad introduction to data communication, networking, internetworking, and client-server applications that examines the hardware and software components used to create networks. The text covers transmission, LANs, WANs, protocols (including TCP/IP), and network applications. A CD-ROM features animations and data sets.

Internetworking With TCP/IP Volume I: Principles, Protocols and Architecture, 5th edition: 2006, ISBN 0-13-187671-6

One of the best-selling TCP/IP texts of all time, Volume I explains technical details of the Internet protocols. Intended for someone with a technical background, Volume I goes into depth by examining the function of each protocol and showing how the suite of protocols works together.

Internetworking With TCP/IP Volume II: Design, Implementation, and Internals (with David Stevens), 3rd edition: 1999, ISBN 0-13-973843-6

Volume II continues the discussion of Volume I by using code from a running implementation of TCP/IP to illustrate all the details. The text shows, for example, how TCP's slow start algorithm interacts with the Partridge-Karn exponential retransmission backoff algorithm and how routing updates interact with datagram forwarding.

Internetworking With TCP/IP Volume III: Client-Server Programming and Applications (with David Stevens)

Linux/POSIX Socket Version, 2000. ISBN 0-13-032071-4
AT&T TLI Version: 1994, ISBN 0-13-474230-3
Windows Sockets Version: 1997, ISBN 0-13-848714-6

Volume III describes the fundamental concept of client-server computing used to build all distributed computing systems. The text discusses various server designs as well as tools and techniques. It contains examples of running programs that illustrate each of the designs. Three versions of Volume III are available for the socket API (Linux), the TLI API (AT&T System V), and the Windows Sockets API (Microsoft).

**To order, visit the Prentice Hall web page at www.prenhall.com
or contact your local bookstore or Prentice Hall representative.
In North America, call 1-515-284-6751, or send a FAX to 1-515-284-6719.**

1

The Internet Has Arrived

The World Has Changed

A revolution has occurred. It started quietly, and has grown to involve most of the world. On an average day, the following events occur:

- A young couple use a computer to plan a road trip from their home in Ohio to a friend's house in San Francisco, California. Within seconds, they receive a description of the shortest route along with maps and detailed descriptions of distances and each turn.
- An investment broker in Houston, Texas sits down at a personal computer and runs a program that accesses current prices on the New York Stock Exchange. After looking at the list, the broker purchases shares of two stocks and sells shares of another.
- Children in an elementary school in Chicago, Illinois use a computer network to read a newspaper article from the New York Times.
- A mother living in Maryland uses a computer to view the weather in North Carolina where her daughter lives. After seeing that the storm has passed, she sends a note expressing her relief.
- A teenager in Seattle, Washington uses a computer to listen to a sample of music. Later, he uses the computer to purchase and download a copy of the song.
- A grandparent in Boston, Massachusetts uses a computer to inquire about airline flights, make a reservation, and purchase a ticket for a trip to visit a grandchild.
- A group of company executives hold a meeting. One executive is in New

York, another in Florida, and a third is on vacation in Colorado. Each sits in front of a computer that has both a camera and microphone attached. They see pictures of one another on the screen and hear each others' voices.

- A computer program runs at 6:00 PM in Atlanta, Georgia to send a copy of a company's daily sales receipts to a branch office in London, England.

- A high school student in Taiwan uses a computer to see and hear a tour of the campus at a university in Hawaii, including a live video showing students walking across campus with palm trees swaying in the breeze. Later, the student uses the computer to send a fax to a relative who is visiting Australia.

What do all these events have in common? In each, people are using the Internet, a communication system that has revolutionized the way we work and play.

If you have not yet encountered the Internet, you will soon. Let's look at some statistics:

- The Internet currently reaches hundreds of millions of people in over 209 countries (every populated area on the planet).

- Two-year and four-year U.S. colleges and universities have access to the Internet; public schools also have access.

- The U.S. military has been using Internet technology for over twenty years; it played a role in military actions as early as Operation Desert Storm in the early 1990s.

- Scientists have been using the Internet since 1980.

- The U.S. President and the White House are accessible via the Internet as are other government agencies in many countries.

Numbers Do Not Tell The Story

The most common assessment of the Internet's significance measures the number of computers that connect to it. However, conventional computer connections tell only part of the story. The Internet reaches ships at sea, planes in the air, and mobile vehicles on land. Private companies provide access to Internet services through the telephone and cable television systems, making it possible to reach the Internet from any home or office that has telephone or cable TV wiring.

To assess the impact of the Internet, one might ask, ''What has it affected?'' The answer is, ''Almost everything.'' So, the question becomes:

The Internet has arrived; how does it affect you?

Learning About The Internet

This book answers the question "What is the Internet?" in the broadest sense. It examines the origins of computer networking and its application to everyday problems. It focuses on the services that the Internet provides and helps the reader understand their importance. More important, it removes some of the mystery and helps the reader understand how the technology works.

Learning about the Internet is not something one can complete in an afternoon — learning never stops because the Internet keeps changing. The Internet is similar to a newsstand: when new information appears, it replaces older information. Each time you visit the newsstand or the Internet, you can find something new.

Of course, information on the Internet changes much more rapidly than information in a conventional newsstand. In fact, because information on the Internet comes from computers and automated systems, it can change instantly. For example, if one accesses weather information twice in a single minute, the information obtained from the two accesses can differ because computers can measure weather and change the report constantly.

In addition to resembling a newsstand, the Internet also resembles a library because it has tools that aid the search for information. Historically, libraries provided a card catalog and a reference desk. The Internet has similar services that help one find information electronically.

Understanding The Big Picture

Grasping all the details of the Internet is impossible because the Internet continues to change. Thus, no one can know the locations of all the interesting data or the way to obtain the lowest price for an item. More important, because new applications are being invented, no one can obtain a complete description of all the services available. Finally, because individual computers and software programs differ, one cannot expect the same details to apply to all computers.

To avoid becoming overwhelmed with details, we will examine the fundamentals of the Internet. Instead of focusing on how to use a particular computer, a particular brand of software, or a particular Internet service, we will consider the basics of how the Internet works and how information services use the basic mechanisms. In essence, we will examine the capabilities of the Internet.

Understanding Internet capabilities makes it much easier to read computer manuals and to use the Internet. In particular, because most computer manuals specify the details of how to accomplish a task without describing why one needs to perform the task, beginners often find them difficult to follow. Knowing how the Internet works and the purpose of each service helps put the details in perspective.

Terminology And Technology

A complex technology, the Internet has spawned a terminology that can be daunting. This book clearly explains the Internet technology using analogies and examples. It shows how the pieces fit together, emphasizing basics instead of details. It discusses the services that the Internet offers, explains the flexibility they provide, and describes how they can be used.

More important, this book introduces technical terminology used for computer networking and the Internet. Instead of providing a list of terms, early chapters present definitions in a historical perspective that shows how communication systems evolved. For example, early chapters explain the difference between digital and analog information. Instead of using computer networks as an example, the chapters relate the terminology to everyday experiences.

Growth And Adaptability

Part of the mystique surrounding the Internet arises from its rapid success. While the Internet has grown, dozens of other attempts to provide the same services have failed to deliver. Meanwhile the Internet continues to expand by adapting to change, both technical and political. We will examine why Internet technology has worked so well and how it has adapted to accommodate change.

Another amazing part of the Internet story is its incredible growth. We will look at how the Internet continues to grow and the consequences of such growth.

The Impact Of The Internet

Perhaps the most significant aspect of the Internet is its impact on society. Once restricted to a few scientists, it has quickly become universal. It reaches governments, businesses, schools, and homes worldwide. We will examine how the Internet changes peoples' lives, and what we can expect in the future. In summary, the rest of this book looks at what the Internet is and what it can do for you.

Organization Of The Book

This book is organized into four sections. After a brief tour of web sites in Chapter 2, the first section (Chapters 3 through 7) introduces communication system concepts and terminology. If you already understand digital and analog communication, universal service, and binary data encoding, you may choose to skim this section. The second section (Chapters 8 through 11) reviews the history of the Internet and its incredible growth. The section documents the rate at which the digital revolution occurred, and provides background that will help you appreciate the significance of the underlying design. The third section (Chapters 12 through 20) describes basic Internet technology and capabilities. It examines how Internet hardware is organized and how software provides communication. Be sure to understand this section; it provides the foundation for later chapters. The final section describes services currently available on the Internet. For each service, it explains both how the service works and how it can be used.

A Personal Note

I still remember an occasion several years ago when a colleague bluntly asked me the question, ''What is the Internet?'' I had been involved with Internet research for many years, and had written a popular college textbook that described the Internet and the principles underlying its design. I knew many details about the hardware and software systems that comprised the Internet, how the computers were connected, and the details of communication. I also knew most of the researchers who were working on technical improvements. What puzzled me most was that the person asking already knew basic technical details and had a copy of my textbook. What more could I say?

As I contemplated the question, my colleague guessed that I misunderstood and said, ''I do not want to know about computers and wires. I mean, in a larger sense, what *is* the Internet, and what is it becoming? Have you noticed that it is changing? Who will be using it in ten years? What will they do with it?''

The questions were important because they pointed out a significant shift. Early in its history, most users of the Internet were the experts who helped build it. The Internet has outgrown its research beginnings and has become a powerful tool. It is a facility used by almost everyone. It is being used in ways that the experts had not imagined.

2

Getting Started: Hands-On Experience

Introduction

The material in this text gives a broad, conceptual view of Internet capabilities. It explains what the Internet can do and how the underlying technology operates, without focusing on details. For example, the text does not attempt to provide a catalog of the most interesting items available on the Internet, nor does it discuss how to use any particular computer or particular brand of software. Thus, the entire text can be understood without direct access to a computer.

Despite the emphasis on concepts, readers who have Internet access are encouraged to use the Internet as they read. Hands-on experience provides intuition and familiarity that enhances learning in the same way that access to a car helps one better appreciate learning about highways and destinations reachable on those highways. To aid readers in getting started, this short chapter suggests some possibilities. It describes the concept of a web browser, which is a computer program, and provides a few examples of sites to visit. Chapter 23 revisits the topic of browsers and explains in greater detail how they work. Readers already familiar with the Internet need not spend time reviewing; they can skip directly to the next chapter.

The Web: Sites And Pages

Although many applications have been devised that use the Internet, one particular application has evolved that incorporates the best features of others through a single interface. The application is known as the *World Wide Web* or merely "The Web."

Most large organizations and many smaller ones have a *web site*. We think of an organization's web site as its point of contact — the site contains all the information about the organization that is available to Internet users. For example, the web site for a corporation might contain a catalog of products the company offers, prices, instructions for ordering, a list of the company's employees along with their telephone numbers and a statement of their responsibilities, or information about employment possibilities. In addition to corporations, institutions such as schools and governments also maintain web sites. Finally, individuals maintain web sites that contain personal information.

To prevent a user from being overwhelmed by a large volume of information, the contents of a web site are divided into "pages." In general, an Internet user views one page of information at a time. Consequently, a page is usually designed to fit on a user's screen. When a user moves to a new page, the contents of the previous page are no longer visible; to view the previous page again, the user must explicitly return to it†.

Web Browsers and Browsing

Access to the World Wide Web requires a computer, a connection to the Internet, and special software on the computer. In later chapters, we will learn that two types of software are required: Internet communication software and application software. The communication software speaks the "language" of the Internet, making it possible for the computer to communicate with other computers. The application software handles all interaction with the user. When the user makes a request for information, the application software uses the Internet to access the requested information, and then displays the results on the screen for the user to see.

An application program used to access the World Wide Web is known as a *web browser*, and someone who uses such a program is said to be *browsing* the Web. Although several browser programs exist, two completely dominate the market: Mozilla's Firefox browser and Microsoft's Internet Explorer. The two differ only in minor details. Interestingly, both are free.

---

†Applications that display information can create multiple windows on a user's screen that allow a user to view several pages simultaneously.

Using A Browser

The paradigm for browsing the Web is straightforward. To begin, a user connects his or her computer to the Internet and launches a browser. When the browser runs, it creates a window on the screen. The major portion of the window consists of an area that the browser uses to display a web page (unless a user specifies otherwise, a browser is also likely to display advertisements along with web pages). A small area near the top of the browser's window contains controls that a user invokes to specify a web page. Within the control area, the browser has a small text area labeled *location* that is used to specify a particular web site. Each site is given an identification string called a *URL* (later chapters explain the terminology; for now, the details are unimportant). To visit a web site, the user moves the mouse to the location box, enters the URL for the desired site, and presses the *RETURN* key. The browser contacts the specified site and displays the main page of information. The page can contain a mixture of text, graphic images, and audio.

Once a web page appears on the screen, moving to another page is easy. Some of the items on a page are ''links'' to other pages. Text that corresponds to a link is usually displayed in a different color and is underlined; some images on the page also correspond to links, but they may not have a clear indication. To follow a link, one uses the mouse to move the cursor over the item on the screen and clicks. The browser automatically uses the Internet to obtain the page that corresponds to the link, and then replaces the display with the new page. Thus, browsing consists of entering the URL for a specific site and then following links from one page to another.

Examples Of Web Sites And Services

A few examples will help demonstrate the type of information available on the Web. The selection is not meant to imply that these are preferred sites; it merely gives an idea of the scope and variety of information available. To visit any of the sites, enter the URL that is given.

An Online Newspaper

The *New York Times*, one of the most well-known newspapers in the world, maintains a web site that contains current newspaper articles and stock market information. The URL is:

www.nytimes.com

Weather Information

The Weather Channel has an online service that gives weather information and forecasts. The URL is:

www.weather.com

Driving Directions

Several web sites offer detailed driving directions that specify routes, distances, and turns needed to drive from one address to another. For example, the MapQuest service can be found at:

www.mapquest.com

Satellite Maps

An Internet site exists that has satellite and aerial maps of the earth's surface. You should be able to see a satellite map of your neighborhood. The URL is:

www.terraserver.com

Radio Stations

Many radio stations send audio over the Internet. Stations, categorized by music format, can be found by following the links on the page given by URL:

www.xmradio.com

An Online Fashion Mall

Every large city has a fashion mall with stores that carry well-known brands. An online version can be found at:

www.fashionmall.com

A Retail Bookstore

Amazon is one of the best-known online retailers. Initially an online bookstore, it now offers other merchandise. The URL is:

www.amazon.com

Stock Information

The New York Stock Exchange site provides a description of the investment community as well as information about popular stock index values and stock prices. The URL is:

www.nyse.com

Music Clips

Chapter 28 explains how audio is delivered over the Internet, and notes that MP3 is a popular format used to encode music. A selection of music and other audio encoded in MP3 format can be found at:

www.itunes.com

Electronic Postage

It is possible to purchase postage electronically and use it to send a conventional letter. In essence, electronic postage operates like a postage meter instead of a conventional stamp — after paying for postage, the customer prints a label that the post office honors in place of a stamp. The URL is:

www.e-stamp.com

Satire

Many web sites contain satirical material. A satire of Microsoft arranged to look like a board game can be found at:

www.ms-monopoly.com

Internet Search

As Chapter 27 describes, services exist that allow a user to find web pages that contain a specific item or topic. One such service can be found at:

www.google.com

Summary

This chapter briefly reviewed the most popular Internet service, the World Wide Web. We learned that information found at a given web site is divided into pages; a user views one at a time with a computer program known as a browser. Each page can contain text and pictures, or can connect to audio and video. We also learned that a wide variety of information is accessible through the Web. Chapters 21 through 30 examine web technologies in more detail, and explain how the Internet provides such services.

Before The Internet

A Gentle Introduction To Communication Systems Concepts And Terminology

3

Telephones Everywhere

Introduction

This chapter introduces the concept of *universal service*. It uses a familiar example to show how the assumption of universal service can affect our view of a communication service, and explains why the Internet is becoming a necessity as it becomes universal.

A Communication Service

The Internet is a communication technology. Like the telephone before it, the Internet makes it possible for people to communicate in new ways. However, to the average person living now, digital communication is as novel as telephone communication was to the average person living one hundred years ago. We can learn many lessons from the story of telephone service that apply directly to the Internet.

Selling Communication

To understand how a new communication technology infiltrates society, think back approximately a century. Imagine yourself as a salesperson in an average town in the U.S. who has the job of selling telephone service.

All things considered, the economic times you face are full of promise. Excitement and optimism pervade industry. After all, society is experiencing an industrial revolution. Everywhere you find that mechanization has replaced manual labor. The steam engine has replaced water wheels and animals as a source of power; some industries are starting to use engines that run on gasoline. Factories are producing more goods than ever before.

Of course, a telephone salesperson of a century ago would have had little or no firsthand experience using a telephone. Indeed, he or she may have had only a few demonstrations before going out to sell telephone service.

Imagine that you walk into a small company and talk to the owner about telephone service. What can you say? You could tell the owner that the company needs a telephone because it will allow customers to place orders easily. Or you could say that a telephone will allow employees to check with suppliers, order raw materials, or trace shipments that do not arrive on schedule. Maybe you would ask the owner if he or she goes out to lunch with other business owners, and point out that a luncheon could be arranged in a few seconds over a telephone. You could say that a telephone is easy to use. Or, you might take a more serious approach and point out that if fire struck the business, a telephone could be used to reach the firehouse: it might save property or lives.

How do the owners react to your telephone sales pitch? Some are interested; many are skeptical. A few are delighted, but others are angry. Although some will think the idea has merit, many will laugh. Some want to redesign business practices, but most resist. A few want a telephone just because it is new and lends status to their establishment. Despite what they say, most owners believe that they will continue to conduct business without using a telephone.

Limited Access

Selling telephone service without having used it can be difficult. But let's make the task of selling easier. Suppose that you had grown up in a world with telephone service, and that you had used telephones all your life. Then suppose that you were transported back in time almost 100 years and tried to sell telephone service. You might think that it would be easy to convince people to buy telephone service knowing how it can be used, but you would be surprised by what you face.

The first shock you encounter when trying to sell telephone service is learning that the service of a century ago did not work the same way as modern telephone service. Back then, telephone service meant *local* service. Each town or village decided independently when to run wires, hire a switchboard operator, and establish phone service. More important, each town chose a telephone technology that met its needs and budget. As a result, although many phone systems existed, they were incompatible — running wires from one town to the next did not guarantee that the telephone systems in the two towns could work together. From a business perspective, even if a company installed a telephone, it could not be used to order supplies from other parts of the country. You quickly discover:

> *Having an independent local telephone service in each town limits the usefulness of a telephone.*

High Cost

The second shock you encounter when trying to sell telephone service approximately a century ago is learning that even when it is available, telephone service is expensive. An average family cannot afford a telephone in their home. In addition to buying the telephone itself, many telephone companies charge each subscriber the true cost of installation. The first customer on a given street must pay for running the wires from the telephone office to the street; subsequent customers pay only for running wires to their houses. As a consequence, it is often more difficult to enlist the first subscriber in a given neighborhood than to enlist additional subscribers. More important, for a large part of the population who live in rural areas, telephone service is out of the question.

After many attempts to sell telephone service to individuals fail, you report back to your employer with a conclusion:

> *Telephone service will not be a viable business until the cost of service becomes low enough for an average family to have a phone installed.*

The Difficult Transition

In a world without telephones, convincing a business to install one may seem impossible. If the business cannot use it to call suppliers in remote parts of the country and local customers do not have easy access to a telephone, there is little economic justification for acquiring one. In fact, after thinking about the world of telephone service that we enjoy and the world of telephone service approximately a century ago, you realize:

> *The single most important idea behind a communication service arises from its coverage — if no one else has the service, it is useless; if everyone else has the service, it is a necessity.*

The transition between the two extremes is difficult. It requires businesses and individuals to invest in a new communication technology before the economic benefit is obvious. If they choose a technology that does not catch on, they lose their investment. Even if others adopt the technology, it may have insufficient subscribers to justify economically. Many people remain reticent when a new technology arrives. They wait to see what everyone else will do, hoping to minimize their financial risk. The financial decision is more difficult for a business, which must decide how rapidly to install telephones. If the business has too few phones, callers will receive a busy signal; if the business has too many, the phones sit idle, meaning that the business has wasted resources.

Ubiquitous Access

Why did everyone in the U.S. eventually choose to subscribe to telephone service? If you are a student of history, you know the answer: because the U.S. government decided that ubiquitous telephone service was important for the country. The governments of most other countries reached the same decision. The U.S. government established a regulated monopoly, American Telephone and Telegraph (AT&T). It mandated that telephone service be available to every home and business, and regulated rates to ensure that telephone service was affordable to the average family. It required the telephone system to reach rural areas as well as cities. More important, the government encouraged AT&T to interconnect all the local telephone services, providing a single, large system.

Because one company owned and operated much of the U.S. telephone network, many tasks were easy. For example, AT&T could specify the technical details of how the phone system in one city interconnected with the phone system in another. Having one company own the system made it easy to deploy new technology. A single company also made it easy to define a global numbering system so that a subscriber in one city could directly dial the telephone number of a subscriber in another city.

In short, the result of the government action was universal telephone service available at a price an average family could afford. Within a few decades, most businesses and a large portion of the population could be reached by telephone. Of course, universal telephone service could have occurred without government intervention; we can only speculate about what might have happened. The important point is not that the government intervened, but that popularity of the telephone surged as universal service became a reality. Businesses understood that universal phone service would mean a change in business procedures. As businesses and individuals started acquiring telephones, it became apparent to everyone that telephones were important. Acquiring one became a necessity. Telephone service changed from a luxury reserved for the rich to something expected by the average family.

In the U.S., the telephone system became the communication system of choice in the twentieth century because the government mandate of universal telephone service guaranteed that subscribing would benefit everyone.

Relevance To The Internet

Like the telephone system, the Internet provides communication. Currently, the Internet falls in the awkward transition period between limited access and universal service. Although connections are growing rapidly, the Internet does not reach everyone. Although the U.S. government has contributed to Internet development, it has not decided to mandate universal service. Thus, unlike the phone system, Internet growth has relied on economics. As a result, growth has proceeded in a haphazard manner. In the mid-1990s, major businesses decided that they would benefit from an Internet connection, and began to mention their web pages in general advertising. By 2000, millions of homes had slow-speed Internet access, and businesses were upgrading both their computers and Internet connections to handle the increased traffic. By 2005, higher speed Internet connections to homes had become commonplace.

During the transition, convincing someone who has not used the Internet that it offers exciting new possibilities is like trying to sell telephone service before a universal phone system is in place. Often people who see Internet technology smile politely and nod, while thinking to themselves, "That's all very nice, but how would *I* use it?" The question is the analogy of someone who has never seen a telephone asking, "Yes, I see how it works, but whom would *I* call?"

The answer, of course, is that as more and more people connect to the Internet, you will want to use it to contact businesses, friends, banks, schools, government offices, and relatives. A later chapter discusses Internet growth, and shows that the Internet is becoming universal.

4

The World Was Once Analog

Introduction

The Internet uses digital technology to carry many forms of information. This chapter explains analog information, and shows how analog signals can be encoded in digital form. The discussion uses audio as an example.

Sound, Vibrations, And Analog Recording

Highway engineers use a simple mechanism to warn motorists to slow down. They install a series of small bumps in the roadway. When a car passes the bumps, the tires vibrate. Humans perceive the tire vibration as sound.

The first mechanical phonographs used the same basic idea to reproduce sound. A pointed stylus traveled across the surface of a cylinder or disc that contained small bumps of recorded sound. As the stylus ran across the bumps, it vibrated a flat diaphragm, producing vibrations that humans perceive as sound. Figure 4.1 illustrates the idea.

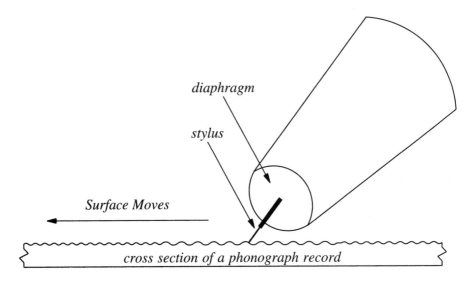

diaphragm

stylus

Surface Moves

cross section of a phonograph record

Figure 4.1 An illustration of how bumps on an early phonograph record cause
a diaphragm to vibrate as the record passes under the stylus.

Devices like a phonograph are called *analog devices* because they record and play
an analog of sound. That is, bumps on a phonograph recording are exactly analogous to
the vibrations that make sounds. For example, the height of the bumps controls the
volume. When the sound is soft, the bumps are nearly flat; when the sound is loud, the
bumps are higher. If there are no bumps at all, a phonograph produces no sound†.

To summarize:

> *An analog device maintains an exact physical analog of information.*
> *For example, bumps on an early phonograph recording correspond to*
> *vibrations that we perceive as sound.*

Analog Electronic Devices

Although early phonographs were entirely mechanical, modern equipment that
reproduces sound uses electronics. For example, an AM radio receiver uses analog
technology. A radio station transmits a signal that is an exact analog of sound. When
the sound is loud, a stronger signal is transmitted than when the sound is soft. In fact,
analog can best be understood by thinking about an amount of one substance being proportional to another: the amount of signal is proportional to the volume of sound.

---

†In practice, a phonograph always produces some noise because the recording surface is not perfectly flat;
it contains minor scratches that become worse each time the record is played.

When a radio receiver is tuned to the same channel as a transmitter, an electronic circuit in the receiver captures incoming radio waves and produces an electric current that is an exact analog of the signal. When the signal corresponds to a soft sound, the current is weak; when the signal corresponds to a loud sound, the current is stronger. Thus,

> *An electronic device is analog if the amount of electrical current it generates is proportional to its input.*

Many Electronic Devices Are Analog

Many familiar electronic devices use analog technologies. For example, in addition to AM and FM radios, stereo systems and televisions use analog electronic circuits. In fact,

> *At one time, most electronic devices used analog techniques to store, amplify, and emit pictures or sounds.*

The First Analog Communication

Analog communication was an important part of early telephone systems. The first telephones had two basic parts: a microphone to convert sound into an analog electrical signal and an earpiece to convert an analog electrical signal into sound. Whenever a person spoke into the microphone, the electrical signals carried an analog of the sound along the wire to another telephone where it was converted back into sound. Because the system used analog signals, a loud sound caused more electric current to flow than a soft sound.

> *Early telephones used an analog scheme to send voice from one place to another; the amount of electrical current sent between two telephones was proportional to the volume of sound.*

Analog Is Simple But Inaccurate

Analog devices are the easiest to understand because most of what we do is analog. When a human uses a muscle to open a door, the door moves in an exact analog of the force exerted on it. The volume of a human voice changes in exact analog to the force exerted by the person's diaphragm. Similarly, the pitch of a human voice is an exact analog of the force a person applies to stretch their vocal cords.

Although analog may be natural and easy for a human to understand, analog devices have drawbacks. In general, it is impossible to produce an exact analog of all
possible inputs. For example, consider recording the sound of a loud drumbeat on a
magnetic tape. The magnetism must be aligned at the place the drumbeat occurs. However, because the alignment is limited by the available magnetic material, it is impossible for the magnetism to be high enough to record an arbitrarily loud sound. Furthermore, because playing a tape wears down the surface, the sound diminishes slightly
each time the tape is played.

Inaccuracies also arise because electronic amplifiers are not perfect. An analog
electronic device changes its input signal in unintended ways. It may mangle the signal,
record it inaccurately, or add background noise. We call the changes *distortion*. For
example, one can hear the background noise produced by an audio amplifier when the
volume is set at maximum and no input is connected. In summary:

An analog device always distorts the input and adds noise.

Sending An Analog Signal Across A Wire

Whenever an electric current passes along a wire, some of the signal disappears.
Although engineers talk about *signal loss*, energy is not really lost. It is simply converted to heat. The consequence for analog electrical signals is important: as electric
current passes along a wire and some of the energy is converted to heat, the signal becomes weaker and weaker. For example, if an electrical signal contains an analog of
sound, the volume of the sound will be lower after the signal passes across a long wire
than it was at the start.

For an analog telephone system, the signal loss causes a problem. It means that
the signal becomes weaker as it travels from one telephone to another. If the telephones
are far apart, the signal will be so weak that the sound cannot be heard. In early telephone systems, the signal loss problem was so severe that telephones only worked in a
small local area.

As telephone service expanded, telephone companies solved the problem of signal
loss by adding amplifiers to the system. Amplifiers were placed periodically along
wires, to boost the signal after it became weak. The amplified signal was given enough
energy to travel to the next amplifier. Eventually, the signal reached its destination.
Figure 4.2 illustrates the idea.

Of course, analog electronic devices are never perfect. Each amplifier along the
path between two telephones distorts the signal and adds a little noise that is amplified,
along with the signal, by the next amplifier. The analog telephone system included special filters to block distortion and noise, but doing so also meant the system blocked
some legitimate sounds. The filters themselves distorted the signal as they eliminated
unwanted sounds.

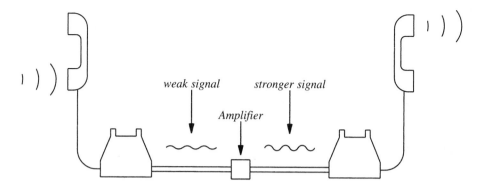

Figure 4.2 Telephone systems that use analog communication need to amplify the signal if it travels a long distance.

Digital Music

In the 1980s, the music industry began selling recordings on a new medium known as a *compact disc* (CD). Advertisements boasted that CDs produce better music than magnetic tapes or vinyl albums because CDs are *digital*. When CDs arrived, most people had no idea what "digital" meant, how digital music would sound, or why it was supposed to be better. If a customer asked what digital meant, he or she received a simple definition:

> *A technology is* digital *if it uses numbers to record information instead of a physical analog like bumps on a record or electric current in a receiver.*

The Digital Revolution

The digital revolution did not start with the compact disc. The current digital world became possible when scientists at Bell Laboratories invented a solid state switch called a *transistor*. The revolution began a short time later when scientists and engineers devised ways to combine transistors in an *integrated circuit*† built out of silicon crystals.

An integrated circuit consists of many electronic components interconnected by wires, built on a square a few tenths of an inch per side. Through intensive research, manufacturers have found ways to reduce the size of transistors and to make integrated

---

†An integrated circuit is informally called a *chip*.

circuits more sophisticated. Currently, a manufacturer can build an integrated circuit that contains several hundred million transistors.

The importance of integrated circuits lies in their economy. Because integrated circuits can be manufactured in mass quantities at low cost, it is now possible to mass produce complex circuits that were too expensive to build using individual components.

Many integrated circuits are designed primarily for use in computers. For example, a microprocessor is an integrated circuit that forms the heart of a modern computer — it contains all the electronic circuitry needed to add, subtract, multiply, divide, or compare numbers. In addition, a microprocessor can fetch numbers from a computer's memory or store results into memory.

Computers Are Digital

Unlike the analog devices discussed earlier, a computer is a *digital device.* It is called "digital" because:

Inside a computer, all information is represented by numbers.

For example, when the user presses a key on a computer keyboard, the keyboard sends a number to the computer. When the computer paints text or graphics on the screen, it does so using numbers.

Because a computer is digital, microprocessors and other integrated circuits built for use in computers work with numbers. Because computer circuits are extremely flexible, they can be used in a variety of ways; because they are inexpensive, engineers have used them in many devices. For example, microprocessors are used in hand-held calculators, automobiles, televisions, refrigerators, microwave ovens, cell phones, and office equipment. They control heating units, airplanes, cameras, and traffic lights.

Digital Recording

Recording sounds in digital form may seem impossible. After all, we know that sound is a sequence of vibrations of varying pitch and volume. Sound seems to have little to do with numbers. Digital recording only works because computer circuits operate at much higher speeds than the human ear and mechanisms exist that translate between analog and digital signals.

Using Digital To Recreate Analog

To understand digital recording, think of the temperature on a summer day. In the early morning it can be cool, but the temperature rises rapidly following sunrise. Around noon it peaks, and begins to fall in early evening. Suppose you wanted to re-create the exact outdoor temperatures of a summer day inside. Let's assume you have a heat lamp, a dimmer switch that controls the amount of heat the lamp produces, and a thermometer.

To recreate the temperatures that occur on a given day, you must record the temperatures that day. You take a thermometer outside and record the temperature periodically (for example, every half hour). The next day, you take the list of temperatures and the thermometer inside to the heat lamp. By adjusting the dimmer control, you can raise or lower the temperature of the lamp every half hour to exactly match the outdoor temperature of the previous day.

Computer circuits use the same technique when they record sound digitally (e.g., on a CD). A conventional microphone generates an analog electrical signal. The signal travels across a wire to a digital recoder. Inside the recorder, a computer circuit periodically measures the incoming signal and generates a number that tells the level of the signal at that instant. Because a computer circuit operates quickly, it can generate thousands of numbers per second. The set of numbers is saved and transferred to a compact disc. When someone plays the compact disc, a computer inside the player reads the numbers. The computer uses the sequence of numbers to recreate an analog electrical signal that matches the original signal. The output passes through a conventional amplifier to a loudspeaker.

The electronic circuit used to convert an analog signal into a sequence of numbers is known as an *Analog-to-Digital converter*, often abbreviated *A-to-D converter*. An A-to-D converter measures an electrical signal and produces a numeric value that corresponds to its level. The computer periodically retrieves numbers from the A-to-D converter and saves them. Figure 4.3 illustrates the conversion.

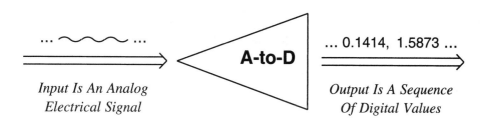

Figure 4.3 An integrated circuit that performs analog-to-digital conversion. The device takes an analog signal as input and produces a sequence of numbers as output.

To play a compact disc, a computer needs an integrated circuit known as a *Digital-to-Analog converter* (D-to-A converter). Figure 4.4 illustrates:

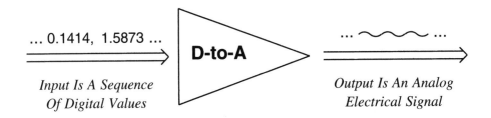

Figure 4.4 An integrated circuit that performs digital-to-analog conversion. The device takes a sequence of numbers as input and produces an analog signal as output.

To reproduce sound from a digital CD, a computer reads the sequence of numbers from the CD and feeds them into the D-to-A converter, which generates an analog electrical signal. The signal can then be amplified and played through a loudspeaker. A computer can send numbers into the converter so quickly that our ears hear the result as continuous sound.

Why Digital Music?

In essence, a compact disc simply contains a long list of numbers that specify how to reconstruct an analog signal. What makes a CD so fascinating is that it does not ''wear down'' as it is played. Numbers are encoded on a CD so they can be sensed with the light from a laser. Thus, nothing touches the CD itself as it is played. Furthermore, the master recording does not wear down as the manufacturer makes copies — each copy is identical to the original. In addition, a CD does not contain as much background noise as an analog scheme. For example, a CD contains zeroes between songs, meaning that no electrical signal will be produced.

Summary

Sounds are vibrations. The most natural representation of audio information is an analog form in which the amount of a physical quantity varies in exact proportion to the sound. In particular, the height of bumps on a phonograph record and the amount of electrical current generated by a radio receiver each correspond to the loudness of the recorded sound.

Audio information can also be represented using a digital form, which means using a sequence of numbers to represent the sounds. A digital representation is the most convenient form for computers because computers represent everything as numbers.

There are two important ideas to keep in mind throughout the remainder of the book:

- *Information, including text, photos, audio and video, can be encoded in digital form.*

- *The chief advantage of using a digital representation arises because the information does not become distorted while being stored, copied, or communicated.*

5

The Once And Future Digital Network

Introduction

This chapter discusses the concept of digital communication, and shows how digital information can be encoded for transmission using only two basic symbols.

The World Was Previously Digital

Chapter 4 asserts that, at one time, most of the electronic devices in the world were analog. Indeed, they were. Before the compact disc appeared, AM and FM radios, stereos, telephones, and televisions all used analog electronic circuits. Surprisingly, the earliest electronic communication devices were not analog. Decades before the first telephones made analog communication popular, the world used digital communication!

Nearly 150 years ago, it was possible to send a message from one town to another in a matter of minutes. The technology was known as a *telegraph*, and became so popular that telegraph lines spread quickly across the country.

A telegraph operates on the same principle as a wall switch that controls an electric lamp. The switch is located at a convenient height on the wall, remote from both the source of power and the lamp itself. A pair of wires that reach the switch carry power to the switch and current back to the lamp. When the switch is in the ''off'' position, the circuit is open and no current flows to the lamp. When the switch is in the ''on'' position, the circuit is complete and current flows to the lamp.

The basic telegraph also uses a switch with wires running to it. In the telegraph, however, distances are much longer: the switch is located in one town, and the device it operates is located in another. In addition, a telegraph does not use light. Instead, a telegraph uses a small electrically operated device that makes an audible click when it receives electric power. To send a message across the telegraph, a person in one town must move a switch back and forth, while a person in another town listens to the clicks generated by a local device.

To an untrained person, a telegraph sounds like an unending series of clicks with no perceptible pattern. Some of the clicks have a short duration (i.e., the switch was held down a very short time), while other clicks are longer. Sometimes, short pauses occur before the clicks begin again. A trained telegraph operator can distinguish individual letters among the clicks, and can transcribe a message on paper as fast as it arrives.

A Telegraph Is Digital

A telegraph is a digital device because instead of sending a continuous signal that is an exact analog of the input, the telegraph uses clicks to send the individual characters of a message. Although telegraph clicks may seem unrelated to numbers, to mathematicians, the set of clicks represent digits of a number system. In fact, we can now define *digital* more precisely: any device that uses a fixed set of discrete values is digital. To summarize:

> *The telegraph is a digital technology because it transfers discrete clicks instead of a continuously varying signal.*

Morse Code

Samuel Morse invented a code that became popular among telegraph operators. Morse code is simply a way to represent letters and words using a series of clicks and pauses. For example, Morse code uses one short click followed by one long click to represent the letter *A*.

When assigning code values, Morse tried to use short sequences for letters that occurred frequently. The result is that one can send a message faster using Morse's code than codes that are not planned as carefully. For example, in common English text, the letter *E* occurs more frequently than any other letter. Morse code uses a single, short click to encode *E*.

Short clicks are called *dots*, and long clicks are called *dashes*. During transmission, a short pause occurs after the dots and dashes that comprise a single letter, and a longer pause occurs after each word. A trained operator uses the pauses to detect when each letter and word ends.

Letters And Digits In Morse Code

In addition to codes for all the letters, Morse specified codes for the digits zero through nine and a few punctuation symbols as Figure 5.1 shows.

A	● —		X	— ● ● —
B	— ● ● ●		Y	— ● — —
C	— ● — ●		Z	— — ● ●
D	— ● ●		0	— — — — —
E	●		1	● — — — —
F	● ● — ●		2	● ● — — —
G	— — ●		3	● ● ● — —
H	● ● ● ●		4	● ● ● ● —
I	● ●		5	● ● ● ● ●
J	● — — —		6	— ● ● ● ●
K	— ● —		7	— — ● ● ●
L	● — ● ●		8	— — — ● ●
M	— —		9	— — — — ●
N	— ●		,	— — ● ● — —
O	— — —		.	● — ● — ● —
P	● — — ●		?	● ● — — ● ●
Q	— — ● —		;	— ● — ● — ●
R	● — ●		:	— — — ● ● ●
S	● ● ●		'	● — — — — ●
T	—		—	— ● ● ● ● —
U	● ● —		/	— ● ● — ●
V	● ● ● —		) or (	● ● — — ● —
W	● — —			

Figure 5.1 Examples of Morse code, which uses a unique sequence of dots and dashes to represent each letter, digit, and punctuation symbol.

Morse did not assign a code to all possible symbols. For example, there is no code for a dollar sign or for a percent sign, even though such characters do occur in written text.

Users Did Not Encounter Morse Code

Although all messages passed across a telegraph in Morse code, only telegraph operators needed to know it. A person who wanted to send a telegram wrote the message on a piece of paper and handed it to an operator. The message itself could be written in any language. In fact, people often abbreviated words because the amount of money a telegraph provider charged to deliver a telegram depended on the length of the message sent.

A skilled telegraph operator could translate between Morse code and text quickly; two operators were required for transmission across a telegraph system. At the sending end, the operator read a message from paper and tapped out Morse code. At the receiving end, the operator listened to the Morse code and wrote the text. After the message was received, it was delivered to the intended recipient.

Three ideas from the telegraph are relevant to the Internet:

- It is possible to encode all letters and digits using only two basic code values: dot and dash.

- A code used for message transmission defines a basic alphabet of characters that can be sent; the code can be useful even if it does not include all possible characters.

- A customer of a telegraph service never encountered or understood the underlying encoding scheme.

Virtually Instant Communication

When the telegraph was invented, it seemed like magic. Until then, sending a message to a remote location meant using a human courier, usually on horseback. Suddenly, the world changed, and it became possible to learn about events as they occurred. With a telegraph, for example, people located far away from a financial market could learn about current stock prices and could send orders to buy or sell stock. People far from the location where ballots were counted could learn the results of an election immediately. Travelers could stay in touch with friends or family at home.

Speed Is Relative

Although the telegraph changed the world because it was so fast compared to a courier, we would think of communication by telegraph as relatively slow. Imagine communicating with a friend via telegraph instead of telephone. After writing a message, you must hand it to a telegraph operator and wait while the operator translates it into Morse code. Only the best operators can send more than a dozen words per minute. Furthermore, both the sending and receiving operators must be equally adept for a transfer to succeed. If the receiver misses a character or word, he or she must ask the sender to transmit it again. As a result, holding a dialogue via telegraph is inconvenient and slow.

It should be obvious why the telephone caused so much excitement. Instead of writing a message and passing it to an operator, a person on one end of a telephone call can speak directly to the other party. The telephone system immediately carries the speaker's voice to the other end, and conveys something that cannot easily be expressed in written form: emotions. Hearing a voice, it is possible to distinguish anger from humor or reticence from excitement.

Telephone communication became popular quickly. Many engineers working on communication systems abandoned the slow, digital telegraph, and spent their time working on analog technology for telephones.

The Telephone Became Digital

Although voice communication may seem inherently analog, many modern telephone systems use digital encoding for voice transfer. At one end, the system converts an analog voice signal into a series of numbers similar to the numbers on a compact disc. Computers transfer the numbers across the phone network, where they are converted back into an analog signal.

Using digital technology to carry voice has a significant advantage for the telephone company. To understand why, consider a phone call. Initially, a long-distance telephone call required a human operator in one town to contact an operator in another, and for them to agree to hook wires together to complete the call. AT&T replaced the manual scheme with a mechanism that used dialing to connect wires automatically. To place a call, a subscriber only needed to dial the destination number. As the subscriber dialed, the telephone sent digital pulses that the dialing system used to connect the call to the specified destination.

When the dialing mechanism was first built, the telephone company used two sets of wires, one set carried the digital signals used for dialing and the other set carried analog signals used for voice communication. Over time, engineers merged the voice and dialing systems. As a result, modern telephone systems are almost entirely digital.

Relevance To The Internet

Like the early telegraph, the Internet provides digital communication. Because computers store information in digital form, digital communication works well in a computer network. When the information moves from one computer to another, a digital mechanism saves time and effort.

Binary Encoding Of Data On The Internet

The Internet is like a telegraph in another way: it uses exactly two values to encode all data items. While the values used in Morse code are commonly called dot and dash, we usually think of the values used in the Internet as zero and one, the two "digits" of the binary number system. In the Internet, as in most computer systems, the values are known as *bits*†. The next chapter explains the modern equivalent of Morse code used on the Internet. It describes the sequences of bits used to represent individual letters.

Why Use Two Symbols?

Using two symbols for digital encoding is not limited to the Internet — all digital electronic devices use bits to encode data. To understand why, think of communicating through a light fog. Suppose you have a flashlight. It would be easiest for another person to tell whether the flashlight is "on" or "off"; it would be much more difficult for the person to distinguish among "off," "dim," "medium," and "bright." Similarly, electronic circuits can sense "off" and "on" much easier than they can distinguish multiple levels of signal.

Even though the Internet encodes data in bits, the details are completely hidden from the user. Like a person who sent a message using a telegraph or a person who plays a music CD, someone who uses the Internet never sees the underlying binary encoding.

> *Although the Internet uses a binary encoding for all data transferred, users usually remain completely unaware of the encoding.*

Summary

The Internet is similar to its early predecessor, the telegraph, in three ways. First, the Internet provides digital communication service. It allows one to transfer a set of numbers from one computer to another. Numbers stored in a computer can be used to encode almost any information including the letters in a document, sounds, or pictures.

---

†The term *bit* is an abbreviation for *binary digit*.

Second, like the telegraph, at the lowest level the Internet encodes all data using two values. The Internet uses zero and one, the two binary digits. Third, the Internet hides the details of data encoding from the user.

6

Basic Communication

Introduction

Computer networks interconnect computers so they can exchange data. Although modern computer networks are complex combinations of hardware and software, early computer networks were much less sophisticated.

This chapter outlines the development of basic communication technologies, and shows how networks evolved. It introduces terminology, and explains how modems work. The concepts defined here are important throughout remaining chapters.

Communication Using Electricity

Since the discovery of electricity, inventors, scientists, and engineers have worked on ways to use electrical signals for communication. The principles discovered have resulted in fast, reliable communication systems. Our knowledge of digital communication can be divided into roughly three historical stages. The first stage focused on the properties of signals on wires. The second stage focused on how to use signals to send bits and how to organize the bits into characters. The third stage focused on how to detect and correct errors that occur during transmission.

Signals On Wires

Researchers first studied how electrical signals pass across wires. They learned, for example, that an electrical signal reflects from the end of a metal wire the same way that light reflects from a mirror (the reason that many modern networks require a terminator device at the end of every wire). They also learned that electrical signals lose energy as they pass across a wire (the reason that modern networks either limit the length of interconnecting wires or use electronic devices to amplify signals). They learned that an electrical signal in a wire emits electromagnetic radiation that can interfere with signals in nearby wires (the reason that high-speed networks and cable TV connections use a special cable that encloses the wire in a metal shield).

Information Coding

Once researchers understood sending electrical signals on wires, they studied ways to encode information in electrical signals. Much of the work focused on finding ways to encode the human voice for transmission across telephone lines with minimum distortion, but many of the techniques apply to communication in general.

Researchers discovered a technique known as *modulation* that transmits voice well. To use modulation, the sender must have a device called a *modulator*. The modulator begins with a basic electrical signal that oscillates back and forth regularly. The basic oscillating signal is called a *carrier*. The modulator uses a second signal (e.g., one generated by a human voice speaking into a telephone) to change the carrier slightly. At the receiving end of the wire, a *demodulator* performs the reverse function, which is known as *demodulation*. The demodulator is tuned to expect the carrier. By measuring how much the incoming signal deviates from a perfect carrier, the receiver can recover the second signal (the human voice). After they determined the range of pitch for the human voice, scientists found a carrier signal sufficient to carry audible information.

MODEM: A Modulator And A Demodulator

The principle of modulation is still in use in modern communication systems — before two computers in the Internet can communicate across a long cable, they need a modulator at one end and a demodulator at the other. A customer can install wires within a building, or lease wires from a telephone company between two buildings, across a town, or across a country. Electrically, the leased wires do not connect to the phone system; whoever leases the wires can only use them for private communication. When a customer uses a set of wires for communication, the customer must install a device at each end of the connection. The device is called a *modem* (an abbreviation for *mo*dulator/*dem*odulator). In fact, a leased communication circuit always contains two independent sets of wires, one set for data traveling in each direction. A modem contains both a modulator that it uses to send information, and a demodulator that it uses for arriving information. Figure 6.1 illustrates the concept.

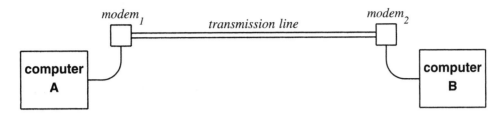

Figure 6.1 Illustration of modems that use modulation to send data across a transmission line. When a computer interacts with a modem, it sends and receives digital data; the modem encodes the data for transmission.

Modems are also available that allow communication over an ordinary dial-up telephone connection. A dial-up modem contains additional circuitry that can dial a phone number or answer an incoming call. The user must instruct a modem on one end to dial a phone number and a modem on the other end to answer the call. Once a call has been accepted, both modems can begin transferring data.

A dial-up modem uses an audible tone as the carrier when it encodes data (the carrier is the high-pitched sound one hears in a telephone handset when a modem is in use on the phone line). Whenever a computer sends data, the sending modem modulates the carrier tone by changing the pitch. The receiving modem monitors the carrier, and decodes the data when the carrier changes.

Modems Allow Two-Way Traffic

Modems permit data to be sent between them in both directions. Recall that each modem contains both a modulator and a demodulator. Furthermore, the modems are designed so they either use two different carrier signals or agree to take turns sending data. In either case, data appears to flow in both directions simultaneously.

To summarize:

A modem is a device needed for communication across a dial-up telephone connection or for long distance communication across a wire. A modem supports two-way communication because it contains a modulator for the signal being sent and a demodulator for the signal being received.

A Character Code For Digital Information

As they studied voice transmission, researchers also considered transmission of digital information. They found ways to encode the basic values of a bit in an electrical signal (e.g., using a positive voltage to encode *1* and a negative voltage to encode *0*). In addition, they devised a sequence of bits to represent each letter and digit.

Although the character codes used on modern computer networks use two basic values, they differ from Morse code because each character is assigned a code with the same number of bits. For example, Morse code uses a single dot for the letter *E* and three dots for the letter *S*. By contrast, many modern character codes assign a sequence of seven 0's and 1's to each letter. Having a uniform number of bits for all characters makes character processing faster and the hardware less expensive. It also simplifies character storage because each character occupies a constant number of bits regardless of the specific character.

The *American Standard Code for Information Interchange (ASCII)* is among the most popular and widespread character codes used throughout the computer and network industry. ASCII defines a bit sequence for most characters used in English: upper and lower case letters, digits, punctuation, and a few miscellaneous symbols such as the mathematical symbols for less than, greater than, equal, plus, and minus.

The details of the ASCII encoding are unimportant because most people who use computers or networks never see the encodings. However, the examples shown in Figure 6.2 will help clarify the idea. ASCII uses the 7-bit sequence 1000101 to represent the letter "E", the sequence 1010011 to represent the letter "S", and the sequence 0101100 to represent a comma.

To summarize:

> *Many networks use the ASCII code when sending textual information in digital form. ASCII assigns a 7-bit code to each letter and digit. Most users never see ASCII because it is an internal detail that remains hidden.*

A 1000001	S 1010011	a 1100001	s 1110011
B 1000010	T 1010100	b 1100010	t 1110100
C 1000011	U 1010101	c 1100011	u 1110101
D 1000100	V 1010110	d 1100100	v 1110110
E 1000101	W 1010111	e 1100101	w 1110111
F 1000110	X 1011000	f 1100110	x 1111000
G 1000111	Y 1011001	g 1100111	y 1111001
H 1001000	Z 1011010	h 1101000	z 1111010
I 1001001	0 0110000	i 1101001	. 0101110
J 1001010	1 0110001	j 1101010	, 0101100
K 1001011	2 0110010	k 1101011	? 0111111
L 1001100	3 0110011	l 1101100	) 0101001
M 1001101	4 0110100	m 1101101	{ 1111011
N 1001110	5 0110101	n 1101110	/ 0101111
O 1001111	6 0110110	o 1101111	& 0100110
P 1010000	7 0110111	p 1110000	+ 0101011
Q 1010001	8 0111000	q 1110001	- 0101101
R 1010010	9 0111001	r 1110010	= 0111101

Figure 6.2 Examples of the ASCII encoding. The upper and lower case letters each have a code. Users never see the encoding.

Detecting Errors

Much of the early work on digital communication focused on error detection and correction. Researchers studied the errors that occur when sending electrical signals across a wire, and found ways to detect the errors. For example, they knew that natural phenomena like lightning can cause random electrical signals to appear on wires and become confused with signals that carry information. They also found that electrical signals on wires can become distorted when the wire carrying them passes through a strong magnetic field (e.g., near an electric motor in a household appliance).

When electric or magnetic interference disrupts signals on a wire, data can be damaged or lost. For example, if voltage is used to represent a bit, a bolt of lightning that strikes near a wire can cause the voltage to change even if lightning does not hit the wire directly. The point to remember is:

When using electrical signals to communicate digital information, electrical or magnetic interference can cause the value of one or more bits to be changed.

To guard against corruption of information caused by random electrical noise, researchers devised mechanisms to detect and correct the problem. For example, they found that they could detect small errors if they added an extra bit to a character's code and set the extra bit to *1* if the character had an odd number of *1*s, or to *0* if it had an even number of *1*s. In essence, the sender sets the extra bit so that each character has an even number of bits set to *1*.

The extra bit is called a *parity bit*. Character *E* will be assigned parity bit *1* because its 7-bit code, 1000101, contains an odd number of *1* bits. However, character *S* will be assigned parity bit *0* because its 7-bit code, 1010011, contains an even number of *1* bits.

To make parity checking work, a receiver must test the parity of each incoming character. The receiver examines all bits that arrived, including the parity bit. The receiver declares that an error occurred if it finds an odd number of bits turned on, and declares that the character arrived undamaged otherwise. If electrical interference changes one of the bits during transmission, the receiver rejects the character as damaged because it will find an odd number of bits turned on.

Although parity checking helps find minor problems, it does not guarantee that all errors will be detected. To understand why, think of the bits for a character traveling across a wire. Random electrical interference can cause some bits that start out as *1* to change to *0*, or it can cause some bits that start out as *0* to change to *1*. If it happens that in a given character, the electrical interference changes an even number of *1* bits to *0*s, the parity bit will still appear to be correct. Similarly, if the noise changes an even number of *0* bits to *1*s the parity will also appear to be correct. As an extreme case, think of what happens if a strong magnetic field changes all bits of a character to zero. The result appears to have correct parity. The point is:

Adding a parity bit to each character code before transmission can help the hardware detect errors that occur when transmitting the character across a network. However, parity alone is not sufficient to detect all possible errors; more powerful techniques are needed.

Indeed, the Internet error checking techniques detect errors that parity alone cannot. In the rare case that bits become damaged in transit, the receiver declares that an error occurred, and the communication software handles the problem.

How does Internet software detect damaged bits? The software uses a technique called a *checksum*. Instead of sending one extra parity bit, the software sends the sum of the numbers in the message. For example, if a message consists of the numbers *1*, *3*, and *5*, the software sends four values — the message followed by the sum of the values in the message:

$$1 \quad 3 \quad 5 \quad 9$$

When the message arrives, the receiving software sums all the values except the last, and then checks to ensure the sum equals the last value. If any of the values are damaged during transmission, the sum will not compare equal.

Summary

Researchers have studied the properties of electrical signals on wires, and have learned how to use electrical signals to encode information like voice. In addition, researchers have found ways to use electrical signals to encode digital information by sending bits. They devised codes that assign each character a unique string of bits. In particular, they devised the ASCII code that many computers and computer networks use.

Researchers devised a transmission scheme of particular importance that uses modulation to encode information for transmission. Modulation starts with a carrier, an oscillating signal such as an audible tone, and uses information to change the carrier slightly before transmission. The receiver extracts the information by measuring how the incoming signal deviates from a perfect carrier.

A device that provides modulation and demodulation is called a modem; modems are used for sending information a long distance across wires or when sending information across a dial-up telephone connection. Modems are currently used on almost all transmission lines throughout the Internet.

Researchers also studied transmission errors and found mechanisms like the parity scheme that hardware can use to detect when electrical interference has damaged bits during transfer. Although parity can help detect errors, it does not solve the problem completely. The Internet uses more powerful error detection techniques like a checksum.

7

The Local Area Network Arrives

Introduction

Motivated by the need for better telephone communication, much of the early work on communication focused on ways to span large geographic distances. Indeed, researchers still study the problem of long-distance communication and look for ways to improve transmission. In the late 1960s and early 1970s, new networking technologies emerged that had a more immediate impact on the average person. This chapter examines the new technologies, and describes how they changed the economics of computing.

Motivation

Known as *Local Area Network* (LAN) technologies, the new networks were motivated by two trends. First, computers had grown smaller and less expensive. In place of large bulky mainframe computers that cost several million dollars, groups began acquiring smaller, less expensive computers called *minicomputers*. Second, people began to understand that computers could help with many of the tasks in an ordinary office.

Low-cost minicomputers changed computing. When each computer cost more than a million dollars, most organizations could only aspire to have a single computer. As computers became inexpensive, however, it became obvious that each organization could benefit from having several computers. It became equally obvious that organizations with many computers needed to move data among them to facilitate information sharing.

Interchangeable Media

The first data transfers from one computer to another involved removable media storage devices, usually magnetic tapes or disks. Although the early disks were physically large and bulky, they worked like modern DVDs. An operator placed a blank disk into a disk drive attached to a computer, and arranged for the computer to write data on it. The operator then moved the disk to a disk drive attached to another computer, and instructed a second computer to read the data.

A Computer Consists Of Circuit Boards

To understand how computer networks were formed, one must understand the basics of how computers are built. Inside a computer, electronic components reside on thin, flat rectangular boards called *circuit boards*. Each circuit board contains both electronic components and the wires that connect them.

Not all computers have the same circuit boards. Typically, a computer has a large circuit board that is known as a *motherboard*. When someone buys a computer, he or she must choose among various options; the options selected determine which additional circuit boards, called *daughter boards*, the computer will contain. For example, one person can choose to purchase a printer and a video camera for their computer, while another person chooses a CD player and two disks. A vendor installs the appropriate daughter boards to create the computer that the customer ordered.

Circuit Boards Plug Into A Computer

To make installing daughter boards easy, computer manufacturers build a computer so it contains a set of sockets. Wires on the motherboard connect the sockets to each other and to other parts of the computer. For example, some of the wires in each socket carry electric power to the circuit board. The computer uses other wires to carry data. Figure 7.1 illustrates the sockets one might see in a computer.

Each daughter board contains a plug that exactly matches a socket on the motherboard. In addition, each daughter board that controls an external device (e.g., a printer) has an additional cable that connects to the device. Assembling a computer means plugging a set of daughter boards into the computer's sockets. Plugging in a daughter board is not difficult — many people who own personal computers add or replace daughter boards to upgrade their computers.

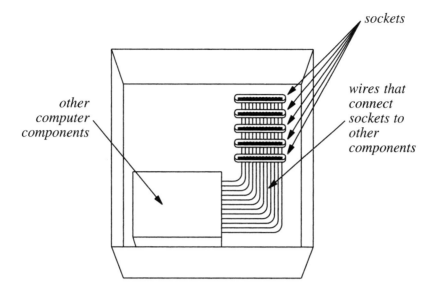

Figure 7.1 Illustration of the components visible in a computer when the cover has been removed. A daughter board can plug into each socket; wires connect the sockets to other components.

Connecting One Computer To Another

The first hardware that engineers built to transfer data between two computers electronically consisted of two daughter boards connected by a cable as Figure 7.2 illustrates.

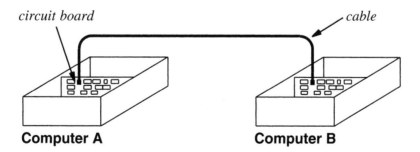

Figure 7.2 Illustration of an early computer communication system formed using two daughter boards plugged into sockets in two computers.

Once communication circuits have been plugged into the computers and connected by a cable, the computers use them to transfer data electronically. The daughter boards operate like an Input/Output (I/O) device (e.g., like a disk). To communicate, one computer writes data to its daughter board as if it were writing the data to a disk. The electronic circuits on the two daughter boards cooperate to move the data between them, and then the other computer reads data from its daughter board as if it were reading the data from a disk.

The chief advantage of a direct connection from one computer to another is speed. Because the sockets in a computer provide the fastest path to the computer's memory, daughter boards can be built that move data from one computer to another quickly.

The chief disadvantages of a direct connection are inconvenience and cost. The method is expensive because one must install costly new circuit boards in each pair of computers that are interconnected. It is inconvenient because it requires considerable effort to add a new computer to the set. Furthermore, if two computers are not the same, it may be impossible to find a pair of daughter boards to interconnect them. Connecting computers directly is also inconvenient because the computers must be running to make communication possible. For example, Figure 7.3 shows three computers connected by two communication links. In the figure, computer *B* must be running before computer *A* can send a message to computer *C*.

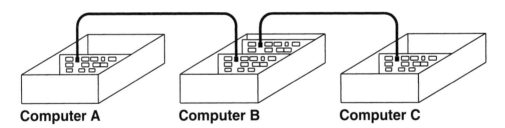

Computer A   **Computer B**   **Computer C**

Figure 7.3 Two pairs of daughter boards connecting three computers. Each new computer added to the set requires a new pair of daughter boards and an additional cable.

LAN Technologies

LAN (Local Area Network) technologies solve the problem of computer communication in a way that is convenient, inexpensive, and reliable. Instead of connecting one computer directly to another, LAN technologies use hardware to interconnect multiple computers. The ''network'' exists independent of the computers themselves. If one computer connected to a LAN is down, other computers can still communicate.

LAN technologies are designed for use across short distances. In general, one can think of *LAN* as meaning ''within a building.'' Because LANs only need to span short distances, it is possible to transmit an electrical signal that remains strong enough to reach the end of the LAN before it experiences any significant loss. Therefore, LANs do not need amplifiers to boost signal strength.

In many LAN systems, a cable connects each computer to a small electronic device called a *hub* or *switch*† that forms the ''center'' of the LAN. Figure 7.4 illustrates how multiple computers connect to a LAN.

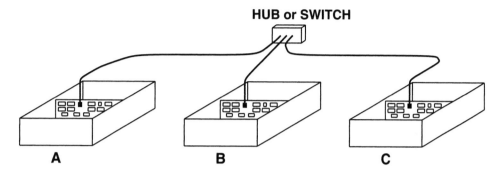

Figure 7.4 Computers connected to a LAN. Each computer attaches to a hub or switch with a cable; the computers can then communicate directly.

In an office building, the cables connecting computers to a LAN usually run in hallway ceilings. Each cable plugs into a hub or switch.

LAN hardware is engineered for reliability. To make the system more robust, correct operation does not depend on all computers running or all hardware working. Even if the daughter board in an individual computer fails or the connection between a computer and the LAN breaks, the remaining computers can continue to communicate.

To summarize:

> *A computer communication technology is classified as a* Local Area Network (LAN) *if it provides a way to interconnect multiple computers across short distances. LANs are inexpensive, highly reliable, and convenient to install and manage.*

Connecting A Computer To A LAN

To connect to a LAN, a computer needs network interface hardware. From the computer's point of view, a LAN interface operates like the interface for an I/O device. Physically, the network interface hardware consists of two parts: a daughter board popu-

---

†Conceptually, a hub and switch operate exactly the same. A switch costs more, and under some circumstances can send data faster.

larly called a *Network Interface Card* (*NIC*) that plugs into the computer and a cable that connects the NIC to the LAN.

The processor in a computer uses the NIC to access the LAN. It can request that the NIC send a message to another computer over the LAN or read the next incoming message.

> *A computer needs additional hardware to connect it to a local area network. The hardware consists of a Network Interface Card that plugs into the computer's motherboard and a cable that attaches the NIC to the LAN. Once connected, a computer uses the NIC to send and receive data.*

A LAN remains independent from the computers it connects. For example, the format of data and the speed at which data traverses the LAN does not depend on the computers that attach. In each computer, the network interface card places data in the form required by the LAN, and compensates for differences in speed between the computer and the network. To do so, the NIC usually contains a microprocessor and a small amount of high-speed random access memory. The NIC uses the high-speed memory to hold each incoming or outgoing message so it can be transferred to the LAN at the speed the network uses, and can be transferred to the computer at the speed the computer uses.

For example, when computer *A* sends a message to computer *B*, it does not send the message directly from its memory across the LAN. Instead, computer *A* moves a copy of the message to its network interface card. The NIC in *A* transmits the message across the LAN to the NIC in computer *B* at the speed the LAN uses. After the NIC on *B* has received the message, it moves a copy into *B*'s memory. The two computers do not need to operate at the same speed as each other or as fast as the LAN because only the network interface cards are used during transmission or reception of data. The important idea is:

> *Because each computer attached to a LAN contains interface hardware that isolates the computer from the LAN, the speed of the LAN does not depend on the speed of computers that attach to it. As a result, heterogeneous computers can communicate across a LAN.*

The Importance Of LAN Technology

LAN technologies changed the way people used computer networks. Before LAN technologies were available, people thought of computer communication as a way to cross large geographic boundaries. Once LAN technologies emerged, people began to use networks to connect machines within a room or within a building.

The most significant change that LAN technologies produced was resource sharing. Before LAN technologies, a computer existed in a self-contained island. Each computer had a specific set of I/O devices like printers and disks, and each computer had one copy of the software that users could access. Once LAN technologies became available, a set of computers could share resources like printers.

The ability to share resources changed the economics of computing dramatically. Because a network connection was much less expensive than a set of I/O devices, it became sensible to hook many computers to a network and to use the network to provide shared access to the I/O devices. To summarize:

> *Local area networks changed the economics of computing because they made it possible to use inexpensive computers that shared access to resources like printers and disks.*

Relationship To The Internet

When the Internet project began, Local Area Network technologies were just emerging. Xerox Corporation had given several universities a prototype version of a new LAN technology that had been developed in one of its research labs. Called *Ethernet*, the technology was destined to become the leading LAN technology.

Internet researchers imagined a future in which LAN technology would become inexpensive and widely available. They assumed, for example, that each organization would use one or more LANs to interconnect all its computers. They designed the Internet with the assumed future in mind. It turned out that their assumption was correct.

A Brief History Of The Internet

...how the Internet grew from its humble beginnings to become the largest network in the world

8

Internet: The Early Years

Many Independent Networks

By the late 1970s, computer networking began to blossom. Several computer manufacturers introduced small minicomputers with sufficient computational power to handle many users. Because such computers are inexpensive, each department in a large organization can afford one.

To interconnect minicomputers and to permit the rapid transfer of information among them, many organizations began installing Local Area Networks. Because LAN technology is both inexpensive and easy to install, an individual department can purchase, install, and operate a LAN for their machines without consulting a central administration.

The Proliferation Of LANs

Allowing each group within an organization to build and operate a computer network has both advantages and disadvantages. When granted independence, a group can choose a network technology appropriate for their needs. They can budget funds to pay for the LAN installation and operation, can decide who has access, and can devise policies regarding network use.

Allowing autonomy can also have severe disadvantages. Most important, because not all computer vendors supply interface hardware for all types of networks, allowing groups to act independently can encourage a proliferation of many LAN technologies.

Facts About LANs

To understand how and why local area networks have proliferated, one must understand three facts:

1. Engineers have devised many LAN technologies.

   LAN hardware can be designed to achieve a combination of speed, reliability, ease of installation, capacity, and cost. Engineers have designed network hardware for several combinations.

2. LAN performance determines cost; high performance LANs are more expensive.

   As one might expect, hardware that transfers data faster costs more money. The consequence is that a given group may choose to save money by acquiring a LAN that has lower performance. Indeed, it is possible to install a LAN with only trivial cost.

3. A particular LAN technology may only work with specific computers.

   Recall that network interface hardware is needed to connect a given computer to a LAN. A computer vendor may not offer interface hardware for all types of LANs. In particular, when a computer vendor develops a LAN technology, the vendor usually sells interfaces only for its computers. Even when the LAN technology is developed by a company that does not sell computers, the company usually sells bus interface hardware only for the most popular computer brands.

Fact *3* suggests that when a group decides to acquire and install a LAN, choices may be limited by the availability of products. If the group owns a set of computers, they must verify that interface hardware is available for each computer. Fact *2* suggests that the choice of a LAN technology may depend on economics. Two groups within an organization can choose different LAN technologies if they have different amounts of money to spend. Finally, Fact *1* suggests that there are many possible technologies from which to choose.

The consequence of the above facts is simple: because each group in an organization can choose a technology that best meets its needs, most large organizations have many LAN technologies in use. Some are chosen for speed, others for ease of installation or maintenance, and still others for minimum cost. To summarize:

> *A LAN technology is chosen for its speed, ease of use, and the availability of interfaces for specific computers. Most large organizations use many LAN technologies.*

LANs Are Incompatible

The disappointing news about LAN technologies can be summed up succinctly:

Various LAN technologies are completely incompatible.

That is, multiple LANs cannot just be plugged together. For example, suppose a given organization has two LANs, one in the shipping department and one in the accounting department. Further suppose that someone needs to transfer information that is stored on a computer in the shipping department to a computer in the accounting department. Connecting the two LAN cables does not solve the problem.

There are several technical reasons why one cannot plug together multiple LANs. First, a given LAN technology is engineered to operate over a limited distance. Each technology specifies a maximum cable length (e.g., one popular technology specifies that the cable must be 500 meters or less). Adding more distance to a LAN can result in a malfunction. Second, each LAN technology has its own specification for electrical signals like voltage and frequency; different LAN technologies may be electrically incompatible. Third, each technology has a way of encoding information (e.g., a form of modulation); the encoding used by one LAN system does not make sense to another.

Wide Area Technologies Exist

In addition to LAN technologies, another form of computer networking emerged in the 1960s and 1970s. Scientists and engineers devised ways to build networks that connected multiple computers across large geographic distances. Called *Wide Area Networks (WANs)* or *long-haul networks*, the long-distance technologies use the same basic mechanisms as earlier long-distance systems. For example, WANs use modems to send signals across long-distance transmission lines. However, WANs do more than connect two computers across a single transmission channel – a WAN uses computers to unify a set of transmission lines into a coordinated system. To do so, a WAN includes a small, dedicated computer at each site that attaches to the transmission line and keeps the network operating independently from the computers that use it. The dedicated computer receives an incoming message from another site and delivers it to one of the local computers. It accepts a message from any of the local computers and sends the message across a transmission line toward the destination. To summarize:

A Wide Area Network technology (WAN) differs from a set of disjoint transmission lines because the WAN includes an additional special-purpose computer at each site that connects to the transmission lines and keeps communication independent of the computers that use the WAN.

To understand how a WAN can be useful, imagine a company with offices in four cities: New York, Chicago, Los Angeles, and Austin. The company can install a WAN that links computers in each office. Physically, the WAN might consist of three leased transmission lines: one from Chicago to New York, another from Chicago to Los Angeles, and a third from Chicago to Austin, plus a small, dedicated computer at each site. Conceptually, the WAN functions much like a LAN except that it operates more slowly. It allows all the attached computers to communicate.

A WAN understands how transmission lines interconnect computers, and handles the details of passing messages automatically. In the example above, when a computer in Los Angeles sends a message to a computer in Austin, the message must pass through Chicago. However, the message does not pass through all the company's computers in Chicago – it only passes through the special purpose computer that is part of the WAN hardware. From the company's point of view, a computer in Los Angeles can communicate with a computer in Austin even when the company's computers in Chicago are temporarily shut down.

Few WANs, Many LANs

Although WAN technologies have been available for many years, WANs cost much more than LANs. To compare, think of the cost of a LAN. By installing a few cables in a single building, a company can create a LAN that interconnects its computers. Furthermore, once the cables are in place, the company can add connections to new computers, incrementally growing the LAN as needed.

Unlike the low cost LAN, a WAN requires more planning and significantly more hardware. To install a WAN, a company must lease long-distance transmission lines as well as acquire modems, special-purpose hardware devices, and the software used by a WAN. The company also needs interface hardware that connects each of the company's computers to the WAN. Because transmission lines and hardware devices that form a WAN are expensive, only a few companies build their own WAN. As a result, LANs are much more popular than WANs.

WANs and LANs Are Incompatible

Engineers have invented a variety of WAN technologies. Each technology has an independent design, chosen for reliability, speed, distance spanned, and cost. Each technology chooses the details of ways to encode data. Thus, most WAN technologies are electrically incompatible with one another; one cannot create a larger network merely by plugging wires from one type of WAN into another.

Companies that use WANs often choose a single WAN technology to link all their sites, so incompatibility among WANs is not usually a severe problem within a company. However, a serious problem can arise because WANs are electrically incompatible with LANs. Most companies that have a WAN connecting their sites also use a LAN to connect the computers within each site. Unfortunately, incompatibility means that the company's WAN cannot connect directly to any of the company's LANs.

To summarize:

> *Many Local Area Network and Wide Area Network technologies exist, and most are incompatible with each other. One cannot produce a usable, large network merely by interconnecting the wires from two different networks.*

The Desirability Of A Single Network

Anyone who uses multiple computers that connect to two or more separate network systems understands how inconvenient the scheme can be. For example, if one computer attaches to a LAN and another attaches to a WAN, neither has access to all resources in the organization. A computer attached to a WAN can access resources and information on remote machines, but cannot easily access information on local machines. A computer attached to a LAN can access resources and information on local machines, but cannot access information on remote machines. Simple tasks that require local access (e.g., printing output on a local printer) are tedious or impossible for machines that only connect to a WAN. At the same time, tasks that require access to remote parts of the company (e.g., access to a remote database) are impossible for machines that only connect to a LAN. In some organizations, a user who needs access to both local and remote services must have two keyboards and two display screens on their desk. Transferring data between the two computer systems can be awkward and time consuming.

In the best of all worlds, each computer in an organization has access to all resources. Of course, policies on use may restrict the set of resources a given computer or user can access, and systems try to keep resources secure from unauthorized use.

However, it should be unnecessary to manually transfer data from one network to another. It should also be unnecessary to force users to move from one computer to another merely to access different resources.

The Department Of Defense Had Multiple Networks

By the late 1960s, the U.S. Department Of Defense became interested in using computer networks. Because the idea of computer networking was new, little was known about how to build networks or how they could be used. Through the *Defense Advanced Research Projects Agency (DARPA)*†, the military funded research on networking using a variety of technologies. By the late 1970s, ARPA had several operational computer networks and had begun to pass technology on to the military. ARPA projects included a Wide Area Network called the *ARPANET* as well as networks that used satellites and radio transmission for communication.

ARPA realized the military would face a problem that many organizations with multiple network systems faced: each network connected a set of computers, but no path existed between computers on separate networks. In essence, each network formed an isolated island that connected a set of computers, with no path between the islands.

Connecting Disconnected Machines

ARPA research examined how to interconnect all machines from a large organization. ARPA started with a few basic ideas, awarded grants to researchers in both industry and academia, and arranged for the researchers to cooperate in solving the problem. Researchers discussed their findings, and generated new ideas at regular meetings.

Instead of allowing researchers to engage in theoretical discussions, ARPA encouraged them to apply their ideas to real computers. ARPA chose researchers interested in experimental work, and insisted that they build prototype software to test their ideas.

The Internet Emerges

A key idea in the ARPA research was a new approach to interconnecting LANs and WANs that became known as an *internetwork*. The term is usually abbreviated *internet*‡, and is applied to both the project and to the prototype network that was built. To distinguish their internet from other internets, researchers working on the ARPA project adopted the convention of writing *internet* in lower case when referring to inter-

---

†At various times during the latter 1980s and early 1990s, DARPA has been called the *Advanced Research Projects Agency (ARPA)*.

‡Chapter 13 discusses the structure of an internet in detail and shows how the Internet connects multiple networks.

networks in general, and writing *Internet* with an uppercase I when referring to their experimental prototype. The convention persists. The key point is:

> *ARPA funded research to investigate ways to solve the problem of incompatible networks. Both the project and the prototype system that researchers built became known by the name* Internet.

The ARPANET Backbone

The ARPANET was especially important to the Internet project, and was often called the *backbone* network because it was the central WAN that tied researchers together. Each researcher working on the Internet project had a computer connected to the ARPANET.

Although having a Wide Area Network in place helped researchers communicate, the ARPANET became a key part of the Internet project because it allowed researchers to attach more than one computer at each site. Researchers took advantage of the feature and used ARPANET for two purposes. First, they used the ARPANET like a conventional WAN to connect a computer at each site. Second, they added an additional connection at each site, and arranged to use the additional connection to experiment with new ideas. Thus, the ARPANET served as both a standard network that permitted researchers to move data among sites involved in the project, and as an experimental network that allowed researchers to evaluate new network software and applications.

Internet Software

Computer software forms an important part of the technology that makes it possible to interconnect networks†. ARPA's Internet project produced many innovations to make networking more general and efficient. Researchers worked individually and in groups to invent, test, and refine new ways of making computers communicate. The research produced software that made communication possible and useful.

Although the software consists of many programs that interact in complex ways, researchers wanted the software to form an integrated system. They studied the interactions among various programs to ensure that the actions taken by one program did not conflict with actions taken by others. The end result is a smooth, apparently seamless software design. The parts work together so well that most users do not sense the underlying complexity.

---

†Chapters 15 through 18 discuss the software that makes internetworking possible and efficient.

The Name Is TCP/IP

Two pieces of the Internet software stand out as particularly important and innovative. The *Internet Protocol* (*IP*) software provides basic communication. The *Transmission Control Protocol* (*TCP*) software provides additional facilities that applications need. In informal discussions, researchers identify the entire set of Internet communication software by the initials of these two important parts; usually the term is written with a slash between the names: *TCP/IP*†.

When a more formal name is needed for the set of software specifications, researchers use *The TCP/IP Internet Protocol Suite*. The formal name is more accurate because it points out that the entire set contains more than just the two protocols. In the end, however, the simpler name has persisted – both vendors who sell the technology as well as users who acquire and install it use the term *TCP/IP*.

The Shock Of An Open System

To encourage vendors to adopt Internet technology, ARPA decided to make the research results public. Whenever a researcher discovered a new technique, measured network performance, or extended the TCP/IP software, ARPA asked that the researcher document the results in a report. All the specifications needed to build TCP/IP software, and all the experience installing and using it were documented. ARPA made the reports available to everyone.

ARPA's practice of publishing network specifications was surprising because most commercial companies that devise network technologies keep their discoveries private. In fact, many companies file patent applications to guarantee that no other company can use the same techniques. The idea derives from standard business practice:

> *Prevailing business opinion suggests that a company selling computer networks can achieve maximum profits by protecting their technology with patents.*

The idea seems to make sense. After all, if a vendor only allows its own brand of computers to attach to its brand of network, sales should increase. The vendor merely needs to convince an organization to use its network technology, and the organization will be forced to buy the vendor's computers.

In the mid-1970s, major computer companies that sold network systems only offered interface hardware that could connect to their own computers. The technologies included various combinations of LANs and WANs. Computer professionals apply the term *closed* to proprietary systems to suggest that they are closed to outsiders (i.e., they exclude computers designed by other vendors).

---

†One pronounces the name by spelling out the letters ''T-C-P-I-P''.

From its inception, the Internet project aspired to produce an *open* system that permitted computers from all vendors to communicate. The open philosophy meant that researchers published all discoveries about the Internet and all specifications needed to build TCP/IP software.

> *A network system is* closed *if a company owns the technology and uses patents and trade secrets to prevent other companies from building products that use it. By contrast, the Internet is an* open *system because all specifications are publicly available and any company can build a compatible technology.*

Open Systems Are Necessary

Computer companies found that, despite their efforts to sell closed systems, customers began to acquire several brands of computers. Advances in processor and memory hardware made new computer designs possible. Plummeting costs made personal computers affordable. Organizations like the U.S. military realized that as computer technology evolved, vendors would continually offer new models. Furthermore, not all software worked on all computers. A large organization usually has many brands and models of computers because it needs software systems and computers for many purposes. Only an open network system can be used to interconnect computers from multiple vendors. In summary:

> *A large organization needs an open network system because it acquires computers from multiple vendors; using a closed network system restricts the computers that can connect to the network.*

TCP/IP Documentation Is Online

Most of the researchers that ARPA chose for the Internet project already had experience using computer networks. They had helped design and build the ARPANET, and had devised applications that used it. They knew they could use the ARPANET to exchange technical information. Soon after the Internet project began, they decided to keep all technical documents in computer files accessible over the ARPANET.

Initially, the researchers planned to issue reports in two steps. When a report was first written, it would be made available to other researchers for comments. After a short time, the author would incorporate all comments and issue a final version of the report. To implement the two steps, researchers established two series of reports: *Requests For Comments* (*RFCs*) and *Internet Engineering Notes* (*IENs*).

Unfortunately, the best laid plans often go astray. Researchers found that some of the initial reports were sufficient and did not need revision or improvement. Other reports were rewritten completely, but reissued as an RFC for another round of comments. Most researchers found it more productive to continue investigating new ideas than to edit old reports. In the end, RFC reports became the official record of the project and the IEN series was dropped. The irony is that each of the documents that specifies the technology of the largest, most successful computer network in history has a label that implies the work is unfinished and the author is still waiting tenuously for comments. To summarize:

> *For historical reasons, the documents that define TCP/IP and related Internet technology are called* Requests For Comments.

Researchers working on the Internet project had access to all Requests For Comments documents because they were stored on a computer attached to the ARPANET. Each RFC was assigned an integer number, and an index was kept that listed the title of each number. At any time, a researcher who wanted to know the details of a particular piece of Internet software could use the ARPANET to retrieve the RFC that contained the information. If the researcher did not remember which RFC was needed, they could retrieve the index.

Keeping the project documentation accessible across the network enabled everyone working on the project to coordinate their activities and keep software up-to-date with the specifications. More important, rapid communication among the researchers increased the speed at which the project progressed.

> *Because RFCs that documented the technical details of TCP/IP and the Internet project were accessible over the ARPANET, work on the project proceeded more quickly.*

As the Internet project progressed, the technology reached a stage where prototype software could be deployed and tested. A fledgling Internet was born. One of the first applications that researchers devised for the new Internet was a mechanism that could be used to access RFCs. In fact, almost all the initial applications for the Internet provided some form of communication among the researchers building it.

The Military Adopts TCP/IP

By 1982, a prototype Internet was in place and the TCP/IP technology had been tested. A few dozen academic and industrial research sites had been using TCP/IP regularly. The U.S. military started to use TCP/IP on its networks.

In the beginning of 1983, ARPA expanded the Internet to include all military sites that connected to the ARPANET. The date marked a transition for the Internet as it began to change from an experiment to a useful network.

Summary

The Internet began as a research project funded by ARPA. Researchers studied ways to interconnect computers that used various kinds of networks. The name *Internet* refers to both the project and the prototype network system that researchers built.

Known by the name *TCP/IP*, the software used to make the Internet operate contains many complex computer programs that work together to provide communication. The software works so well that it hides the details of the underlying hardware and provides the illusion of a seamless system.

The Internet is an *open* system because the specifications needed to build TCP/IP software or use the Internet are available to everyone. Researchers who devised the Internet published technical information in a series of reports that describe the Internet and the TCP/IP software it uses. For historical reasons, each document in the series is labeled *Requests For Comments*.

A Personal Note

In the late 1990s while I was attending a technical conference, two attendees stepped into a crowded elevator carrying on a loud, animated conversation. One of them explained to the other that the Internet had been started as a secret government project to upgrade the ''hot line'' (the telephone system that ran between Washington and the Soviet Union during the years of the cold war). I wanted to interrupt the conversation, but I hesitated. The attendee doing most of the talking explained for the benefit of everyone in the elevator that the military had to cover up the project when Congress heard about it and decided to investigate the cost. He suggested that the military worked out an agreement with a large corporation. He said that the corporation paid money that was put into the treasury and, in exchange, the corporation received the technology. I wanted to interrupt and explain, but the attendee concluded emphatically that the whole episode clearly explained why the corporation's stock prices dropped rapidly during the preceding year. The pair left chattering and nodding in agreement.

When I stepped off the elevator, I was amused and puzzled. Later, I realized that something significant had happened. The Internet had become a powerful force quickly. To newcomers, it seemed vast, strange, and intimidating. Novices were shocked and ready to believe almost anything, including preposterous tales. Others were ready to invent a mythology that could explain it. Such tales would soon seep into urban legend.

FOR FURTHER STUDY

Many groups have attempted to compile histories of the Internet. As unfortunately happens, however, attempts to gather an accurate history in retrospect are difficult because memories tend to fade and individuals' self-interests tend to bias their recollections. Thus, many web pages contain specious or exaggerated claims about who started the Internet or who was involved in the early work.

One attempt to compile an accurate history can be found at:

www.nethistory.info

As a lighter, fun alternative, consider the hilarious spoof of Internet history found at:

http://dogme.burningman.com/~jeremymb/ioih

9

Two Decades Of Incredible Growth

Introduction

During the decades between 1980 to 2000, the Internet changed from a small, experimental research project into the world's largest computer network. In 1981, the Internet connected approximately one hundred computers at research sites and universities. Twenty years later, over sixty million computers were attached. This chapter chronicles the phenomenal growth of the Internet and the changes that accompanied it. It concludes by explaining some of the consequences that arise from the Internet's incredible rate of growth.

Disseminating The Software

In 1980, the Internet was merely a research project, but by 1985 it was becoming a viable network system. Experimental TCP/IP software was available for several brands of computers. A handful of universities and research labs had copies of the TCP/IP software, and were using it every day. The Internet reached researchers at a dozen academic and industrial research labs.

Before the U.S. military could use the Internet for production work, however, the technology needed to become more robust. The software needed to be polished and tested, and the whole system needed more tuning. ARPA considered the next step in its research program carefully.

Meanwhile, Back In Computer Science

While ARPA worked on the Internet research project, another technology came from a research lab and swept the computer science community: the *UNIX Operating System*. Although vendors use the term *operating system* to refer to the simple support software that comes with a personal computer, computer scientists use the term to describe the complex software that manages the computer, controls I/O devices, and provides file storage on multi-user computers. Operating systems are so complex that scientists and engineers spent years in the 1960s trying to understand them. Computer vendors sold proprietary operating systems for each of their computers.

A team of computer scientists at Bell Laboratories built a new operating system in the early 1970s. They called it *The UNIX Timesharing System*. Because Bell Laboratories used a variety of computers, the researchers built the system to be general — they designed the software carefully so it could be moved to new computers easily.

Bell Labs allowed universities to obtain copies of the UNIX system for use in teaching and research. Because they were interested in measuring its portability, Bell Labs gave away the system and encouraged universities to try running it on new machines. As a result, the UNIX system became one of the first operating systems that students could study.

A group of faculty and graduate students from the University of California at Berkeley became interested in the UNIX system. They wrote application programs and modified the system itself. They added new features and experimented with programs that used a Local Area Network. To make the work available to other universities, researchers at Berkeley established a software distribution facility to mail out computer tapes that contained a copy of their software. The Berkeley version of the UNIX system, often called *BSD UNIX*†, became popular at other universities.

The Internet Meets UNIX

ARPA realized that the Berkeley software distributions reached many universities, and decided to use it to disseminate Internet software. They negotiated a research contract with Berkeley. Under the terms of the contract, ARPA gave researchers at Berkeley a copy of the TCP/IP software that had been developed as part of the Internet project. Berkeley incorporated the software into their version of the UNIX system, and modified application programs to use TCP/IP.

When Berkeley issued its next major software distribution, most computer science departments received TCP/IP software at virtually no cost. Although only a few computer science departments had computers connected to the Internet, most of them had a Local Area Network or were about to install one. They knew that their students needed to study networking. They also knew that using a network would make computing easier because it would allow users to share resources like printers.

---

†The acronym BSD stands for *Berkeley Software Distribution*.

For many departments, TCP/IP was the first viable networking software they had encountered. It offered a low-cost, efficient way to provide a departmental network and a technology that could be studied in classes. Thus, in a short time, most computer science departments had TCP/IP software running on their Local Area Networks. The point is:

> *Computer science departments in universities received TCP/IP software along with a release of UNIX system software from U. C. Berkeley. Although only a few departments had computers connected to the Internet, most of them used TCP/IP on their Local Area Networks for teaching, research, and production computing.*

The U.S. Military Makes A Commitment

In the early 1980s, the Internet operated reliably. It interconnected academic and research sites. More important, the Internet demonstrated that the basic principles of internetworking were sound. Convinced of the Internet's viability, the U.S. military started to connect computers to the Internet and to use TCP/IP software.

In 1982, the U.S. military chose the Internet as its primary computer communication system. Consequently, a cutoff date was planned. At the beginning of 1983, the ARPANET and associated military networks stopped running old communication software. All connections were switched to use TCP/IP, and any computer that did not understand TCP/IP could not communicate. The point is:

> *Although the U.S. military funded Internet research and eventually chose to use the Internet, internetworking was developed and tested at civilian sites.*

The Internet Doubles In Size In One Year

Before the U.S. military started switching its computers to TCP/IP, the Internet interconnected approximately two hundred computers. One year later, it had doubled in size. In retrospect, the increase seems trivial. It involved hundreds, not thousands of computers. At the time, however, the increase was significant.

As one might expect, the increase in Internet size uncovered limits in the computer software. For example, some parts of TCP/IP contain lists of other computers and the addresses used to access them. As new computers joined the Internet, the lists became too large; the software had to be changed to accommodate longer lists. Unlike modern computers, the computers in use in the early 1980s had a small amount of memory; researchers could not increase sizes arbitrarily. Any computer memory devoted to a list was unavailable for use with network devices or other programs. As a result, using more memory for lists meant the computer system ran slower.

At first, researchers made small increments to the software. They increased the capacity by ten or twenty percent. Soon, they found that it was insufficient, and further increases were needed. As the Internet continued to grow, the process of changing the software kept pace.

In addition to uncovering limitations in the software, the Internet growth revealed limits in manual and clerical procedures. For example, each time a new computer was added to the Internet, several people had to take action. Someone had to review the reasons for the connection and its relationship to the project before approving the connection. Someone else had to assign a name to the computer and then enter it in a database. Finally, someone had to make a physical connection between the computer and the network.

During the period of rapid growth, researchers were busy updating the software and had little spare time to help with manual procedures like registration; the duties began to pass to a professional staff. We can summarize what happened:

> As new computers were added to the Internet, it doubled in size in a single year. The rapid growth forced researchers to tune administrative procedures as well as the software.

Every Computer Science Department

In the late 1970s, many computer scientists recognized the importance of networking. A small group of researchers proposed a networking project to the *National Science Foundation (NSF)*†. Their goal was to devise a network that could connect all computer science researchers.

After reviewing the proposal and asking the group to revise it, the National Science Foundation funded a project to build the Computer Science Network. The project, which also had support from ARPA, became known as *CSNET*.

To reach all computer scientists in the country, CSNET had to contend with the problem of providing network service to a variety of institutions. Because large institutions could afford to pay more, CSNET encouraged them to run TCP/IP software and connect to the Internet. For smaller institutions that could not afford direct connections, CSNET devised ways to provide limited network services at much lower cost.

By the time the U.S. military selected the Internet as a primary computer communication system, many of the top computer science groups in industry and academia were already using it. Over the next few years, CSNET worked to provide Internet connections to computer science departments. As a result, by the mid-1980s, many computer scientists had Internet access.

---

†NSF, a U.S. federal agency, is responsible for funding research and education in science and engineering.

Graduate Students Volunteer Their Time

Connecting major computer science research groups to the Internet had an interesting effect. Although some computer scientists work in industrial research labs, many are professors who work in universities, where they also teach classes and advise students. The professors talked to students about the Internet project, the technology and software that it used, its success, and the remaining research problems. The professors' enthusiasm was contagious.

Students became interested in learning more about TCP/IP and the Internet. Graduate students who were searching for research topics began to investigate the technical details of TCP/IP software. They studied ways to extend the Internet technology, and devised experiments to measure its capabilities. They considered new applications, and found ways to extend the functionality. The result was synergistic: students gained valuable knowledge and experience with computer networks, while their creative energies helped advance Internet technologies.

The IAB evolves

Research scientists working on the Internet held regular meetings to discuss new ideas, review the technology, share discoveries, and exchange technical information. ARPA decided that with the Internet growing rapidly, the group of scientists should have a more formal structure and more responsibility for coordinating TCP/IP research and Internet development. It renamed the group the *Internet Activities Board*. Following military tradition, the board became known by its acronym, IAB.

ARPA appointed a chairman of the IAB, who was given the title *Internet Architect* (although the Internet was already growing too rapidly for a single person to seriously consider devising an architectural plan). Another member of the IAB was designated as the *RFC Editor* and given responsibility for reviewing and editing all RFCs before they were published. Others scientists on the IAB were each assigned a specific problem to investigate.

To study an assigned problem, each member of the IAB gathered volunteers from the research community to serve on a *task force*. The IAB member served as the task force chairperson, interacted with the task force members, and represented the task force at meetings of the IAB. Each task force held meetings to discuss ideas, resolve issues, generate new approaches, and report on experiments. If a task force reached a consensus on a new approach, members would build prototype software to demonstrate how their ideas worked in practice, and then would generate and submit a specification as an RFC.

The IAB guided the development of the Internet for many years. In 1989, it was reorganized to add representatives from commercial organizations. The IAB's duties and interactions with other groups were reorganized again in 1992, when it became part of the *Internet Society*. The IAB divested some of its technical responsibilities, passing more control to subordinate groups, and leaving the board as the ultimate arbiter of policies and standards. At the time of its second reorganization, the IAB kept the acronym, but changed its name to the *Internet Architecture Board*.

The IETF

Among all the task forces established by the IAB, one stands out: the *Internet Engineering Task Force (IETF)*. The IETF has survived reorganizations, and remains active. In fact, the IETF has grown so large that its subgroups have been partitioned into a dozen areas of interest, with a manager assigned to coordinate groups within each area. The IETF holds open meetings approximately three times per year, rotating the location among Europe, the U.S., and the Pacific rim. When it holds a meeting, hundreds of people attend, most from commercial companies. They are all volunteers who attend to hear about the latest developments and participate in efforts to refine and improve the software.

The IETF had as its original charter the problem of short-term Internet development. It now has responsibility for much of the technical direction, including adoption of specifications for new communication software or revisions of old software. Most RFCs now originate within the IETF from committees called *working groups*. To summarize:

> *The group responsible for guiding the research and development of the Internet is known as the* Internet Architecture Board *(IAB). The primary subgroup responsible for technical matters is known as the* Internet Engineering Task Force *(IETF)*.

Doubling Again In A Year

During the years following the military's decision to use the Internet, growth continued. In 1984, the Internet almost doubled in size again. However, size alone does not tell the story: government agencies other than ARPA began to use the Internet and to support research. For example, the *Department of Defense (DOD)* and the *National Aeronautics And Space Administration (NASA)* used TCP/IP on some of their networks, and would soon connect more networks to the Internet.

The Internet Improves Science

By the mid-1980s, the National Science Foundation (NSF) recognized that eminence in science would soon demand computer communication. Before computer networks, scientists exchanged ideas by publishing them in scientific journals. It took many months, sometimes years, between the time a scientist submitted a manuscript and the time a final version appeared in print.

Computer communication changed the way scientists do research. Scientists connected to the Internet can exchange documents or experimental data instantly. In fact, scientists can use the Internet to disseminate data as an experiment proceeds, making it possible for many other scientists to analyze the results without traveling to the site of the experiment. More important, scientists can use the Internet for informal discussions that are not published.

NSF Takes A Leadership Role

Recognizing how important the Internet was becoming to science, NSF decided to use some of its money to fund Internet growth and the TCP/IP technology. In 1985, NSF announced that it intended to connect researchers at *100* universities to the Internet. They advised the U.S. Congress of their plan, and received additional money to support networking. NSF consulted experts in the field, devised a plan, and began a program that resulted in major changes to the Internet.

Scientists often use sophisticated, high-speed computers called *supercomputers* to analyze data from their experiments. Because supercomputers are expensive, NSF had previously established five supercomputer centers around the country. A scientist working on an NSF project could use the nearest supercomputer center to analyze data.

NSF took the first step by building a Wide Area Network that interconnected computers at its five supercomputer centers. The network used TCP/IP, and provided a connection to the Internet. Named *NSFNET*, the network was much smaller, and not any faster, than the ARPANET. Scientists found the network useful, but not exciting.

Target: All Of Science And Engineering

NSF knew that the small network they built would not replace the ARPANET; it was only the beginning. While scientists began using the initial network to access the supercomputers, NSF made plans for a major new program. The program had an ambitious goal:

*NSF decided that to keep the U.S. competitive, it needed to extend net-
work access to every science and engineering researcher.*

Although NSF was impressed with the functionality that the Internet provided, it
knew that the ARPANET did not have sufficient capacity to achieve the goal. Clearly,
the Internet needed a new Wide Area Network.

NSF's Approach

NSF decided to use its funds to create a major new Internet that had significantly
more capacity than the existing Internet. After examining available technologies and reviewing its budget, NSF decided that it could not afford to pay for the entire project.
Instead, it decided to offer partial support, in the form of federal grants. Companies and
other organizations submitted written proposals to NSF to request funding to work on
the project.

NSF divided the grants into two types. First, NSF funded a group that wanted to
build and operate a new high-speed Wide Area Network to connect parts of the Internet.
The new WAN had to replace parts of the ARPANET as well as the original NSFNET.
Second, NSF funded groups that wanted to interconnect computers in a small region
and attach them to the new WAN. For example, NSF thought that each state might
choose to apply as a group. Originally, the groups were referred to as *NSF Regional
Networks*. Later, when it became clear that some of the groups spanned large geographic areas, NSF began referring to them as *NSF Mid-Level Networks*.

Because most universities or companies already had LANs connecting their computers, NSF decided to use its funds to help pay for long-distance connections; individual companies and schools paid for their own internal networks.

The NSFNET Backbone

NSF used a competitive bidding process when it awarded a grant for the new Internet WAN, which became known as the *NSFNET backbone*. In 1987, it asked for proposals and used a panel of scientists to help assess them. After considering the alternatives, NSF selected a joint proposal from three organizations: IBM, a computer
manufacturer; MCI, a long-distance telephone company; and MERIT, an organization
that built and operated a network connecting schools in Michigan.

The three groups cooperated to establish a new Wide Area Network that became
the backbone of the Internet in the summer of 1988. MCI provided long-distance
transmission lines, IBM provided the dedicated computers and software used in the
WAN, and MERIT operated the network. Most people referred to the new backbone
using the same name applied to its predecessor, *NSFNET*.

The ANS Backbone

Eventually, as traffic on the new WAN reached capacity, NSF approved reorganizing the network slightly and tripled the capacity of each transmission line. By the end of 1991, it became clear that the Internet was growing so fast that the NSFNET backbone would soon reach its capacity. NSF realized that the federal government could not afford to pay for the Internet indefinitely. They wanted private industry to assume some responsibility. To solve the problem, IBM, MERIT, and MCI formed a nonprofit company called *Advanced Networks and Services (ANS)*.

During 1992, ANS built a new Wide Area Network to serve as the Internet backbone. Known as *ANSNET*, the WAN used transmission lines with 30 times the capacity of the NSFNET backbone it replaced. Figure 9.1 illustrates the major ANSNET connections.

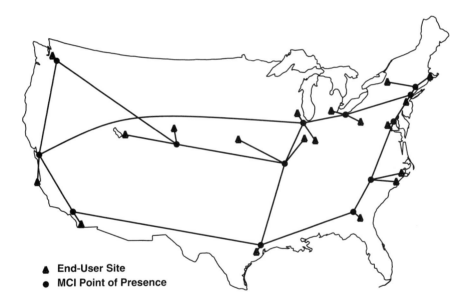

▲ **End-User Site**
● **MCI Point of Presence**

Figure 9.1 The Wide Area Network that formed the backbone of the Internet in 1995. Funding came from NSF, IBM, MCI, and MERIT.

ANSNET differed from the former NSFNET backbone in a significant way. ANS, not the federal government, owned the transmission lines and computers that comprised the network. Transferring ownership to a private company was one of the first steps toward commercialization and privatization of the Internet.

In 1995, MCI Corporation began work on a WAN with even higher capacity that was known as the very high-speed Backbone Network System (*vBNS*). Subsequently, NSF funded a backbone known as *Internet2* that is used to support research.

Exponential Growth

As NSF connected scientists and engineers, the Internet grew incredibly fast. In 1983, the Internet connected 562 computers. Ten years later, it connected over 1,200,000 computers and was growing quickly. Such staggering growth can best be understood by considering individual computers:

> *By 1999, the Internet was growing so fast that, on the average, a computer was added to the Internet every second; by 2006 the average exceeded ten computers per second.*

Although the Internet did not grow at exactly the same rate in all years and most of the computers were added in recent years, a trend of doubling can be identified. In round numbers the Internet has experienced sustained growth of approximately *10* percent per month, doubling in size approximately every *10* months. Mathematicians call such growth *exponential*. The table in Figure 9.2 illustrates growth from 1983 through 2006.

Exponential growth has some interesting properties. For example, although the Internet has been around for many years, exponential growth means that approximately half the people connected to the Internet have gained access in the past year. Interestingly, that same statement could have been made in any previous year. In fact, the following summarizes the incredible growth:

> *At any time from 1983 through 2005, approximately half the Internet growth occurred in the previous 12 to 14 months.*

Another way to look at exponential growth puts it in terms of an individual. In the beginning, a person who acquires access to the Internet feels like a novice. It seems as if many people have had access for a long time. After a year, the individual can feel content knowing that slightly over half the Internet users have gained access more recently.

Extending the time scale for exponential growth makes one appreciate it more. If exponential growth continues, three years after an individual gains access, over *87%* of all Internet users have gained access more recently. In six years, the figure reaches *98%*. Six years ago, we thought the Internet was huge; it represents less than 10% of the current Internet.

Year	Approximate Number Of Computers On The Internet
1983	562
1984	1,024
1985	1,961
1986	2,308
1987	5,089
1988	28,174
1989	80,000
1990	290,000
1991	500,000
1992	727,000
1993	1,200,000
1994	2,217,000
1995	4,852,000
1996	9,472,000
1997	16,146,000
1998	29,670,000
1999	43,230,000
2000	73,000,000
2001	109,574,429
2002	147,344,723
2003	171,638,297
2004	233,101,481
2005	317,646,084

Figure 9.2 Estimates of computers connected to the Internet each year from 1983 through 2005. Starting around 2000, NAT technology made it difficult to obtain an accurate count; by 2005, a majority of computers on the Internet were hidden†.

A Commercial Assessment

Phenomenal growth has been both a curse and an opportunity. On one hand, it haunts groups who are responsible for operating the Internet and pushes engineers who must plan new technologies that accommodate expansion. On the other hand, it provides an incredible opportunity for vendors who sell TCP/IP and Internet technologies.

In the mid 1980s, most implementations of TCP/IP software were found in universities or computer science research laboratories. Now, businesses and individuals use TCP/IP. Entire new industries have arisen; they sell products and services that connect

---

†Chapter 19 explains how NAT technology allows multiple computers to share a single address.

homes and businesses to the Internet. More important, companies sell services that deliver information across the Internet.

The End Of Growth

The Internet cannot continue to grow indefinitely. Although the technologies have managed to accommodate an incredible expansion, exponential growth must end soon. At its current growth rate, for example, the Internet will outpace worldwide production of computers. Furthermore, current Internet technology can connect a maximum of 4,294,967,295 computers†, which is several times larger than the number of computers in existence, but only about two-thirds of the world's population. When will growth slow to less than exponential? When will it stop?

At various times in the past, people have predicted the imminent collapse of the Internet by observing that some small piece of the technology was reaching its limit. By 1990, for example, someone had predicted that the Internet could not survive past March of 1993. In 1995, a group predicted that the Internet would collapse in the summer of 1997; in 1999, another group predicted collapse in 2004. The predictions of doom have been incorrect; the Internet keeps growing. Each time the traffic has approached the capacity of a backbone network, a new backbone technology has been developed with significantly more capacity. When the traffic approached the capacity of the dedicated switching computers that comprise the Internet, faster computers were created with significantly more processing power. While researchers agree that growth cannot continue unchecked, no one can predict when it will begin to slow down.

FOR FURTHER STUDY

The Internet Systems Consortium, Inc. uses the domain name system (described in Chapter 18) to obtain counts of computers with registered names. A summary can be found at:

http://www.isc.org/index.pl?/ops/ds

In addition to measuring the number of computers on the Internet, several groups attempt to estimate the number of individuals with Internet access. For example, estimates of users given by geographic area can be found at:

http://www.internetworldstats.com/stats.htm

---

†The limit arises because the numeric addresses TCP/IP uses to identify computers must be less than 4,294,967,296; new technologies allow multiple computers to ''share'' an address, and a new version of IP is being developed that overcomes the limitation.

10

The Global Internet

Introduction

Because it spans many countries, people often refer to the Internet as *The Global Internet*. This chapter describes the scope of the Internet, and gives examples of how it expanded to reach much of the world.

Early ARPA Networks

Most of the early network research ARPA funded focused on U.S. participants, a few of the research networks included connections to other countries. For example, ARPA used satellites to experiment with communication to sites in Norway and England.

As ARPA concentrated research funding on the Internet project, it used existing connections outside the U.S. to test Internet technology on a larger scale. Thus, those sites became the first foreign sites to have Internet access.

Electronic Mail Among Computers

While ARPA researchers worked on the Internet, other U.S. researchers also experimented with networking. Many of them had used electronic mail for communication with other users on a single timesharing computer. They realized that if a computer had access to basic communication, its electronic mail system could be extended to send messages to users on other machines. The researchers built software that used the dial-up telephone system to connect computers, and soon had electronic mail systems on multiple machines interconnected.

Extending electronic mail connections to machines outside the U.S. was trivial. Because the voice telephone network adheres to a set of standards, systems in multiple countries all interoperate. Thus, researchers did not need to add additional hardware to make communication possible. Like its U.S. counterpart, a foreign computer required only a modem and a copy of the software to enable communication.

One early computer network technology that offered electronic mail over the dial-up telephone system came with the UNIX system from Bell Laboratories. Called the *Unix to Unix Copy Program* or *UUCP*, the program handled the details of interacting with a modem, dialing the destination computer's telephone number or accepting incoming calls, and transferring electronic mail messages across the connection. UUCP ''networks'' arose as owners of machines agreed to cooperate in the exchange of electronic mail.

BITNET And FIDONET

Not everyone had a UNIX system. Researchers who used IBM mainframe computers invented a network that permitted those systems to exchange electronic mail as well. Called *BITNET*, the network grew from a grass roots effort. An alternative, known as FIDONET, also allowed computers to send electronic mail. Technologies like UUCP, BITNET and FIDONET were adopted in many countries, and examples of such networks survived into the late 1990s. For example, as late as 1997, the following countries did not have an Internet connection; they used FIDONET to send electronic mail:

Chad Gambia Malawi Sierra Leone

Figure 10.1 lists the entire set of countries that did not have an Internet connection in 1997, but could send and receive electronic mail with each other and with sites on the Internet.

Networks In Europe

As computer technology emerged, Europeans began to establish computer networks. Most countries of Europe have an organization known as the *Post, Telegraph, and Telephone* (*PTT*). The PTTs are agencies of the government, and have control over many forms of communication including computer networking.

PTTs and other telephone companies have experience working together. To ensure that all telephone systems throughout the world are compatible, they formed an organization to create standards. Officially, named the International Telecommunication Union, the organization usually is known by its acronym, *ITU*. The ITU publishes documents that contain technical specifications for telephone systems. For example, the documents specify such details as voltages used on telephone lines as well as international agreements for the assignment of telephone numbers.

Angola	Grenada	Samoa
Anguilla	Guadeloupe	Seychelles
Bahamas	Guinea	Sierra Leone
Bangladesh	Guyana	Solomon Islands
Bosnia-Herzegovina	Haiti	St. Vincent & Grenadines
Botswana	Kiribati	Sudan
Burkina Faso	Lao Democratic R.	Swaziland
Cambodia	Lesotho	Tajikistan
Cameroon	Malawi	Tanzania
Chad	Mali	Togo
Cook Islands	Marshall Islands	Tonga
Cote d'Ivoire	Nauru	Turkmenistan
Cuba	Netherlands Antilles	Tuvalu
Eritrea	New Caledonia	Vanuatu
Ethiopia	Niger	Vietnam
French Guiana	Nigeria	Yugoslavia
French Polynesia	Niue	
Gambia	Papua New Guinea	

Figure 10.1 Countries in 1997 that could send or receive electronic mail over computer networks, but did not have direct connections to the Internet.

When the PTTs became interested in computer networks, they asked the ITU to create a network standard that would guarantee compatibility. The ITU convened a committee that produced a standard for computer networking. The result is a network technology known as *X.25*, that was widely used throughout Europe.

Because the PTTs in Europe followed the ITU recommendation, it was difficult for European groups to experiment with alternatives like TCP/IP, which is used in the Internet. The point is:

Many countries in Europe adopted the X.25 technology for computer networks because PTTs controlled networking and followed ITU's recommendation for computer networks in the same way that they followed ITU's recommendations for voice networks.

Despite the restrictions imposed on networking, European researchers in universities and research labs developed experimental networks. In the United Kingdom, for example, a network known as the *Joint Academic NETwork* (*JANET*) became operational in the 1970s. With funding from IBM, universities in several European countries established a network called the *European Academic And Research Network* (*EARN*).

EBONE: The Internet In Europe

In 1991, several European countries had experimental networks using TCP/IP; a few had connections to the Internet. Most of the experimental networks connected computers at universities or research labs. Groups throughout Europe organized themselves into a cooperative. Their goal was to form a high-speed European backbone network that connected the members and extended the Internet to each. Figure 10.2 shows a diagram of the resulting European backbone network, called the *EBONE*.

By the mid 1990s, the European backbone organization consisted of *25* members, each of whom paid an annual fee. In exchange for its fee, a member received reliable network connectivity to other sites and to the US portion of the Internet. The central organization used the fees to pay the costs associated with maintaining the backbone network. For example, the organization had to pay for leased transmission lines (including transmission lines that connect to the U.S.), hardware, and a staff to operate the backbone. To summarize:

The EBONE was a WAN that spanned Europe and connected sites to the global Internet.

Backbones And Internet Hierarchy

As in the U.S., the European portion of the Internet was organized in a three-level hierarchy. The EBONE provided the top level of the hierarchy that interconnected regions of Europe. In addition, each region had one or more networks that formed the second level of the hierarchy. Multiple sites attached to each regional network, which then connected the sites to the backbone. At the third level, an individual site usually had multiple local area networks connecting the computers at the site.

Hierarchy is still used in the Internet. When two computers at a single site communicate, they use the local network at the site. Communication between computers at two sites within a single region relies on a regional network that connects the sites. Finally, when a computer in one region communicates with a computer in another, the data passes across a backbone network on its way from one region to another.

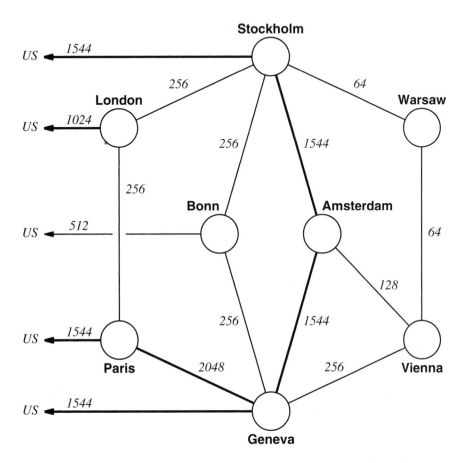

Figure 10.2 The European backbone, EBONE, and the transmission lines that connected it to the U.S. portion of the Internet in 1995. Each transmission line is labeled with its capacity in thousands of bits per second. High-capacity lines are darkened. By 2000, commercial services had developed additional backbones, and the EBONE gradually became obsolete.

Internet On All Continents

By 1997, the Internet reached countries on all seven continents, including Antarctica. Figure 10.3 lists the 172 countries that were connected.

Albania	Dominican R.	Kyrgyz R.	Russian Federation
Algeria	Ecuador	Latvia	San Marino
Andorra	Egypt	Lebanon	Saudi Arabia
Antarctica	El Salvador	Liechtenstein	Senegal
Antigua & Barbuda	Estonia	Lithuania	Singapore
Argentina	Faroe Islands	Luxembourg	Slovakia
Armenia	Fiji	Macau	Slovenia
Aruba	Finland	Macedonia	South Africa
Australia	France	Madagascar	Spain
Austria	Georgia	Malaysia	Sri Lanka
Azerbaijan	Germany	Malta	St. Lucia
Bahrain	Ghana	Mauritius	Suriname
Barbados	Gibraltar	Mexico	Svalbard & Jan Mayen
Belarus	Greece	Moldova	Sweden
Belgium	Greenland	Monaco	Switzerland
Belize	Guam	Mongolia	Taiwan
Benin	Guatemala	Morocco	Thailand
Bermuda	Honduras	Mozambique	Trinidad and Tobago
Bolivia	Hong Kong	Namibia	Tunisia
Brazil	Hungary	Nepal	Turkey
Brunei Darussalam	Iceland	Netherlands	Uganda
Bulgaria	India	New Zealand	Ukraine
Canada	Indonesia	Nicaragua	United Arab Emirates
Cayman Islands	Iran	Norway	United Kingdom
Central African R.	Ireland	Pakistan	United States
Chile	Israel	Panama	Uruguay
China	Italy	Paraguay	Uzbekistan
Colombia	Jamaica	Peru	Vatican City State
Costa Rica	Japan	Philippines	Venezuela
Croatia	Jordan	Poland	Virgin Islands
Cyprus	Kazakhstan	Portugal	Zambia
Czech R.	Kenya	Puerto Rico	Zimbabwe
Denmark	Korea	Re'union	
Djibouti	Kuwait	Romania	

Figure 10.3 Countries or regions with computers connected to the global Internet in 1997, the last year before the Internet reached all countries.

The World Of Internet after 1998

Interestingly, 1998 represents another milestone in the growth of the Internet. During 1998, the Internet reached every populated country on the planet. Of course, some countries had only a few computers connected, and many had slow-speed connections. Despite the details, the Internet was present.

> *By the end of 1998, the Internet reached every populated country in the world.*

A Personal Note

As the Internet grows, I receive messages from many places around the world. In the early 1980s, I was pleased to receive messages from England and Canada because it was thrilling to imagine network connections that reached to foreign countries. I was surprised the first time someone in the Soviet Union sent me electronic mail because I assumed that such communication was forbidden during the cold war. I was also pleased the first time I heard from someone in far away places like Australia, Japan, India, China, and Taiwan. Communication still arrives from around the world.

Although the thrill of foreign communication has faded over the years, I am still occasionally astonished at the penetration of the Internet. To lure commuters into using its facilities, a bus service in California offers wireless Internet connections to customers. Although I expect business hotels to provide Internet connectivity, it's still surprising to find small inns and bed-and-breakfasts in resort areas offering high-speed Internet services. I shouldn't be surprised. After all, the Internet is global.

11

A Global Information Infrastructure

Introduction

The previous chapter describes some of the long-distance connections that comprise the Internet, and illustrates how it expanded around the world. The Internet's significance does not arise from size alone, however, it arises because the Internet offers a global infrastructure that is changing the way people interact. This chapter reviews how previous advances in infrastructure have changed society, and describes the potential impact of the Internet.

Existing Infrastructure

Originally, the term *infrastructure* referred to permanent installations established by the military, usually fortifications used for defense. Currently, it refers to any basic foundation on which society depends. For example, a power distribution system that supplies electricity to homes and businesses is an important part of the infrastructure in industrialized nations.

Each new infrastructure changes society. Before currency was invented, all business transactions involved barter. A person with goods or services for sale had to trade for other goods or services. Each transaction required two parties to negotiate terms for an exchange. Currency introduced the concept of price, and allowed everyone to translate the value of goods or services into a common form.

Overland transportation infrastructures changed the way businesses operate. Before society had such an infrastructure, companies could only choose locations close to raw materials, workers, and customers. Railroads changed society because they made it economical to ship raw materials or manufactured goods long distances. The railroad infrastructure meant companies could locate factories far from the raw materials they use and far from the customers they serve.

A second major change to the U.S. transportation infrastructure occurred when the U.S. government installed an interstate highway system across the country. Originally designed to provide mobility for military equipment, the Interstate system provides high-speed highways that span multiple states, and make it possible to travel to any part of the country quickly. Although railroads existed previously, the interstate system added fundamental new infrastructure because it dramatically improved flexibility by allowing each individual to choose a destination and the most direct route to that destination. As a result, long-distance travel over roads became an economical alternative to travel via railroad; the trucking industry expanded. The point is:

> *New infrastructure makes new industries possible; the interstate highway system provides an example.*

Communication Infrastructure

Communication infrastructure has been dominated by a series of advances. In ancient civilizations, messengers carried all communication by foot. Later, messengers rode on animals. Modern civilizations replaced messengers with a postal mail system that delivers letters. Two advances in infrastructure accompanied the adoption of postal systems. First, because postal mail permits a message to be addressed to an individual, it means that any individual served by the mail system can receive a letter. The idea has become known as *universal delivery*. Second, in most modern societies the postal system permits any individual to send a letter; communication is no longer reserved for heads of state or other dignitaries. To summarize:

> *Modern postal mail service adopted the notion of universal access and delivery; any individual can send a letter to any other individual.*

Of course, "universal" may be limited. For example, a given country can decide to limit postal mail to those individuals within the country. The result of such limitation is a closed community: individuals in the country share the benefits of easy communication, while individuals outside the country do not have easy access to it. In general:

> *The scope of an infrastructure defines a closed community that shares the benefits it offers.*

Telegraph

The telegraph introduced a major change in communication technology because it used electricity to carry information. More important, it changed the basic communication infrastructure because it dramatically increased the speed of message delivery. Instead of days or weeks, an intercity transfer via telegraph required only minutes. High-speed delivery made it possible to conduct business in ways that were impossible by mail.

> *The telegraph changed the basic communication infrastructure because it introduced high-speed delivery.*

Telephone

The modern telephone system introduced additional changes in the communication infrastructure by making communication direct and instantaneous. Unlike a telegraph system that uses a single telegraph machine to serve an entire town, a modern telephone system has one or more telephones in each home or office and permits an individual to communicate directly with another. To understand the advantage of direct communication, compare using a telephone to sending a telegram. Instead of going to a telegraph office and relying on an operator to send a message, a user can place a call directly. To understand the significance of instantaneous access, imagine trying to hold a conversation using a telegraph. A sender cannot know whether the intended recipient is currently available (e.g., whether the recipient is out of town), whether the recipient needs time to think about an answer, or whether the recipient did not receive the message. With a telephone, a person communicates with another party directly. Instantaneous communication makes conversation possible, just as if the two parties were physically adjacent.

> *Telephones changed the communication infrastructure by extending communication services to individual homes and offices, and by providing the instantaneous communication needed for interactive conversations.*

The Internet Infrastructure

The Internet has introduced another significant change in communication infrastructure: generality. Unlike most of the previous communication systems, the Internet was not designed for a specific set of services or a specific set of users. Instead, software that provides services over the Internet is built in two functional parts. The first part contains basic software needed to allow computers to communicate. It can be used by any service. The second part consists of applications that provide high-level services. As a result:

> *Because the basic Internet communication facilities are both general-purpose and efficient, almost any network application can use the Internet.*

The Internet Offers Diverse Information Services

When an individual first encounters the Internet, they usually use a specific service. Sometimes, people expect the Internet to be completely different from anything they have used before, and are surprised to learn that the Internet offers many of the same services available in other networks. One can send electronic mail or receive a text message sent from a cellular telephone. In addition, one can obtain information ranging from weather maps to a list of recent jokes. Finally, one can listen to music or see a video.

Although an individual user examines the information and services available on the Internet at a given time, people who invented the Internet understood that the technology could not be designed for a specific set of services. It had to support a wide variety of services, many of which had not been invented when the basic technology was created. In short,

> *The Internet offers a wide variety of services. Most of the services currently available had not been invented when the Internet was designed.*

TCP/IP Provides Communication Facilities

TCP/IP software provides the basic communication facilities used on the Internet, and forms the base on which all services depend. Its flexibility is the key to Internet success. Because TCP/IP is general purpose and efficient, it can support many services. Because TCP/IP is flexible and robust, it can be used with many underlying communication technologies. Most important, its flexibility has allowed scientists and engineers to use TCP/IP with computers, networking technologies, and services that did not exist when TCP/IP was designed.

In essence, TCP/IP provides a general-purpose communication mechanism on which many services have been built. It has been flexible enough to withstand exponential growth for over two decades, to tolerate computers and network technologies that were unimaginable when it was defined, and to support constantly changing services. In summary:

> *The Internet is a global information infrastructure. Although it offers many services, the Internet's chief advantage lies in the design of TCP/IP software that has accommodated changes in computers, networks, and services.*

A Personal Note

We live in a university town, so it did not surprise me in the early 1990s when my teenage daughter found a summer job in one of the physics labs at the university. At dinner one evening shortly after she started work, she announced that as part of her summer job she was learning to use a computer program that worked over the Internet.

I was surprised at the casual way that she talked about the Internet. Unlike me, she did not view the Internet as a grand computer science research project; she viewed it as a service, exactly the same way one views a telephone system. She used the Internet without understanding the history or the underlying technology.

Today, users expect the Internet to be ubiquitous and easily accessible. Services, such as email and instant messaging, are commonplace, and no longer require special expertise. In short, the Internet has become part of the infrastructure.

Inside The Internet

An Explanation Of The Underlying Technology And Basic Capabilities Of The Infrastructure

12

Packet Switching

Introduction

This chapter begins an exploration of the basic communication technology that the Internet uses. It describes the fundamental mechanism all computer networks use to transfer data, and explains why the scheme works well. Succeeding chapters show how the Internet uses the mechanism. Understanding how networks function is important because it explains which high-level services are possible.

Sharing Saves Money

Computer networks do not usually dedicate a single wire to each pair of communicating computers. Instead, the network system arranges for multiple computers to share the underlying hardware facilities. Economics motivates sharing:

> *Arranging for multiple devices to share a single transmission path lowers cost because it uses fewer wires and fewer switching machines.*

Sharing Introduces Delays

Sharing a transmission path is not a new idea, and is not limited to computer networks. For example, some stores require customers to share a transport mechanism. The store is divided into two sections, a main showroom for customers and a warehouse for the inventory. A slow-moving conveyor belt connects the two areas.

When a customer places an order, the order is sent to the warehouse where a clerk assembles the ordered items onto the conveyor belt, which carries them to the showroom. Such stores often require a clerk to finish sending items from one order before moving to the next one.

Normally, the shared conveyor system works well because each order is small. If one customer orders a chess set and then another orders a toaster, the chess set will arrive on the conveyor before the toaster. When a large order appears, however, the shared conveyor can delay many orders. Imagine, for example, that after ordering a toaster, a customer finds the conveyor belt busy transporting *48* folding chairs. Because the store does not permit mixing orders on the conveyor, the customer must wait for all the chairs to arrive before receiving the toaster.

The point is:

> *Granting one party exclusive access of a shared transport path can be impractical because it can delay all other parties.*

Sharing Wires

In a computer network, the transmission path between two computers consists of wires†. Many years ago, engineers designing computer hardware and telephone systems came to the same realization: because only one data transfer can occur on a given wire at a given time, multiple devices that share a wire must wait to use it. For example, in some early telephone systems, subscribers on a street all shared one telephone line. If two neighbors were talking to each other, their conversation prevented a third person from making a call. Similarly, when two computers attached to a given network transfer data, all other computers are forced to wait until the transfer completes.

Selectable Channels

Engineers have devised several solutions to the problem of shared resources. Cable television systems use one of them. A cable company transmits multiple signals on a single wire by using multiple *channels*. Technically, the encoding uses a scheme similar to the one described for modems in Chapter 6: each channel is assigned a unique

---

†Although optical glass fiber can also be used and the path may contain small electronic devices, we will use the term ''wire'' to simplify the explanations.

frequency, and a carrier at that frequency is modulated to encode information for the channel. The cable company then mixes the encoded signals for all channels and transmits them across the cable.

A television receiver contains the electronic circuitry needed to separate incoming signals by frequency. At any time, a person watching the television tunes it to a specific channel. The television receiver extracts the signal for the selected channel from those that arrive over the cable, and ignores signals on other channels.

Sharing By Taking Turns

While it is possible to build a computer network technology that uses multiple channels to mix signals on a shared wire, most network technologies do not. Instead, they use a variation of the conventional idea of taking turns. Access to the shared resource proceeds by allowing one computer to use the network at a time. As we can see from the conveyor belt example above, the rules of sharing must be defined carefully or a single computer can delay others by using the shared cable for an arbitrarily long time.

To avoid long delays, network technologies limit the amount of data that a computer can transfer on each turn. The idea, which was invented in the 1960s, is called *packet switching*, and the unit of data that can be transferred at one time is called a *packet*. Figure 12.1 illustrates how computers use packet switching.

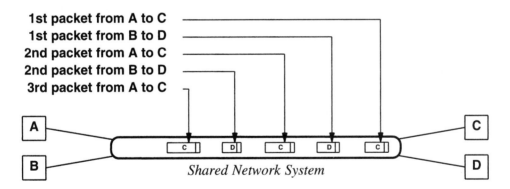

Figure 12.1 An example sequence of packets transferred across a packet switching network as computer *A* communicates with computer *C*, while computer *B* communicates with computer *D*.

In the figure, four computers attach to a network. Assume that computer *B* is sending data to computer *D* while computer *A* is sending data to computer *C*. Both *A* and *B* divide outgoing messages into packets, and then take turns sending the packets.

First *A* sends one packet to *C*, then *B* sends one packet to *D*. After *B* sends its packet, *A* sends a second packet, and so on. If *A* has less data to send than *B*, its transfer will complete and *B* can send remaining packets without interruption.

Packet Switching Avoids Delays

Both LANs and WANs use packet switching. To understand how packet switching avoids delays, think of the conveyor belt analogy. Suppose that clerks in the warehouse fill orders by sending an item from one order, then an item from another order, and so on. If a customer orders one small item, it will be placed on the conveyor quickly. If a customer orders 48 folding chairs, only one chair from that order will be entered on the conveyor before an item from each of the other orders is entered.

The same idea holds for computers. A computer can divide data into pieces easily. If *A* needs to send a long message to *C*, the computer divides the message into many packets. If *B* has a short message for *D*, the message will fit into a single packet or a few packets. After *A* sends one packet of its message, *B* can send its packet. Thus, *B* need not wait for *A* to finish before it has an opportunity to send packets. Consequently, short messages need not wait for long transfers to complete.

Each Packet Must Be Labeled

Each packet sent across a network originates at one computer and is destined for another. The hardware watches as packets pass across the network. Whenever the hardware detects a packet destined for its local machine, it captures the packet. The hardware places a copy of the packet in the computer's memory, and informs the computer that a packet arrived.

To enable network hardware to distinguish among packets, each packet follows the same format. The packet includes a *header* at the beginning and data at the end. Think of the header as a label that specifies which computer sent the packet and which computer should receive the packet.

Computers Have Addresses

Each computer on a network has a unique number known as the computer's *address*. To identify the pair of communicating computers, the header at the beginning of a packet contains two important addresses: the address of the computer that sent the packet and the address of the computer to which the packet has been sent. The sender's address is called the *source address*, while the receiver's address is called the *destina-*

tion address. Network hardware always uses the numeric addresses to send or receive packets.

The numbers used for addresses depend on the specific network technology. Some technologies use numbers containing a few digits, while others use numbers of sixteen digits. The important idea is:

> *Each computer attached to a network is assigned a unique number called its* address. *A packet contains the address of the computer that sent it and the address of the computer to which it is sent.*

Packets Are Not All The Same Size

Although packet switching technologies limit the amount of data in a packet, they allow the sender to transmit any size packet up to the maximum. For example, some network applications allow a user to interact with a remote system by sending keystrokes. Such applications often send a single keystroke in a packet as soon as the user types it on the keyboard. Other applications that have larger amounts of data to transfer choose larger packets.

Packet Transmission Seems Instantaneous

In most packet switching networks, packet transfer occurs quickly. For example, an inexpensive LAN can transfer one thousand large packets between two computers in a second; it takes slightly less time to send small packets. To a human, events that require thousandths of a second seem instantaneous. For example, several people can use computers that attach to a single, shared network without perceiving delay. While one user runs a word processing application on a remote computer, another can access a remote database. Each user types input, uses a mouse, and experiences exactly the same response as if the program were run locally.

To summarize:

> *A packet switching system permits multiple pairs of computers to communicate across a shared network with minimal delay because it divides each conversation into small packets and arranges for the computers that share a network to take turns sending packets.*

Sharing Is Automatic

Packet switching technologies allow computers to send data at any time. One computer can begin to send packets before others are ready to use the network. As long as only one computer needs to use the network, it can send packets continuously. As soon as a second computer becomes ready to send data, sharing begins. Both computers take turns so each receives a fair share of the network. If a third computer becomes ready, all three share the network equally. The network also adjusts sharing when a computer stops sending data. For example, if three computers share a network equally and one of them finishes sending data, the remaining two computers take turns.

More important, a computer does not need to know how many other computers are using the network simultaneously. The key point is:

> *Because packet switching systems adapt instantly as computers become ready to send data or others finish sending data, each computer receives a fair share of network resources at any given time.*

Network Hardware Handles Sharing

Interface hardware handles sharing automatically. That is, network sharing does not require any "computation," nor do computers need to coordinate before they begin using a network. Instead, a computer can generate a packet at any time. When a packet is ready, the computer's interface hardware waits its turn and then transfers the packet. Thus,

> *From a computer's point of view obtaining fair access to a shared network is automatic — the network hardware handles all the details.*

Many Devices Can Use Packet Switching

Devices such as cash registers, video cameras, bar code scanners, and magnetic strip readers can all connect to a packet switching network. Many vendors also sell printers that connect to a network. Because a single network printer can be accessed by all computers on a network, using network printers can reduce costs: each computer does not need a separate printer.

A device like a printer requires special hardware to attach it to a network. In particular, each device attached to a network must contain a small computer, usually a microprocessor. The computer receives packets from the network that contain instructions to control the device. Conceptually,

Although many types of devices can connect directly to a computer network, each such device must contain a small computer that handles communication.

Relevance To The Internet

Like most computer networks, the Internet is a packet switching system. Internet hardware includes physical wires shared among multiple users. Packet switching allows many communications to proceed simultaneously, without requiring an application to wait for all other communication to complete. As a consequence, whenever a user transfers data across the Internet, network software on the sending machine divides the data into packets, and network software on the receiving machine must reassemble the packets to produce the data. For example, a document from a word processor must be divided into packets for transfer across the Internet, and then reassembled into a complete document at the receiving side. To summarize:

All data is transferred across the Internet in packets. A sender divides a message or document into packets and transfers the packets across the Internet. A receiver reassembles the original message from the packets that arrive. Packets from many machines traverse the Internet at the same time.

Summary

The fundamental technique that computer networks use to ensure fair access to shared network resources is known as packet switching. Before data can be transferred across a network it must be divided into packets. Each packet contains a header that specifies the computer to which the packet should be delivered; the destination is specified using a number known as the computer's address. Computers that share access to a network take turns sending packets. On each turn, a given computer sends one packet. Although devices like printers can connect to a network, such devices must contain a microprocessor to handle network communication.

13

Internet: A Network Of Networks

Introduction

The previous chapter describes packet switching and shows why dividing long messages into short packets lowers delays for computers that share a transmission path. This chapter describes how multiple packet switching networks can be interconnected to form an Internet that functions like a single, large network.

Network Technologies Are Incompatible

Many packet switching technologies exist because each has been designed to meet constraints of speed, distance, and cost. Inexpensive networks usually operate at lower speeds than expensive networks. Designers do not attempt to make all designs compatible — details such as the electrical voltages and the numbers assigned as computer addresses often differ. Consequently, one cannot form a large network merely by connecting the wires of two or more smaller networks.

To understand the consequences of incompatible technologies, consider a large enterprise that has two, incompatible local area networks in use. For example, suppose the accounting department uses one type of network and the production department uses another. When the accounting department needs information that resides on a computer in the production department, the information must be written to an external storage device (e.g., a flash ROM), and transferred manually. If both networks could be interconnected, the information could be transferred from one computer to another at electronic speed without requiring a person to transport a flash ROM; interconnecting networks saves time and money.

Coping With Incompatibility

There are two possible solutions to the problem of network incompatibility:

- Choose a network technology that suffices for the entire enterprise, and mandate that the enterprise use the chosen technology.

- Allow groups to choose the network technology that best fits their needs and budget, and then find a way to interconnect all types of networks.

The first solution has several drawbacks. It can be impossible to find a single network technology that handles all the needs of an enterprise. Even if such a technology exists, cost may be prohibitive. More important, requirements can change when a new group within an enterprise needs a network. If every group in the enterprise must use the same type of network, changing the technology to accommodate one group means replacing all existing installations. We can conclude:

> *It is impractical, and may be economically infeasible, to require all computers in an enterprise to use the same network technology.*

The Internet uses an approach that allows each group to select the network technology that best meets the group's needs. To accommodate multiple network types, the Internet provides a mechanism to interconnect arbitrary networks and the software to transfer data across the connections.

Two Fundamental Concepts

Two simple ideas will help explain some of the technology used to interconnect networks within the Internet. The first reveals how it is possible to solve the problem of distant connections; the second reveals how it is possible to connect networks that are incompatible.

A Connection To A Network Can Be Extended

Each computer that attaches to a Local Area Network needs a cable that connects from the computer to the LAN. Although the cable between a computer and a LAN is usually short (e.g., a few inches or the distance of one hallway in an office building), it can be extended. Figure 13.1 illustrates three ways that a computer can connect to a remote network.

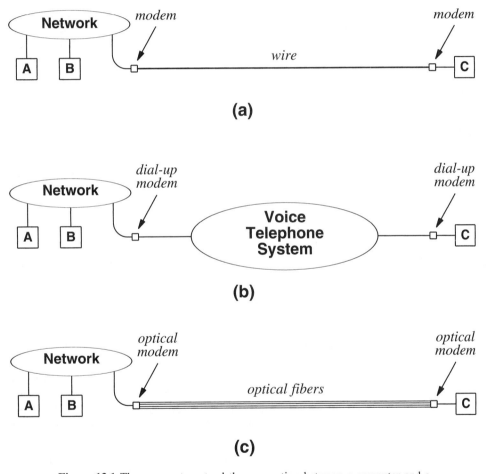

Figure 13.1 Three ways to extend the connection between a computer and a network: (a) two modems with wires connecting them, (b) two modems that communicate across the voice telephone system, and (c) two optical modems with glass fibers connecting them.

Chapter 6 discusses how modems can be used to send data across a wire or across the telephone system. Instead of wires or telephone connections, many modern communication systems use flexible glass fiber to provide connections across long distances. Called a *fiber optic* connection, the technology requires optical modems that use light instead of electricity to carry data. At the sending end, an optical modem contains a laser that converts data from a computer into pulses of light and sends the pulses down the fiber. At the receiving end, an optical modem senses the pulses of light and turns them back into data for a computer.

The fiber optic approach has the advantage of permitting long distances (e.g., across a campus or between towns). An optical fiber has three interesting properties that explain why it is so useful. First, because the fiber is flexible, it can be installed similar to any cable. Second, because the fiber is made from glass, light can travel through it. Third, because the fiber is constructed to reflect light inward, the light intensity does not diminish much as it travels along (i.e., almost no light escapes from the sides of the fiber).

A Computer Can Have Multiple Connections

The second idea that will help explain Internet technology is straightforward: a given computer can connect to two or more networks. Chapter 7 explains that a computer contains a Network Interface Card (NIC) that connects the computer to a network. In fact, a computer can have multiple NICs that each connect to a network; the networks do not all need to use the same technology. After a computer has been connected to multiple networks, it can send or receive packets from any of them.

Using A Computer To Interconnect Networks

The Internet uses special-purpose computers to interconnect networks. Figure 13.2 illustrates the concept. Computers used to interconnect networks resemble conventional computers. Like a conventional computer, they include a central processor, memory, and network interfaces. Also like conventional computers, they come in a variety of sizes and speeds. The smallest, least powerful models cost less than one hundred dollars; powerful models that can interconnect multiple networks cost tens of thousands of dollars.

Although they can use conventional hardware, computers that interconnect networks do not use conventional software. Because they are busy handling network interconnections, such computers do not include application programs. For example, an interconnecting computer does not run word processing spreadsheet applications. Instead, such a computer has only special-purpose software that performs tasks related to the job of interconnecting networks. In fact, interconnecting computers are configured so they start the needed software automatically whenever they are powered on. As a result, they automatically restart after a power failure, and normally do not require any human intervention.

To summarize:

> *Computers that interconnect networks are dedicated to the interconnection task. Although they can use conventional hardware, they run special-purpose software that starts automatically when the system is powered on and remains operating at all times.*

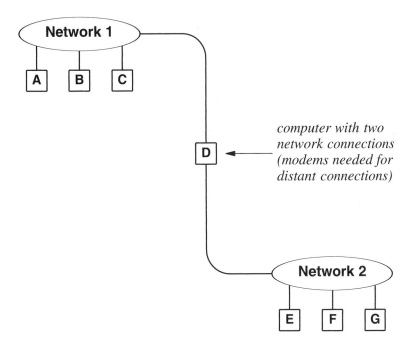

Figure 13.2 A computer, *D*, used to interconnect two networks. The networks can be the same type or different types.

Interconnecting Computers Pass Packets

A computer that interconnects networks has one major task to perform: it forwards packets from one network to the other. The next chapter describes how packet forwarding works, but the idea is simple: the computer receives a packet sent to it across one network, and sends the packet on to its destination across the other network. For example, in Figure 13.2, computers *A* and *G* do not attach to the same network. If computer *A* generates a packet for computer *G*, it sends the packet to *D*, the computer that interconnects the networks. *D* receives the packet from Network *1*, and then uses Network *2* to send the packet to *G*.

Interconnecting Computers Are Called Routers

Software on a computer that interconnects networks needs to know to which network each computer connects so it can determine where to send packets. In the case of two networks, the decision is straightforward — when a packet arrives over one network, it should be sent over the other. In the case of a computer that interconnects three networks, however, the decision is complex. When a packet arrives over one network, software on the computer must choose one of the other two networks.

The process of selecting a network over which to send a packet is called *routing*, and the dedicated computers that interconnect networks and perform the task are called *routers*. The next chapter discusses the details of routing in the Internet.

Routers Are The Building Blocks Of The Internet

Although many people think of the Internet as a single, giant network to which many computers attach, it is not. Instead, the Internet consists of thousands of computer networks, interconnected by routers. Each computer attaches to one of the individual networks. When a computer on one network communicates with a computer on another network, it sends packets through a router. To summarize:

> *The Internet is not a single computer network. Instead, it consists of thousands of computer networks interconnected by dedicated, special-purpose computers called* routers.

Routers are used in many ways throughout the Internet. For example, a router can interconnect two Local Area Networks in a single building or even in a room. Using a pair of modems to reach a distant network, a router can interconnect the Local Area Networks in two buildings or across a campus. Because a router can interconnect diverse technologies, it can interconnect a Local Area Network and a Wide Area Network.

The Internet Includes Multiple Types Of Networks

Because a given router can interconnect networks that use different hardware technologies, the router architecture permits the Internet to contain multiple types of networks. Each small group can use whichever LAN technology is best suited to its performance needs and budget. It then uses a router to connect its network to the Internet. A large organization can purchase routers to interconnect its networks into a private internet. By adding one additional router, the organization can connect its private internet to the global Internet.

Connecting multiple types of networks is important for two reasons. First, because the Internet connects many organizations of diverse size, networking needs, and budgets, the organizations use diverse network technologies. Second, and more important, because computer networking is an active area of research, technologies keep changing. Many of the hardware technologies currently used in the Internet did not exist when the Internet began, and many technologies in use now will be replaced in the future. The Internet could not survive if it did not permit multiple types of networks.

Routers Can Interconnect WANs And LANs

Routers explain how the Internet can use both Wide Area Networks and Local Area Networks. For example, a large Wide Area Network owned by a major ISP provides an efficient long-distance technology that connects many sites. Often, the term *backbone network* is used to describe a major WAN to which other networks attach. The backbone reaches some, but not all sites; such locations are called *backbone sites*. Figure 13.3 illustrates the architecture.

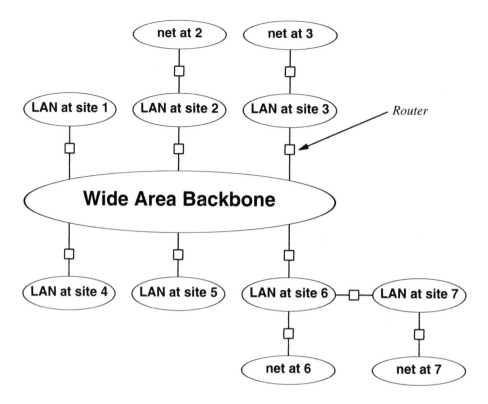

Figure 13.3 An example of a wide area backbone. At each backbone site, a
router connects a local area network to the backbone. At some
sites, additional routers connect additional networks. Networks
at site 7 do not connect directly to the backbone.

As Figure 13.3 illustrates, a router at each backbone site connects the backbone
WAN to a Local Area Network. The router at a site provides a path between computers
attached to the site's LAN and computers attached to LANs at other sites. A given site
can also use additional routers to connect additional networks either at the site or at other sites. In Figure 13.3, for example, site 2 has two routers and two networks. Three
routers attach to the LAN at site 6: one connects to the backbone, another connects to a
second network at the site, and a third connects to a LAN at site 7.

Usually, the least expensive way to connect a new network to the Internet involves
finding the closest Internet site and connecting a router between one of its networks and
the new network. However, not all sites are authorized to provide connections. In addition, it may be impossible to cross political boundaries (e.g., to form a connection
between networks in two different countries).

The Hierarchical Structure Of The Internet

Figure 13.3 gives a simplified view of the Internet. In practice, even a medium-size ISP contains several networks interconnected by routers. Large ISPs have even more complex structure. In addition to running a backbone, a large ISP usually has a set of *regional networks* that each cover a large geographic region and *access networks* that provide connections to individual businesses or residences. So, the question arises: how is the Internet structured?

To help understand the structure without becoming overwhelmed by details, networking professionals draw diagrams in which a cloud denotes a set of networks. For example, Figure 13.4 illustrates the overall hierarchy of ISPs, with major ISPs shown near the top, regional ISPs in the middle, and local ISPs near customers.

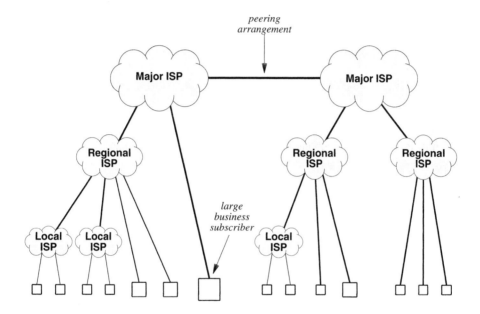

Figure 13.4 Illustration of the structure of the Internet with each ISP denoted by a cloud. Boxes at the bottom of the diagram correspond to subscribers — a small box corresponds to a residence or small business, and a large box corresponds to a larger business.

Major ISPs (i.e., ISPs that operate a backbone network) are known as *tier 1 providers*, regional ISPs are known as *tier 2 providers*, and local ISPs are known as *tier 3 providers*. Thus, providers such as AT&T or Sprint that run a large backbone network are classified as tier 1.

As the figure indicates, a connection between a pair of tier 1 providers is called a *peering* arrangement. The two providers are "peers" in the sense that they each have approximately the same number and type of customers beneath them. Peering is reserved for the largest ISPs around the world; as the figure illustrates, a small local ISP is merely a customer of a medium-size regional ISP, and a regional ISP is a customer of a large tier 1 provider.

As Figure 13.4 shows, some residential customers connect to a regional ISP and others connect to a local ISP. In general, a local ISP cannot provide service to large businesses because the connection between a local ISP and a regional ISP does not have sufficient capacity to handle large amounts of traffic. Consequently, a large business usually chooses to connect directly to a regional or large tier 1 ISP.

Where Packets Travel

To understand the hierarchy, consider two subscribers that are geographically distant. Assume that each subscriber connects to a local ISP in his or her area, and consider what happens when they communicate. When a message is sent, a packet travels from the sender's computer across an access network to the subscriber's local ISP. The local ISP forwards the packet to a regional ISP, which, in turn, forwards the packet to a tier 1 provider. If the destination is reachable through the same tier 1 provider, the packet travels across the backbone to a regional ISP near the destination. If the destination is only reachable through another tier 1 provider, the packet passes across a peering point, and across a second tier 1 backbone. Once a packet reaches a regional ISP near the destination, the regional ISP forwards the packet to the correct local ISP, which then delivers the packet to its destination over an access network. Of course, each ISP along the path contains multiple networks and routers, and a packet may traverse many networks as it travels through an ISP.

The point is:

> The Internet's network of networks is arranged in a hierarchy with major tier 1 ISPs that provide backbone networks at the top, regional ISPs in the middle, and local ISPs at lower levels.

Interconnecting Networks Was Revolutionary

The idea of using a router to interconnect two networks may not seem like a fundamental idea, but it is. Before Internet technology appeared, a company needed to choose one network technology for all computers or needed multiple, independent networks. Routers enable a company to allow each group to choose an appropriate network technology, while providing a way to interconnect the networks.

Summary

Although to a user it appears to be a single, large network, the Internet consists of thousands of computer networks interconnected by dedicated devices called routers. Because a router can interconnect networks that use different technologies, a router can connect a LAN to another LAN, a LAN to a WAN, or a WAN to another WAN. Because it is made up of networks interconnected by routers, many people refer to the Internet as a *network of networks*.

Networks in the Internet are arranged in a conceptual hierarchy of ISPs. Tier 1 ISPs form the core of the Internet, regional ISPs form the next level, and local ISPs form the last level. At each level of the hierarchy, a smaller ISP is a customer of a larger ISP; when two tier 1 ISPs agree to exchange traffic, they are said to peer.

Using routers to interconnect networks produced a revolution. It permits connections among multiple types of networks, and allows each group in an organization to choose a network technology that best suits the group's needs and budget.

14

ISPs: Broadband And Wireless Access

Introduction

The previous chapter described the Internet as a network of networks. For most individuals, however, the main question is not how the Internet is built, but how their computer can connect and use it. This chapter describes technologies used for Internet connections, and explains what each provides.

Internet Service Providers And Fees

A company that provides Internet access is known as an *Internet Service Provider* (*ISP*). Like any company, an ISP charges for its services. In general, ISPs levy two types of fees:

- A charge for using the Internet
- A charge for a physical connection to the Internet

In the United States, charges for use of the Internet are usually billed at a flat rate. That is, the ISP charges each customer a fixed rate per month, independent of the number of minutes a customer uses the service, the destinations with which the customer communicates, or the amount of data transferred. In return for the use charges, the ISP agrees to forward packets from the customer's computer to destinations on the Internet and from computers on the Internet back to the customer's computer.

Although use charges are billed at a fixed rate, ISPs do discriminate among classes of users. For example, an ISP usually charges a business more than an individual because businesses tend to use the Internet heavily, and individuals tend to use the Internet casually. In addition, an ISP may make the fee depend on the type of physical connection a customer has — a customer whose connection is capable of transferring larger volumes of data is charged more than a customer with a lower-capacity connection.

The second type, a charge for a connection, applies to a customer who has a dedicated connection between their site and the ISP. The next sections discuss and explain several technologies that are used for such connections.

Customer Connections Form The Last Mile

Although the Internet consists of interconnected networks, providing direct connections between an ISP and its customers is difficult. First, because a single ISP can have many customers, the technologies must accommodate a large number of physical locations. Second, because most customers are individuals or families, the technologies must be inexpensive to adopt. Third, because customers are dissatisfied when they wait a long time to view information, the technologies must provide data transfer at high speeds. Thus, engineers face conflicting goals of trying to create technologies that perform well, but have low cost. In the industry, the problem is known as the *last mile problem*, and the technologies are called *access technologies*.

Until the mid-1990s, only one technology was available that offered a dedicated connection to the Internet: a digital circuit leased from a common carrier. In essence, a phone company forms a leased circuit by renting unused wires in phone cables. Because leased circuits are expensive, the option is most often used by business customers who contract to lease a circuit between their business and an ISP. A customer pays an initial fee to have a circuit installed, and then pays a monthly fee to use the circuit. Some ISPs require each customer to contract directly with a carrier (e.g., a telephone company) for a circuit, while other ISPs handle the contract on the customer's behalf. In any case, the customer must pay a monthly fee for the circuit, either to the ISP or to the public utility.

Leased Circuits Are Expensive

The chief advantages of a leased circuit are availability and control. A circuit remains available twenty-four hours a day, seven days a week. Thus, a business that needs to keep its Internet site online at all times will choose a leased circuit. More important, because each circuit is dedicated to one customer, the only traffic on a circuit belongs to the customer that leases the circuit. Consequently, a business might choose a dedicated circuit merely to guarantee that no one interferes with their packets — only traffic to and from the customer travels across the circuit.

The chief disadvantage of a leased circuit is high cost; a leased circuit is extremely expensive. For example, one of the circuits leased to the author's university costs over several thousand dollars a month. Thus, few individuals can afford to lease a dedicated circuit.

The monthly cost for a circuit depends on the length (i.e., the geographic distance from a subscriber to the ISP) and the capacity. The circuits that businesses use are classified as *broadband* because they have high capacity. One of the leased circuit types is known as a *T1 circuit†*, the name of a telephone company standard that specifies the circuit's electrical specifications as well as the bit rate.

Dial-up Access Is Inexpensive, But Slow

How can someone access the Internet if they cannot afford a leased circuit? Fortunately, several alternatives are available. The least expensive technology used to access Internet services consists of the conventional telephone system. Most ISPs offer a telephone-based service, which is known as *dial-up access.*

To use dial-up access, a computer must have a modem that connects to the phone system like an ordinary telephone. In addition, the computer must have software that uses the modem. When the software runs, it instructs the modem to place a telephone call to the telephone number provided by the ISP. At the ISP, another modem answers the call and agrees to accept Internet packets. Figure 14.1 illustrates the idea.

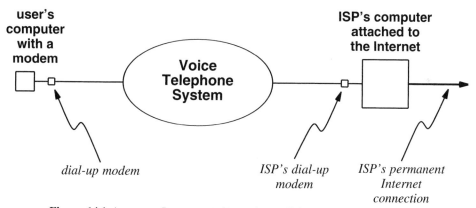

Figure 14.1 Access to Internet services using a dial-up modem and the telephone network. Dial-up access is less expensive than a permanent Internet connection.

Although dial-up connections provide full service, response times can be slow. To summarize:

---

†An apartment complex in the author's town advertises "T1 to every bedroom".

Using the conventional telephone system to access the Internet is the least expensive access technology, but has lower speed.

Broadband Connections Offer High Speed

Users desire data to be delivered quickly. After all, faster delivery means less time waiting. The difference between dial-up and dedicated access can be dramatic. The speedup is most obvious when an image is being transferred. For example, a high-resolution photograph sent to the author contained 3,523,353 bytes of data. To transfer the image over a dial-up connection running at 33.3 Kbps requires approximately fourteen minutes. The same image can be sent across a T1 circuit in eighteen seconds.

We use the term *broadband* to characterize a technology that enables data to move at high speeds. For example, a T1 circuit is classified as broadband because it can transport over a million bits per second. A dialup connection is not classified as broadband because dialup is limited to less than 56 thousand bits per second. The high speeds offered by broadband allow users to view more data without long delays. Thus, a user who has broadband access is more likely to wait for an entire image to appear than a user who has dial-up access.

The Important Concept Of Continuous Connectivity

In the broadest sense, dial-up Internet access appears to provide users with exactly the same Internet services as a dedicated circuit. Once a dial-up connection has been established, the user's computer can send or receive packets, and the user can communicate with any destination on the Internet. Despite appearances, however, there are two fundamental differences between dial-up access and dedicated access. A dedicated connection offers:

- Higher-speed data delivery

- Instantaneous access and continuous availability

Although higher-speed data transfers make a difference in users' perceptions, dedicated circuits provide an even more significant improvement over dial-up: instantaneous access and continuous availability. To understand the effect, consider the tedious procedure a dial-up user follows when using the Internet. The user must wait until the telephone is free before he or she can begin. In most cases, the user must also turn on the computer, wait for it to start, and then invoke software that uses the modem to dial the user's ISP. At the ISP, a modem answers the phone call, and begins to communicate with the user's modem. The user must wait for the two modems to exchange test messages that verify the quality of the phone connection and negotiate a communication speed. Once the modems have synchronized, other Internet software can begin to send packets. Finally, after waiting through the preliminaries, the user can run applications that access Internet services. Typically, the user launches a browser, which also takes time to start.

Now consider the astounding difference a dedicated Internet connection makes. Because a dedicated connection remains in place at all times, a user does not need to wait for a modem to dial a phone number, a modem to answer, the modems to synchronize, or other Internet software to start running. Instead, the computer remains permanently connected to the Internet and ready to send or receive packets at all times. Thus, the user never waits for a connection. To make Internet access even faster, users who have dedicated connections often leave their computer running and leave a browser ready in background. Thus, the computer is continuously available for Internet access — all delays are eliminated. A user needs only to enter a few keystrokes or click the mouse to begin access.

Instantaneous Access Changes Use

Instantaneous access and continuous availability have an interesting effect on the way people use the Internet. Instead of perceiving access as a time-consuming activity, users think of it as a trivial amount of effort. A user who has dial-up access usually plans Internet use at a particular time during the day. With a dedicated connection, a user can simply invoke an Internet service whenever it is needed. Thus, instead of scheduling all their Internet use in a single session, users who have a dedicated connection become casual — they use the Internet for one task at a time whenever the need arises. For example, dedicated access makes it trivial for someone to view current weather conditions. Similarly, dedicated access makes checking email trivial — an icon on the screen can tell the user when email is available, and a single click of the mouse is sufficient to read and display messages. As a result:

> *A dedicated Internet connection that provides instantaneous access twenty-four hours per day changes the way an individual views the Internet because it encourages frequent and casual use.*

Modern Technologies Offer Inexpensive Dedicated Access

ISPs and engineers are aware that customers desire higher-speed data transfer and dedicated Internet connections. Consequently, during the 1990s, engineers worked to find technologies that offer the advantages of a high-speed, dedicated connection at lower cost than a leased digital circuit. Three technologies emerged which are now in widespread use by ISPs:

- *Cable Modem technologies* that use the same wiring as cable television

- *DSL technologies* that use the same wiring as conventional telephones

- *Wireless access technologies* that use radio transmissions

Cable Modems

Before the Internet became popular, the cable television industry already had wiring in place to most homes. Although coaxial cable was originally designed to deliver analog video signals instead of digital data and the hardware was only designed to send information in one direction (toward the customer), the system has been modified. A technology, known as a *cable modem*, was invented that uses cable wiring to provide Internet service. A cable modem consists of a small electronic box that connects a customer's computer to the cable system. In addition to the cable modem at each customer's site, the cable company needs cable modems at its end. The modems encode data and transmit it over the coaxial cable. Cable modems are specifically designed so that data transmission does not interfere with television signals, making it possible to send data over the existing wiring at the same time as cable television signals.

Cable modems have four advantages over other technologies. First, they deliver data much faster than a dial-up connection. Second, they provide continuous and instantaneous connectivity. Third, they are not as expensive as a leased data circuit. Fourth, they use existing wiring.

The chief disadvantage of cable modems arises because they require many customers to ''share'' the wiring. A cable company connects a group of approximately one hundred customers (i.e., the modems from one hundred residences) to the same underlying cable system, and then arranges for the modems to take turns sending packets. If only one customer in a group uses their computer at a given time, the customer has all the bandwidth; data transmission proceeds at the highest possible speed. If all customers use their cable modems at the same time, however, the modems take turns sending, which means data transmission slows down. Even at the slowest speed, a cable modem can operate faster than dial-up, but the effective rate does change significantly when many customers access the Internet simultaneously. Thus, the service a customer receives depends on how other customers (e.g., in the same neighborhood) are using the Internet.

DSL Technology And Telephones

The telephone industry also has wiring in place to most homes, and phone companies have investigated ways their wiring can be used to transfer digital data. Originally designed to carry analog voice signals, the telephone system was extended. A technology, known as *Digital Subscriber Line (DSL)*†, was invented to provide high-speed Internet access over telephone wiring.

It may seem that we already discussed how the dial-up telephone system can be used for Internet access, but DSL technology does not use the telephone system at all. Instead, it only uses the underlying wires.

To understand DSL, you must know that a separate pair of copper wires connects each residence or business to the telephone office. Instead of using a dial-up modem to encode data in sounds, DSL technology sends electrical signals on the wires to transfer data at high speed. The design is ingenious because the electrical signals used by DSL are carefully chosen so they do not interfere with telephone signals; *filters* are installed to insure that there is no accidental interference. As a result, it is possible to transfer data over a pair of wires at the same time as a standard telephone transfers voice signals.

In a sense, DSL signals are invisible — they travel over phone wires without affecting normal telephone service in any way. Thus, while someone is using the Internet, the telephone can ring and be answered. Similarly, someone can make a call without affecting Internet use. The point is:

> *Although DSL technology sends digital data over the same wires that are used for conventional telephone service, there is no interference. Telephone calls do not interfere with Internet use, and Internet use does not interfere with telephone calls.*

Besides allowing simultaneous use of the Internet and a telephone, DSL technology offers several advantages. First, DSL provides high data rates similar to those available with cable modems. More important, a DSL customer does not share bandwidth with other subscribers — the data traveling over the wires from a customer's house to the telephone company is unaffected by data traveling between other customers' houses and the phone company. Second, also like cable modems, DSL provides continuous and instantaneous connectivity. Third, DSL is not as expensive as a leased circuit. Fourth, DSL uses existing wiring.

---

†Several variants of DSL technology exist; residential customers use a specific form known as *Asymmetric Digital Subscriber Line (ADSL)* technology.

Wireless Access Is Available

It may seem that DSL and cable modem technologies solve the last mile problem completely. However, each has limitations. DSL has a distance limitation that prevents the signals from traveling as far as conventional telephone signals. Thus, it cannot reach to rural areas. Similarly, some homes are not served by cable television. Finally, cable and telephone companies may not offer Internet connectivity in all areas for economic reasons.

To provide access to remote areas, engineers have developed a set of *wireless access technologies*. Although all wireless networks use radio waves to carry data, a wide variety of technologies have been developed. Some are point-to-point, meaning that special antennas are used to aim the transmissions in a straight line between two communicating sites (e.g., between a remote residence and an ISP), and some are broadcast (e.g., between a transmitter and a set of houses in a nearby neighborhood). Others use a satellite orbiting the earth to relay data between subscribers at arbitrary locations and an ISP. The point is:

> *A variety of wireless access technologies has been developed to meet various needs.*

Wi-Fi And 3G Wireless Technologies

Two wireless technologies have become extremely popular:

- Wi-Fi Local Area Networks
- 3G wireless cellular networks

A *Wi-Fi* network provides connections among computers in a small area (e.g., inside a house or inside a store). To provide Wi-Fi Internet access, an owner purchases and installs a device known as a *Wi-Fi access point*. An access point attaches to the conventional wired Internet. In essence, an access point acts like a router: it relays packets between the wireless network and the wired network.

Most laptop computers now include a Wi-Fi NIC that allows the laptop to obtain Internet access when the laptop is sufficiently close to an access point. Businesses such as coffee shops provide free Wi-Fi access as a way to entice customers — while on the premises, a customer can use a laptop computer to access the Internet. Other businesses (e.g., airports) offer Wi-Fi access, but require a customer to pay a fee for the service.

Telephone companies worldwide have responded to the demand for Internet services by devising their own data transmission scheme, known as *3rd-Generation wireless* or *3G wireless*. 3G telephones include a screen that can display text or graphics, and the phone company has planned many data services. Although 3G wireless builds on cellular telephone technology rather than an Internet technology, 3G services are interconnected with the Internet. Thus, it is possible to have email messages forwarded to a 3G telephone or to accept a short message from a 3G phone and send it across the Internet.

A Personal Note

As a networking researcher, I have had opportunities to try technologies long before they became commercially available. During the late 1990s, for example, I participated in an experiment that used DSL technology to deliver data to my house at 6 million bits per second. Currently, two dedicated connections run between my lab at the university and my house; each operates at 2.24 million bits per second. In one form or another, my house has had Internet access available twenty-four hours a day since the late 1970s.

Several years ago, I attended a lecture by a distinguished person at a leading high-tech industry. Although the announcement for his lecture said that he would discuss the future of the Internet, the lecture was disappointing because it focused on technologies that were already available. Near the end of the lecture, it became clear that facilities I have enjoyed for many years seemed new to the speaker — he informed the audience that when he converted from slow, clumsy dial-up access to a continuous broadband connection, his perception of the Internet changed. As broadband access becomes standard and Internet services become as commonplace as telephone service, people will wonder how they survived without it.

15

IP: Software To Create A Virtual Network

Introduction

Chapter 13 describes the Internet as a network of networks, formed by using special-purpose computers called routers to interconnect networks. Of course, merely connecting hardware together does not make an Internet. Interconnected computers need software before they can communicate. This chapter describes the basic software that makes the hardware behave like a single, large network.

Protocol: An Agreement For Communication

It is impossible for two humans to communicate unless they agree to speak a common language. The same holds true for computers — two computers cannot communicate unless they share a common language. A *communication protocol* is an agreement that specifies a common language two computers use to exchange messages. The term derives from diplomatic vocabulary, in which a protocol specifies the rules under which a diplomatic exchange occurs.

A computer communication protocol defines communication precisely. For example, a protocol specifies the exact format and meaning of each message that a computer can send. It also specifies the conditions under which a computer should send a given message, and how a computer should respond when a message arrives.

Basic Functionality: The Internet Protocol

A key communication protocol used in the Internet is called, appropriately, the *Internet Protocol*. Usually abbreviated *IP*, the protocol specifies the rules that define the details of how computers communicate. It specifies exactly how a packet must be formed and how a router must forward each packet on toward its destination.

Each computer that connects to the Internet must follow the rules of the Internet Protocol. When it creates a packet, a computer must use the format IP specifies. When a computer receives a packet, the packet will be an exact copy of the packet that was originally sent, still in IP format. Furthermore, each router in the Internet expects packets to adhere to the IP format as they pass from one network to another.

IP Software On Every Machine

Computer hardware does not understand IP. Therefore, attaching a computer to the Internet does not mean it can use Internet services. To communicate on the Internet, a computer needs IP software. Indeed, every computer that uses the Internet must run IP software.

IP is fundamental: all Internet services use IP to send or receive packets. Thus, each computer usually has a single copy of IP software that all applications share. On sophisticated computers, the operating system keeps a copy of the IP software in memory at all times, ready to send or receive packets. In summary,

> *Because all Internet services use the Internet Protocol, a computer must have IP software before it can access the Internet.*

Internet Packets Are Called Datagrams

To distinguish between Internet packets and packets for other networks, we call a packet that follows the IP specification an *IP datagram*. The name was chosen to provide intuition about how the Internet packet delivery service handles packets. As it suggests, the Internet handles datagrams in much the same way that a telegraph office handled telegrams. Once the sending computer creates a datagram and starts it on a trip through the Internet, the sender is free to resume processing in the same way that an individual is free to leave a telegraph office after handing an operator a message to be sent. A datagram travels across the Internet independent of the sender, analogous to the way operators forward a telegram to its destination independent of the person who sent the telegram. To summarize:

> *Each packet sent across the Internet must follow the format specified by the Internet Protocol. Such packets are called IP datagrams.*

The Illusion Of A Giant Network

Although the Internet Protocol defines many communication details, it has an important purpose. Once every computer on the Internet has IP software installed, any computer can create an IP datagram and send it to any other computer. In essence, IP transforms a collection of networks and routers into a seamless communication system by making the Internet function like a single, large network. Figure 15.1 illustrates the idea.

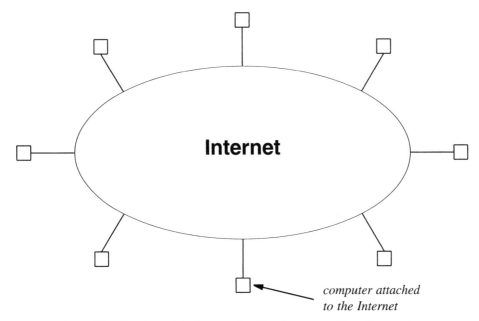

computer attached
to the Internet

Figure 15.1 The view of the Internet that IP software provides. Users and application programs treat the Internet like a single, large network that allows arbitrary numbers of computers to communicate.

Computer scientists use the term *virtual* to describe technologies that present the illusion of larger, more powerful computational facilities than the hardware provides. The Internet is a *virtual network* because it presents the illusion of a single, large network. Although the Internet is a network of networks, IP software takes care of the details and allows users to think of "the Internet" as a single network. Users remain unaware of the Internet's networks and routers, just as telephone subscribers remain oblivious of the wires and switches that comprise the telephone system.

The point is:

The Internet operates like a single network that connects several million computers. IP software allows any computer to send an IP datagram to any other computer.

The Internet's Internal Structure

Although users believe the Internet to be a single, large network, the Internet contains a complex internal physical structure that users never see. Figure 15.2 illustrates the concept.

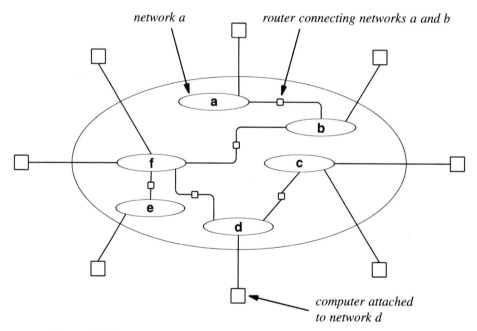

Figure 15.2 A small example of the physical structure that remains hidden inside the Internet. Each computer attaches to a single network; routers interconnect the networks.

When a datagram travels across the Internet from one computer to another, it must follow a physical path. At each step along the path, the datagram either travels across a physical network or through a router to another network. Eventually the datagram reaches its final destination.

Datagrams Travel In Packets

The IP datagram defines a standard format for all Internet packets. Choosing a standard packet format may seem like a wonderful idea because it means an Internet packet is not limited to the packet format used by the underlying network hardware. More important, it means that the Internet packet format does not depend on one particular network technology.

Unfortunately, defining a standard Internet packet format also has a disadvantage. Each network technology defines its own packet format, and a given computer network only accepts and delivers packets that adhere to the format for its technology — network hardware simply does not understand the IP datagram format.

How can the Internet send IP datagrams across networks that do not recognize the IP datagram format? The easiest way to imagine a datagram transfer is to consider how overnight shipping services handle letters. Assume someone has written a letter, placed it in an envelope, and written the name of the intended recipient on the outside. The letter is much like an IP datagram. Suppose the sender asks an overnight shipping service to deliver the letter. The overnight service requires that the letter be placed inside one of their envelopes, and that the name and address of the recipient be written on the outside in the format they specify. The outer envelope is analogous to a *network packet*.

Both the inner and outer envelopes contain a recipient name. Although the names usually agree, they need not be identical. Consider what happens if the sender knows the exact office address of a secretary at the recipient's place of business, but not the exact office address of the individual to whom the letter is addressed. The sender can mail the overnight parcel to the secretary for delivery. In such cases, the inner address and outer address differ. When the parcel arrives at the address on the outer envelope, the secretary named on the outer envelope opens it and forwards the letter.

Datagram transmission follows the same pattern. The Internet sends an IP datagram across a single network by placing it inside a network packet. As far as the network is concerned, the entire IP datagram is data. When the network packet arrives at the next computer, the computer "opens" the packet and extracts the datagram. The receiver examines the destination address on the datagram to determine how to process it. In particular, when a router determines that the datagram must be sent across another network, the router creates a new network packet, "encloses" the datagram inside the packet, and sends the packet across another network toward its destination. When a packet carrying a datagram arrives at its final destination, local software on the machine opens the packet and processes the datagram.

Every Computer Is Assigned A Unique Address

To make datagram routing and delivery possible, each computer attached to the Internet must be assigned a unique address. Like addresses used by conventional networks, the addresses used on the Internet are numeric. One computer must know the address of another computer before it can communicate, just as a person must know someone's telephone number before calling them on the phone.

Internet Addresses

The unique number assigned to a computer is called its *Internet address*, often abbreviated *IP address*. Each computer, including routers, needs to be assigned an IP address before the computer can communicate on the Internet. When an organization connects to the Internet, it obtains a set of IP addresses for the organization's computers from the Internet authority. If the organization acquires a new computer, an address from the set is assigned to the new machine.

An Odd IP Address Syntax

Internally, a computer stores an IP address in four binary units called *bytes*. Although the exact internal form is unimportant, it helps explain why IP addresses are expressed in an odd syntax. When an application program needs to display an IP address for a human or when humans need to type an IP address to a program, the binary address is expressed in a form that is easy for humans to understand: it is written as four decimal numbers separated by periods. For example, the IP address of one particular computer is:

128.10.2.1

The IP address of another computer is:

192.5.48.3

Fortunately, users seldom need to type or see IP addresses; most application programs allow humans to enter an alphabetic name when specifying a computer†.

---

†Chapter 18 describes the format of alphabetic computer names, and explains how each name is translated to an equivalent IP address.

IP Addresses Are Not Random

IP addresses are similar to telephone numbers in another way: the assignment of unique numbers is not random. Like the area codes in the phone system, IP addresses are assigned so that all computers on the same network have the same prefix. The address assignment has been chosen to make it efficient to route IP datagrams through the Internet.

A Trip Through An Example Internet

An example will clarify how IP software works. Consider the sample internet that Figure 15.3 shows.

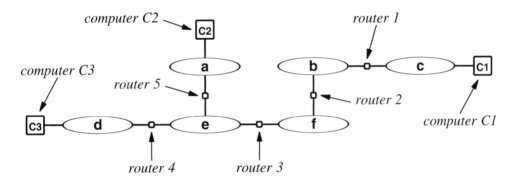

Figure 15.3 An example internet with six networks and three computers attached.

Imagine that computer *C1* needs to communicate with computer *C3*. To begin, IP software on *C1* must create an IP datagram. Each datagram has a field that specifies the sender's IP address and a field that specifies the destination's IP address. The datagram that *C1* creates contains *C3*'s IP address as the destination and *C1*'s IP address as the sender's (source) address.

Because the two computers do not attach to the same network, any datagram traveling between them must pass through a router. *C1* sends the datagram across network *c* to router *1*. Router *1* examines the datagram's destination address, *C3*, to determine where to send it. Because the destination lies beyond network *b*, router *1* sends the datagram across network *b* to router *2*. Router *2* examines the destination address and sends the datagram across network *f* to router *3*. Router *3* must make a choice between routers *4* and *5*. It chooses to send the datagram across network *e* to router *4* because router *4* leads to the destination†. Router *4* finds that it can deliver the datagram to its final destination, *C3*, by sending across network *d*. If *C3* sends a datagram back to *C1*, the new datagram follows the same path in the reverse direction.

Of course, computer networks and routers transfer datagrams at incredibly high speed. If the networks in our example are local area technologies, the entire time required for a datagram to traverse the Internet and a reply to come back takes only a few thousandths of a second. A human perceives the time required for a complete round trip to be instantaneous. Even if some of the networks are distant, the delays can be so short that a human does not notice. As a result, the Internet is so effective when transferring datagrams that it appears to operate like a single, large computer network.

How Fast Is Your Connection?

An interesting program is available that uses web communication to test the speed (bandwidth) of a connection. To run the speed test, follow the directions on‡:

http://www.auditmypc.com/internet–speed–test.asp

The test proceeds by moving data in two directions: from the web site to your computer and then from your computer to the web site. During the data transfer, software keeps track of the rate at which data is transferred. Although the site measures data transferred across the entire Internet, the speed is reported in terms of access technologies (e.g., dial-up, DSL, cable modem). The reason is that the interior of the Internet usually has higher-speed connections. That is:

> *Access is the slowest part of the Internet — the rate of a data transfer is usually limited by the rate at which an access technology operates.*

The test shows the speed in two directions: from the web site to your computer (called *download*) and from your computer to the web site (called *upload*). A difference between download and upload speeds arises because technologies such as DSL are *asymmetric*. That is, to provide faster display of web pages, the technology devotes more channels to data traveling to a user's computer than to data traveling to the Internet.

---

†When a router must choose between two paths that both lead to the destination, the router chooses the shortest path.

‡Because the site is popular, you may need to wait before the site is ready to test your connection's speed.

Summary

The Internet Protocol, IP, specifies the basic rules that a computer must follow to communicate across the Internet. IP defines the format of Internet packets, which are called IP datagrams. IP also defines an address scheme that assigns each computer a unique number used in all communication. More important, IP software makes an interconnected set of networks and routers operate like a single, large network.

Each computer on the Internet must have IP software that allows it to create and send IP datagrams. Each router also has IP software that knows how to forward datagrams to their destination. When a datagram arrives at a router, the IP software chooses the path that will lead to the datagram's destination.

16

TCP: Software For Reliable Communication

Introduction

The previous chapter discusses the Internet Protocol and describes how IP software on computers and routers makes it possible to send an IP datagram from any machine on the Internet to any other. This chapter continues the discussion of basic Internet communication software. It examines the second major communication protocol, TCP.

A Packet Switching System Can Be Overrun

Chapter 12 describes packet switching, the basic technique used by most modern computer networks. Recall that packet switching allows multiple computers to communicate without delay because it requires that the computers divide data into small packets. Packet switching systems, like those used in the Internet, need additional communication software to ensure that data is delivered. To understand why, consider the miniature internet that Figure 16.1 illustrates.

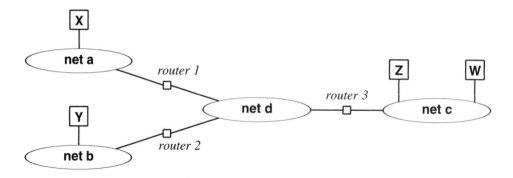

Figure 16.1 An example internet with four networks connected by routers. If each network has the same capacity, packets from networks *a* and *b* cannot flow to network *d* at full speed.

Suppose computer *X* sends packets to computer *W* at the same time computer *Y* sends packets to computer *Z*. Network *d* lies on the path from *X* to *W* as well as on the path from *Y* to *Z*. Furthermore, all four networks have the same capacity. Suppose that each network can handle 5000 packets per second. Also suppose that computers *X* and *Y* each generate 5000 datagrams per second. Router *1* and router *2* each receive 5000 datagrams per second. Both routers need to send all the datagrams they receive across network *d* to router *3*. Unfortunately, network *d* can also handle only 5000 packets per second.

To understand the problem, imagine that each network is a road, that each router is an interchange that connects two roads, and that all roads have the same speed limit. Figure 16.2 illustrates how cars traveling on roads correspond to packets traveling on an internet. Imagine that both roads *a* and *b* are packed with cars traveling at the speed limit. If all the cars from roads *a* and *b* attempt to merge onto road *d*, a traffic jam results.

On a roadway, cars stop when a traffic jam occurs. In the example internet, however, datagrams cannot stop. Each second, 5000 datagrams arrive from one network, 5000 from another, and only 5000 datagrams can be sent to their destinations. Where do the extra 5000 datagrams per second go when they cannot enter network *d*? The routers discard them! Of course, each router has memory, and can store some of the datagrams in memory in case of temporary congestion. However, a router only has enough memory to hold a few thousand datagrams. If datagrams continue to arrive faster than they can leave, the router must discard datagrams as they arrive until the congestion clears.

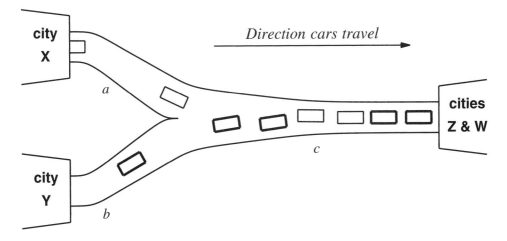

Figure 16.2 Cars from two roads (a and b) merging onto another road (c) are analogous to packets from two networks merging onto a third network. The diagram only shows cars traveling left-to-right, from cities *X* and *Y* to cities *Z* and *W*.

TCP Helps IP Guarantee Delivery

Because the Internet uses packet switching hardware that can become overrun with datagrams, the designers knew that additional communication software was needed. To handle the problem, they invented the *Transmission Control Protocol* (*TCP*). TCP makes the Internet reliable. All computers that attach to the Internet run IP software; most of them also run TCP software. In fact, TCP and IP are so important and work together so well that the entire set of communication protocols the Internet uses is known as the *TCP/IP* protocol suite.

TCP solves several problems that can occur in a packet switching system. If a router becomes overrun with datagrams, it must discard them. As a result, a datagram can be lost on its trip through the Internet. TCP automatically checks for lost datagrams and handles the problem. The Internet has a complex structure with multiple paths that datagrams can travel. When the hardware in a router or network system fails, other routers start sending datagrams along a new path analogous to the way cars detour around a problem on a highway. As a result of the change in routes, some datagrams can arrive at the destination in a different order than they were sent. TCP automatically checks incoming datagrams and puts the data back in order. Finally, network hardware failures sometimes result in duplication of datagrams. As a result, multiple copies of a datagram can arrive at the destination. TCP automatically checks for duplicate datagrams and accepts only the first copy of data that arrives. To summarize:

*Although IP software allows a computer to send and receive da-
tagrams, IP does not handle all the problems that can arise. A computer using the Internet also needs TCP software to provide reliable,
error-free communication.*

TCP Provides A Connection Between Computer Programs

Conceptually, TCP allows computer programs to interact analogous to the way
people interact when they use a telephone. A program on one computer specifies a remote program and initiates contact (the equivalent of using a telephone number to place
a call). The called program must accept the incoming call (the equivalent of answering
the phone). Once contact has been established, the two programs can send data in either direction (the equivalent of holding a telephone conversion). Finally, when the
programs finish, they terminate the session (the equivalent of hanging up the telephones). Of course, because computers operate at much higher speeds than humans,
two programs can establish a connection, exchange a small amount of data, and then
terminate the connection within a few thousandths of a second. To summarize:

*TCP software makes it possible for two computer programs to com-
municate across the Internet in a manner similar to the way humans
use a telephone. Once the programs establish a connection, they can
exchange arbitrary amounts of data, and then terminate communication.*

The Magic Of Recovering Lost Datagrams

Detecting and removing a duplicate copy of a datagram is a relatively easy task.
Because TCP includes an identification of the data in each datagram, the receiver can
compare the identification in an incoming datagram with the identification of data already received. If a duplicate copy of data arrives, the receiver ignores it.

Recovering from datagram loss is more difficult. To understand why, consider the
example internet shown in Figure 16.1; datagrams can be lost in a router in the middle
of the internet while neither the original source computer nor the final destination computer experiences trouble. TCP handles the problem by using timers and acknowledgements. Whenever data arrives at its final destination, TCP software on the receiving
machine sends an *acknowledgement* back to the source. An acknowledgement is a short
message that specifies which data arrived.

A sender uses acknowledgements to guarantee that all data arrives. Whenever TCP
software sends data, it starts a timer using the computer's internal clock. The timer
works like an alarm clock — when the timer expires, it notifies TCP. If an ack-

nowledgement arrives before the timer expires, TCP cancels the timer. If the timer expires before an acknowledgement arrives, TCP assumes the datagram was lost and sends another copy.

TCP Retransmission Is Automatic

Many computer communication protocols use the scheme of starting a timer and resending data if an acknowledgement fails to arrive before the timer expires. TCP's scheme differs from the one used by other protocols because it adapts to work anywhere on the Internet. If the destination computer resides close to the source (e.g., in the same building), TCP only waits a short time before retransmitting the datagram. If the destination computer resides far from the source (e.g., in another country), TCP waits a longer time before retransmitting. Furthermore, the timeout mechanism is completely automatic — TCP measures current delays on the Internet and adjusts the timeout automatically. If many computers begin to send datagrams and the Internet slows down, TCP increases the time it waits before retransmitting. If conditions change and datagrams begin to flow across the Internet quickly, TCP automatically decreases the timeout. Experience has shown that in a large Internet, a communication protocol must change the timeout automatically to achieve efficient data transfer.

TCP's ability to automatically adjust timeout values has contributed much to the success of the Internet. In fact, most Internet applications could not operate without TCP software that adapts to changing conditions. Furthermore, careful measurements and experience have shown that TCP software can adapt to changes in the Internet extremely well — although many scientists have tried to devise improvements, no one has produced a protocol that works better in typical cases.

TCP And IP Work Together

It is not a coincidence that TCP and IP work well together. Although the protocols can be used separately, they were designed at the same time to work as part of a unified system, and were engineered to cooperate and complement each other. Therefore, TCP handles the problems that IP does not handle without duplicating the work that IP does. The point is:

A computer connected to the Internet needs both TCP and IP software. IP provides a way to transfer a packet from its source to its destination, but does not handle problems like datagram loss or delivery out of order. TCP handles the problems that IP does not. Together, they provide a reliable way to send data across the Internet.

Often, vendors sell a single package that includes software for TCP, IP, and a few related communication protocols. Collectively, the set is known as *TCP/IP software*.

Summary

Although IP software provides basic Internet communication, it does not solve all problems that arise. Like any packet switching system, the Internet can become overrun if many computers send data at the same time. When computers send more datagrams than the Internet can handle, routers must discard some of the incoming datagrams.

IP software does not detect missing datagrams. To handle such communication errors, a computer must also have TCP software. TCP eliminates duplicate data, ensures that data is reassembled in exactly the order it was sent, and resends data when a datagram is lost.

The problem of data loss is especially difficult because loss can occur in the middle of the Internet, even when the networks and routers adjacent to both the source and destination computers do not experience problems. TCP uses acknowledgements and timeouts to handle the problem of loss. The sender retransmits data unless an acknowledgement arrives before the timer expires. TCP's scheme for timeout works across the Internet because TCP changes the timeout automatically depending on whether the destination is close or far away from the source.

17

Clients + Servers = Distributed Computing

Introduction

Previous chapters describe the TCP/IP communication protocols that work together to provide reliable data delivery across the Internet. This chapter describes how application programs use TCP/IP software to provide services across the Internet. It shows that, despite their diversity, all applications on the Internet follow a single organizational model. Later chapters discuss specific examples of services, and show how the model applies in practice.

Large Computers Use Networks For Input And Output

Early computers were large and expensive. As a result, most companies could only afford a single computer. When networks first appeared, companies used the technology to connect remote I/O devices to their computer. For example, some remote sites included a printer plus one or more terminals, each with a keyboard and display. Although a remote device connected to the single central computer across a network, the central computer controlled the device completely. The arrangement in which a large, central computer controlled small I/O devices at remote sites led to the term *master-slave* networking.

Small Computers Use Networks To Interact

As newer technologies emerged, computers became inexpensive. Powered by microprocessors, personal computers and scientific workstations appeared. Although small, a personal computer contains much more than a keyboard and a display. It also has the ability to process information.

Because it contains the processing power necessary to send and receive packets, a personal computer can communicate directly with any other computer on its network. Furthermore, because a personal computer does not depend on a large, central computer for control, it can act independently. To emphasize the symmetric relationship among computers that communicate with one another, scientists use the terms *distributed computing* or *peer-to-peer communication*†.

Peer-to-peer networking refers to network technologies that permit arbitrary communication among computers. The Internet supports peer-to-peer communication because it does not distinguish among connected computers. A personal computer can contact another personal computer as easily as it can contact a large mainframe. A large mainframe computer can contact another large mainframe, a medium-size computer, or a small personal computer.

Distributed computing refers to any computation that involves two or more computers communicating over a network. The computation need not involve arithmetic or numbers. For example, when two computers exchange electronic mail, they engage in a form of distributed computing because multiple computers cooperate to send and deliver the message.

To summarize:

> *Because modern computer networks allow large or small computers to initiate interaction and to interact arbitrarily with other computers, we use the term* peer-to-peer *networking. Distributed computing refers to any interaction among computers that share access to a peer-to-peer network.*

Distributed Computing On The Internet

The Internet offers an amazing diversity of services that each involve a form of distributed computation. For example, one can send a message to a friend, retrieve a file, browse through directories, search a database, print a document, transmit a fax, or listen to music.

The diverse variety of available services means the Internet offers equally diverse styles of interaction. In some cases, a user interacts with another human. In other cases, a user interacts with a remote computer program that offers a service. In still

---

†As Chapter 29 explains, the term *peer-to-peer* is applied to music and file sharing applications that take advantage of direct communication among computers.

others, two computer systems communicate without human intervention. Interactive services allow a user to remain connected for hours or days. Other services need only milliseconds to supply requested information, and terminate communication almost immediately. Some services allow users to fetch information, while others allow users to store or update information. Some services involve only two computer systems, one that sends a request and another that supplies a response; other services involve several computers.

A Single Paradigm Explains All Distributed Computing

Despite the wide diversity among Internet services and the apparent differences in their use, the software that implements a service always uses a single scheme. The scheme is called *client-server computing*. Client-server computing is not limited to the Internet — it forms the basis for all distributed computing.

The idea behind client-server computing is quite simple: some computers on the Internet offer services that others access. For example, some servers manage files that contain information. A client program can contact such a server to request a copy of one of the files. Other servers manage multi-user games. An individual who wants to play one of the games must use a client program to contact the server and participate in the game.

To understand how a single paradigm can encompass the diversity of services, one needs to know three basic facts.

- Programs communicate.
  People who use the Internet often say that their computer has communicated with another computer. Although such statements occur frequently in informal conversations, they hide a technical detail. Computers do not communicate with other computers — only programs can communicate. A program running on one computer uses protocol software to contact a program on another computer and exchange messages. On the Internet, the two programs must use TCP/IP protocol software. While the distinction between computers and the programs running on them may seem trivial, it is important because it explains how a single computer can engage in multiple conversations with other computers.

- TCP/IP does not create or run application programs.
  Although the Internet can transfer data from one point to another, it does not automatically start a program on the receiving machine. In a sense, the Internet works like a telephone system — it allows one program to call another, but the called program must answer the call before communication is possible. Thus, two programs can only communicate if one of them starts running and agrees to answer calls *before* the other program contacts it.

- Computers can run multiple programs.
  Even the slowest, smallest computers can run more than one program at a time. It may seem strange to think about a computer running more than one program because most computers contain a single processor. However, an operating system keeps multiple programs running by switching the processor among them rapidly. The operating system allows the processor to work on one program for a short time, then it moves the processor to another program for a short time, and so on. Because a computer's processor can execute several million operations per second, switching it among multiple programs gives a human the impression that the programs all run at the same time. For example, a user can have three activities in three separate windows on the display that each appear to proceed simultaneously.

Knowing that programs communicate and that a computer can run multiple programs at one time explains an apparent mystery: how a single computer can provide service to multiple users at the same time. Many Internet services use multiple copies of a program to permit multiple users to access the service simultaneously. For example, a single computer can receive and store incoming electronic mail from many other computers at the same time. To do so, it creates multiple copies of the program that accepts incoming email. Each computer that sends mail communicates with a single copy of the program. Because the processor can switch among the copies rapidly, all transmissions appear to proceed simultaneously.

To summarize:

> *Communication across the Internet always occurs between a pair of programs; one initiates a conversation, and the other must be waiting to receive it. Because a given computer can run more than one program at the same time, a single computer can appear to engage in multiple conversations simultaneously.*

Communicating Programs Are Clients Or Servers

Each computer program that communicates can be classified in one of two categories. Any program that offers a service belongs in the *server* category; any program that contacts a service belongs in the *client* category.

Usually, people who use Internet services run client software. For example, a typical application program that uses the Internet to access a service becomes a client. The client uses the Internet to communicate with a server. For some services, the client interacts with the server using one request. The client forms a request, sends it to the server, and awaits a reply. For other services, the client engages in a long-term interaction. The client establishes communication with the server, and then continuously displays the data received from the server, while it transmits keystrokes or mouse input to the server.

A Server Must Always Run

Unlike client software, a server program must always be ready to receive requests. A client can contact a server at any time; the server has no warning. Usually, server programs only run on large computers that allow multiple servers to execute simultaneously. When the system first begins execution, it starts one or more copies of each server program running. A server continues to execute as long as the computer continues to run.

If a computer loses power or the operating system crashes, all servers running on the computer are lost. When the computer that offers a service crashes, clients actively using a server on that computer will receive an error message. Any client that attempts to establish communication with a server while the computer is down will also receive an error message.

Summary

Unlike older networks that connected terminals to large, central computers, the Internet provides peer-to-peer networking. It allows an arbitrary computer to communicate with any other computer.

The Internet offers a wide variety of services that use many styles of interaction. Despite apparent differences among the available services, all software on the Internet uses the same general structure. The structure is known as client-server computing.

In a client-server environment, each program must be classified as a client or as a server. A server program offers a service. Usually, computers that offer services start the server software running automatically when the computer is powered on. The server remains running, ready to accept an incoming request at any time. Users usually run client software when they access a service. A client program contacts a server, sends a request, and displays the server's response.

18

Names For Computers

Introduction

The previous chapter describes communication between computer programs that provide and use services. This chapter describes an important Internet facility that allows humans to use alphabetic names for machines in place of numeric addresses. It explains the naming scheme, and describes how software uses client-server interaction to convert a computer's alphabetic name into the computer's numeric address.

People Prefer Names To Numbers

Recall that the Internet assigns each computer a numeric value called an IP address, and that every packet sent across the Internet contains the IP address of the computer to which it has been sent. Like a telephone number, an IP address is a multi-digit number. Also like a telephone number, an IP address can be difficult to remember and enter correctly. When written in decimal, for example, an IP address contains ten digits.

Instead of IP addresses, people prefer to use alphabetic names for computers. The Internet accommodates such names. First, a user is permitted to name their computer. Second, software permits a user to enter a computer's alphabetic name in place of the computer's IP address. Third, the Internet includes a service that automatically translates a computer's alphabetic name to the computer's numeric address. We will explore name translation after considering how computer names are assigned.

Naming A Computer Can Be Challenging Or Fun

The name assigned to a computer can affect the way people react toward it; a name creates a sense of personality. For example, some people choose a name for their computer that conveys a sense of pride in their work. Others choose a name that conveys their sense of frustration. When someone hears a computer's name, they often infer something about the machine or its owner.

Names for computers attached to the Internet vary widely. For example, people have chosen the names of geographic locations, characters in movies, actors, colors, oceans, corporations, characters from mythology, and famous people. The names of planets like *Mercury* or *Saturn* remain popular. In 1996, the most popular name for a computer on the Internet, other than mundane names such as *mailhost* , was *venus*; by 2000, *mars* had surpassed *venus*. By 2005, however, *zeus* had surpassed *mars*.

Of course, using a common word as the name of a computer can seem frivolous. Some people choose names that identify the type of computer, and simply add a suffix to distinguish multiple machines. For example, the series *pc1*, *pc2*, ... ranks among the top names used in the Internet as does the series of *host1*, *host2*, and so on.

A group of co-workers can adopt a naming scheme for their computers. For example, one group uses the names of trees. Their computers are named *birch*, *elm*, *oak*, etc. Often, a naming scheme relates to a group's profession. Computers owned by a group of chemists could be named after the elements (e.g., *hydrogen*, *helium*, and *oxygen*), while a group of computers owned by physicists could be named after particles (e.g., *proton*, *quark*, *neutrino*, and *positron*).

Some people have fun choosing a name for their computer. At one university, computers were named *up* and *down*, making it possible for the statement "down is up today" to be true. Characters from comic strips have also been popular. You may be surprised to learn that *snoopy* has always ranked in the top few hundred names for computers on the Internet; when *Calvin and Hobbes* was a popular comic strip, *calvin* ranked in the top 50 names. Sometimes a computer and its owner share the same name, making it possible to joke about the machine or the person. For example, if both a computer and its owner are named *John*, one can say "John is down today" or "I find it difficult to work with John."

In addition to names chosen for fun, the names given to some computers reflect the computer's main role. A computer that runs an organization's electronic mail service is often named *mail* or *smtp* (the protocol used to send mail). Similarly, a computer that runs an organization's World Wide Web service is often named *www* or *web*. Figure 18.1 shows that by the year 2005, many of the most commonly used computer names were the names of services†. Using service names makes it easier for people who operate or troubleshoot an organization's computers.

---

†Later chapters explain Internet services, including the File Transfer Protocol (FTP) and the World Wide Web (WWW).

rank	name	rank	name	rank	name
1	www	18	www2	35	web
2	mail	19	webmail	36	fw
3	dsl	20	mailgate	37	dns1
4	cpe	21	network	38	host1
5	ns2	22	dns	39	ns3
6	ns	23	mail1	40	e0
7	ns1	24	pc3	41	dns2
8	gw	25	pc4	42	host2
9	ftp	26	secure	43	admin
10	router	27	pc5	44	vpn
11	smtp	28	mailhost	45	mx
12	pc1	29	proxy	46	bcast
13	pc2	30	test	47	server1
14	mail2	31	demon-gw	48	www1
15	gateway	32	pc6	49	szerver4
16	server	33	gate	50	szerver3
17	broadcast	34	net		

Figure 18.1 The fifty most common names assigned to computers on the Internet in 2005.

Computer Names Must Be Unique

Although most people prefer to use a short name for their computer, longer names must be used on the Internet to avoid assigning the same name to multiple computers. Two computers with the same name would create a significant problem because communication software could not distinguish between them. The point is:

> *Each computer on the Internet must have a unique name or the name would not distinguish the computer from all others.*

Suffixes On Computer Names

To make names unique, the Internet naming mechanism uses a familiar idea: it extends each name by adding additional strings. We think of the additional strings as a suffix appended to the name. The full name of a computer consists of its local name followed by a period and the organization's suffix.

Among humans, additional parts of a name identify a person's family or place of birth; additional parts of a name on the Internet identify the organization that owns the computer. Unfortunately, multiple organizations sometimes have similar or related names. To allow multiple organizations to use similar names without conflict, the Internet scheme further qualifies each name by giving the type of the organization. For example, because the Internet authority classifies Purdue University as an *edu*cational institution, it approved the suffix:

purdue.edu

for the names of all computers at Purdue. If a company named *Purdue Gumball Corporation* asks to use *Purdue* in the names of its computers, the Internet naming authority will assign it a suffix that designates it as a *com*mercial enterprise. For example, it might be assigned:

purdue.com

The suffix *purdue.com* clearly distinguishes the company from the university.

If both Purdue University and Purdue Gumball Corporation each name one of their computers *groucho*, the suffixes guarantee that the two computers will have unique full names†:

groucho.purdue.edu

and

groucho.purdue.com

The point is:

> *Because a suffix appended to the name of a computer identifies the organization that owns the computer and the type of the organization, the full names of any two computers owned by separate organizations are guaranteed to differ from one another.*

Names With Many Parts

Although the examples above imply that computer names always have three parts (local, organization, and organization type), they seldom do. The Internet naming scheme allows names to contain multiple parts. Once the Internet assigns a suffix to an organization, the organization can choose to add additional parts to the names of its computers. Often, each organization decides that names for all its computers will contain a computer name and a department name followed by the organization suffix. Adding an additional level to names solves an important problem:

---

†In Internet terminology, a computer is called a *host*, and a computer's full name is called a *hostname*.

Because the Internet permits organizations to add additional parts to computer names, each group in the organization is free to choose the primary names for its computers. The full names of any two computers in separate groups are guaranteed to differ.

Like the computer science departments at many other universities, the Computer Science Department at Purdue University uses the 2-letter abbreviation *cs* to denote the department. Thus, the suffix *cs.purdue.edu* appears on the names of all computers in the CS Department. For example, a computer named *groucho* in Purdue's Computer Science Department has the full name:

groucho.cs.purdue.edu

Similarly, a computer named *www* in the same department has the full name:

www.cs.purdue.edu

The Electrical and Computer Engineering department at Purdue University uses the abbreviation *ece*, so a computer named *www* in that organization has the full name:

www.ece.purdue.edu

Domain Names Outside The US

Although most domain names in the United States end with *.edu* or *.com*, other countries have chosen to follow alternative schemes. Most append the 2-letter country code to each domain name. For example in China, Yahoo is named:

yahoo.com.cn

because *cn* is the internationally recognized 2-letter county code identifier for China. Similarly, domain names for computers in Germany end in *de*, those in Canada end in *ca*, and those in the United Kingdom end in *uk*. Each country chooses how to further divide domain names. For example, because the United Kingdom has chosen *ac* to denote academic institutions, a computer at the University of York in England has the name:

minster.cs.york.ac.uk

Translating A Name To An Equivalent IP Address

Recall that the Internet communication software must use IP addresses when it sends and receives datagrams. Although people can refer to a computer by name, the name must be translated into an IP address before a packet can be sent to the named computer. The Internet includes a facility that translates names to IP addresses automatically. The alphabetic names described above are called *domain names*, and the software that translates a domain name to an IP address is called the *Domain Name System* (*DNS*). Whenever an application program encounters a computer name (e.g., when a user enters the name of a computer on the keyboard), the application uses the domain name system to translate the name into an IP address. It then uses the IP address in all communication.

The domain name system uses the client-server approach described in the previous chapter. Each organization operates a domain name server that contains the list of all computers in that organization along with their IP addresses. When an application program needs to translate a computer's name into the computer's IP address, the application becomes a client of the DNS. It contacts a domain name server, and sends the server an alphabetic computer name. Sending a domain name server a computer's name is equivalent to asking,

What is the IP address for this name?

The server looks up the answer, and returns the correct IP address.

Domain Name System Works Like Directory Assistance

The easiest way to understand the operation of the domain name system is to think about directory assistance in the telephone system. To place a telephone call, the caller must use a telephone number. If the caller knows a person's full name, address, and city, the caller can obtain the person's telephone number from the directory assistance service. To do so, one calls directory assistance for the correct city, and specifies the person's name. The directory assistance operator replies by giving the person's telephone number.

Of course, a single directory assistance operator does not know all the telephone numbers in the world. If one needs the telephone number of a person in another country, for example, local directory assistance does not have an answer. However, the directory assistance in one country can supply the telephone number of directory assistance in a foreign country.

The domain name system works similar to the way directory assistance does. A given server does not store the names and addresses of all possible computers in the Internet. Instead, each server stores the names of local computers (e.g., the computers at one company or enterprise). When an application on a computer in France needs to know the IP address of a computer in California, the application sends its request to a domain name server in France. The server in France does not know the answer, but knows how to contact the appropriate domain name server in California.

Computer Name Lookup Is Automatic

Consider an example. Suppose that a user sitting at a computer in France needs to communicate with computer *calvin* located at company *XYZ* in California. The user must specify the computer's name. For example, the full name might be:

calvin.xyz.com

Before an application program running in France can communicate with computer *calvin*, it needs to obtain *calvin*'s IP address. To find the address, the application uses the Internet's domain name system.

Does an application program in France need to know the address of the domain name server for company *XYZ*? No, the domain name system is completely automated. A computer on the Internet only needs to know the location of one domain name server, usually a local one. The domain name server handles the lookup automatically. Figure 18.2 illustrates the communication.

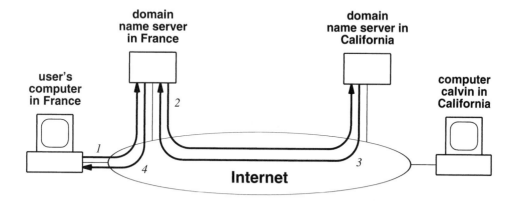

Figure 18.2 To communicate with a remote computer, an application program asks a local domain name server for the remote computer's IP address. If the local domain name server does not know the answer, it contacts a remote domain server automatically. Numbers on the arrows tell the order of the four steps taken.

As the figure shows, finding the IP address for a remote name takes four steps. First, an application program on a computer in France places the name *calvin.xyz.com* in a message and sends it to the local domain name server in France. The application is asking the server,

What is the IP address of the computer named calvin at company XYZ*?*

Second, the domain name server in France contacts the domain name server at company *XYZ*. Third, the server at company *XYZ* responds by sending an answer. Fourth, the local domain name server in France sends the answer back to the original application program. Note that the domain name service performs all four steps without contacting computer *calvin* similar to the way directory assistance can provide someone's telephone number without calling that person.

Although the domain name system may send several messages across the Internet, obtaining a response does not take long. In most cases, a response takes less than a second. Speed is important because domain name lookup often occurs when a user enters the name of a computer to be contacted. The user must wait while the domain name system finds the computer's IP address. As soon as the domain name system responds, the application program can begin sending packets directly to the computer†.

To summarize:

> *A computer on the Internet only needs to know the location of one domain name server. A program becomes a client of the domain name service when it sends a computer's name to the local domain name server. The local server answers the request by translating the name into an IP address. Although the server may contact remote servers to obtain the information, the client receives an answer from the local server.*

IP Addresses And Domain Names Are Unrelated

Syntactically, domain names resemble IP addresses. An IP address is written as four numbers separated by three periods, while a domain name consists of alphabetic strings separated by periods.

Appearances can be deceiving. Although they may look similar, the individual parts of domain names and IP addresses are completely unrelated. An IP address contains four parts because a 32-bit binary number can be divided into four 8-bit sections. A domain name contains multiple parts because an organization can choose to add zero or more items to its suffix to allow individual groups within the organization to choose the same primary names for computers.

---

†To further optimize speed, after a computer looks up a domain name, the computer remembers the answer for a short time. Thus, if a user browses the same web site three times in a row, only the first causes a domain name lookup.

Confusion arises because some domain names contain exactly four parts. For example, the Internet's Domain Name Service translates the name:

arthur.cs.purdue.edu

to the IP address:

128.10.2.1

However, the string *arthur* is not related to *128*, nor are any of the other parts of the name related to parts of the IP address. To keep the distinction clear, think of a person's name and their telephone number. Letters or groups of letters in a person's name have no relationship to groups of digits in their telephone number (e.g., a person's first name is unrelated to the initial group of digits in the person's telephone number).

Summary

Because humans prefer using names instead of numbers, the Internet allows people to assign a name to each computer, and provides an automated system that can translate a name into an equivalent IP address.

Many application programs that use the Internet permit users to enter names for remote computers. The application becomes a client of the domain name service by sending a name to the local domain name server in a request message. The server translates the name to an IP address, automatically contacting other servers if needed.

A computer's name consists of multiple alphabetic strings separated by periods. The computer's primary name comes first, and a suffix that designates the organization that owns a computer comes last. Additional strings can occur in the name if the organization has added supplementary names to identify groups within the organization.

Although both the names used for computers and their IP addresses are written as strings of characters with periods separating them, items in a computer's name are unrelated to items in the computer's IP address just as characters in a person's name are unrelated to digits in their telephone number.

19

NAT: Sharing An Internet Connection

Introduction

Chapter 14 describes technologies such as DSL and cable modems that provide broadband access to the Internet. This chapter examines an extension of basic access — a mechanism that allows a set of computers to ''share'' a single physical connection and a single IP address. The chapter explains both the motivation for sharing and the technology used to achieve it.

High Capacity And Multiple Computers

As Chapter 14 points out, a technology such as a DSL line or a cable modem provides high-speed, dedicated Internet access. In each case, the underlying technology provides a dedicated connection between a subscriber and an ISP. One of the advantages of a broadband connection arises from the speed — a broadband connection can transmit so many bits per second that the capacity is enough for multiple computers.

Unfortunately, many ISPs design their broadband systems with a limitation: a subscriber can only use one computer at a time. Recall, for example, that each computer on the Internet requires an IP address. Many ISP networks are designed to give each subscriber a single address; a request for an additional request is denied. So, merely connecting additional computers to a given DSL line or cable modem does not work — only the first computer that makes a request will receive an address, and others will be prevented from using the Internet.

It Is Possible To Share A Single IP Address

When ISPs began to sell broadband service that restricted each customer to a single IP address, Internet researchers began to ask whether it might be possible to arrange for multiple computers at a residence to "share" a single address. If a mechanism for sharing were invented, each subscriber could use multiple computers at the same time (e.g., children could be looking up information for school, while parents read email).

At first, the whole idea of sharing a connection seemed preposterous. After all, the entire Internet is designed so that each computer is assigned a unique IP address. If multiple computers used the same address, how could datagrams be sent to the correct computer? Some engineers asserted that sharing violated the fundamental design principles.

Clever engineers devised a way to solve the problem: instead of connecting a computer directly to a DSL or cable modem, insert an additional device. The additional device is designed to connect multiple computers without requiring any additional IP addresses.

A Device For Connection Sharing Is Called A NAT Box

The device that allows connection sharing is known as a *Network Address Translation* device; engineers in the industry use the informal term *NAT box*. Figure 19.1 illustrates how a NAT device connects between computers and a broadband modem.

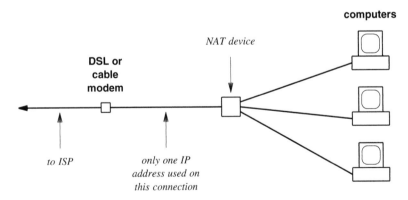

Figure 19.1 Physical connections used to allow multiple computers to share a single IP address. A NAT device is inserted between a broadband modem and a set of computers.

The point is:

A device known informally as a NAT box allows a subscriber to share an Internet connection among multiple computers Sharing is most practical with a broadband connection that has sufficient capacity to handle multiple computers.

A NAT Box Acts Like A Miniature ISP

A NAT device provides an illusion to both the subscriber's ISP and to computers that connect to the NAT box. To an ISP, a NAT box appears to be a single computer. When it is powered on, a NAT box communicates exactly like a computer that has been powered on — the NAT box sends datagrams over a DSL or cable modem to the ISP, and requests an IP address that is used for all future communication. Thus, the subscriber's ISP thinks the subscriber has a single computer.

To a computer, the NAT box appears to be an ISP. When a computer starts, the computer requests an IP address, and the NAT box responds by sending an address. Interestingly, the address that a NAT box assigns to a computer is not valid on the Internet. Instead, a NAT box uses a local address that is restricted to the link between the computer and the NAT device. A special set of IP addresses have been reserved for such purposes; NAT devices usually use addresses of the form:

192.168.1.xxx

where *xxx* is a unique number for each computer that connects to the NAT box. For example, the first computer that requests an IP address might be assigned address:

192.168.1.100

the next computer might be assigned address:

192.168.1.101

and so on.

NAT Changes The Address In Each Datagram

In essence a NAT box acts like a router that can forward datagrams between computers and the Internet. Indeed, vendors that sell NAT devices often use the term *router*. Can a NAT box merely route datagrams between the attached computers and the Internet? No, because the IP addresses the computers are using are not valid on the Internet. To accomplish its magic, a NAT box must alter the addresses in each datagram. In essence, before a datagram goes out to the Internet, the NAT box replaces the "return" address with the one valid IP address that the NAT box knows. When a site on the Internet replies, the reply will be forwarded to the NAT box.

If all outgoing datagrams have the same reply address, how can a NAT box know which computer should receive each datagram that arrives from the Internet? In essence, a NAT boxs keeps a record of what each computer is doing (e.g., which web site is being accessed or which file is being downloaded). When a datagram arrives from the Internet, the NAT box consults its record to determine which computer should receive the datagram. Before sending, the NAT box replaces the "to" address in the datagram with the local address that has been assigned to the destination computer.

We can summarize:

> *Although a* Network Address Translation *device resembles a router and vendors often use the term* router *for commercial products, a NAT box differs from a conventional router because NAT replaces addresses in datagrams.*

Computer Software Can Perform The NAT Function

Many versions of NAT exist. The easiest form to understand consists of a small physical device that connects exactly as Figure 19.1 shows. It is also possible, however, to write a special-purpose computer program that performs the NAT function. Free NAT software that runs under the Linux operating system has been popular among students. For example, if a dorm room has a single Internet connection, it is possible to purchase an extra NIC for a PC, install the Linux operating system plus NAT software on the PC, and then connect additional computers.

Logically, a software version of NAT is no different than the arrangement that Figure 19.1 shows. However, the physical interconnections differ. A small, inexpensive *network hub* provides the physical interconnection, and a PC running NAT software has an extra network connection that attaches to the hub. Figure 19.2 shows the connections.

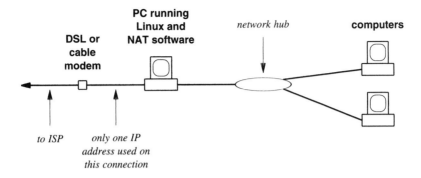

Figure 19.2 The connections used when NAT software runs under the Linux operating system on a PC. Logically, the result is the same as Figure 19.1.

Linux is not the only operating system that can run NAT software. Versions of NAT software are also available for Microsoft Windows and the Apple OS X operating system used on Macs. The Microsoft version is known as *Internet Connection Sharing*, and the Mac version is part of *airport*. Each provides essentially the same functionality as the Linux version.

NAT Can Use A Wireless Network

One of the most interesting aspects of commercial NAT products involves the use of wireless network technology, usually Wi-Fi. Many vendors advertise NAT devices as *wireless routers*. In essence, a wireless router merely extends the idea of NAT to permit a Wi-Fi connection as well as a wired connection. For example, consider Figure 19.1. We can imagine that in addition to the three computers shown in the diagram, the NAT device contains a Wi-Fi transmitter that allows additional computers to communicate.

Chapter 31 discusses an interesting problem that arises from wireless routers. Because they run NAT, such routers can connect an arbitrary wireless computer to the Internet. An incorrectly configured wireless router can allow someone in a nearby location (e.g., an adjacent apartment) to connect to the Internet and share a subscriber's connection.

Summary

Although ISPs often restrict each subscriber to a single IP address, a technology known as Network Address Translation (NAT) allows a subscriber to share a single Internet connection among a set of computers. Sharing makes most sense with a broadband connection because broadband access provides sufficient capacity to handle communication from several computers.

To an ISP, a NAT device gives the illusion of a single computer; to each computer, the NAT box gives the illusion of an ISP. As datagrams pass through, the NAT box translates between local IP addresses and the single externally-valid IP address so the ISP remains unaware that multiple computers exist and the computers remain unaware that they are sharing a connection.

In addition to their use with wired network connections, a NAT box can provide wireless network connections. Correct configuration is needed to ensure that wireless service is not inadvertently extended to neighbors.

20

Why The Internet Works Well

Introduction

Previous chapters describe the basic Internet technology, including TCP/IP software. This chapter considers reasons for the Internet's success and the lessons that can be learned.

The Internet Works Well

The Internet is a marvel of technical accomplishment. The basic TCP/IP technology has accommodated growth and changes that the original designers could not imagine. While the number of computers on the Internet has grown exponentially, TCP/IP technology has accommodated the increase in size. Traffic on the Internet has also grown exponentially, and TCP/IP technology has tolerated the additional packets. Although computers now operate several thousand times faster than the computers that existed when TCP/IP was first built, new computers can communicate across the Internet with each other and with older computers. Despite a 150,000-fold increase in the speed of circuits at the center of the Internet, basic TCP/IP protocols have not changed; the same design continues to operate correctly at the higher speed.

Why is TCP/IP technology so successful? How could a technology from a research project become the foundation of the world's largest computer network system? What lessons have we learned from the Internet project? Obviously, no single technical decision results in the overwhelming success of a complex system like the Internet. However, a poor design choice can ruin an otherwise excellent plan. Remaining sections of this chapter examine some of the best design choices in TCP/IP and draw lessons from the Internet project.

IP Provides Flexibility

The Internet Protocol provides the flexibility needed to accommodate a wide range of underlying network hardware. For example, IP can use:

- Wide Area Network technologies or Local Area Network technologies
- Networks that operate at the highest speeds or networks that operate at the slowest speeds
- Networks that guarantee no packet loss or networks that provide only best-effort delivery
- Wireless networks that use radio for communication, networks that send signals across wires, or networks that send signals across glass fibers
- Combinations of the above

In summary, IP allows the Internet to include almost any type of computer communication technology.

The secret of IP's success stems from a tolerant approach. Because it does not demand much from the network hardware, IP tolerates almost any mechanism that can send bits from one location to another. In terms of the design:

> *The Internet Protocol accommodates many types of hardware because it makes almost no assumptions about the underlying network hardware.*

Although IP makes minimal assumptions about network hardware, all implementations of IP must use exactly the same rules for communication. To ensure compatibility among implementations of TCP/IP, complete specifications for the protocols have been written in documents informally called *standards*. TCP/IP standards include an exact specification of how to send IP datagrams on each type of network. Whenever a new network technology appears, a new Internet standards document is written that describes how to use the technology with TCP/IP. The specifications form an important part of Internet literature because they guarantee that all computers and all routers use exactly the same format when sending a datagram across a network. Thus,

Because TCP/IP standards documents specify the exact way to send IP datagrams on a given type of network, computers and routers from multiple vendors always agree on the details.

TCP Provides Reliability

TCP and IP form a complementary pair that work together well. TCP handles communication problems that IP does not handle, and provides applications with reliable communication.

Interestingly, TCP needs to compensate for differences among the various types of network hardware that IP can use. For example, although sending a datagram across a satellite channel takes tenths of seconds, sending a datagram across a LAN takes only one or two thousandths of a second. A single copy of the TCP software must handle both. Similarly, although a LAN seldom or never drops packets, a Wide Area Network can lose a significant percentage of packets. TCP software must be able to use either technology efficiently.

TCP also handles the most difficult problem found in packet switching systems: rapid changes in the performance. Computers tend to send information in bursts — the computer remains quiet for awhile, then emits a burst of data for a short time, and then resumes its quiet state. For example, when a user first starts an application, the application may need to interact with a server (e.g., to fetch a file or to obtain the first screen of information). If the user stops to think, move the mouse, or enter data on the keyboard, the application stops communicating with the server. Although the Internet has sufficient capacity to handle datagrams sent among many computers, it can become temporarily overloaded and slow down if too many computers send a burst of datagrams at exactly the same time. TCP watches for delays and knows to wait until the congestion clears.

The secret of TCP's success arises from the way it automatically adapts to change.

Because it constantly monitors conditions on the Internet and automatically adapts, TCP makes reliable communication possible even when the Internet experiences temporary congestion.

TCP/IP Software Was Engineered For Efficiency

In any complex computer system, engineers must choose among a variety of possible designs, TCP/IP protocols have been carefully designed to run efficiently. For example, TCP/IP is designed so it does not require extensive computation when sending or receiving a packet. In addition, TCP/IP is designed so it does not send more than the minimum network packets required to communicate.

The efficient design permits TCP/IP software to run on small, slow computers as well as on fast, large computers. Thus, TCP/IP works well on personal computers that do not have as much processing power or memory as large computers.

TCP/IP Research Emphasized Practical Results

Scientists and engineers working on the Internet project took a practical approach to research. Instead of discussing vague possibilities, they decided to build, test, and measure a working communication system. They used experimental evidence to judge all new proposals and ideas. For example, before any new addition to the TCP/IP specifications was approved, two programmers had to build and test software on at least two types of computers. Furthermore, the programmers had to demonstrate that the two implementations could communicate.

In a keynote address at the *INTEROP 92* conference, David Clark† characterized the style of development used for TCP/IP and the Internet as *rough consensus and working code*. The phrase captures a simple idea: although much of TCP/IP arose from a consensus among researchers, no idea was accepted until it had been implemented and demonstrated.

To emphasize pragmatics and to make implementations interoperate, researchers working on the Internet project urged one another to design software that tolerated errors or unexpected packets. They challenged one another to build software that would anticipate possible mistakes or flaws in the software on other computers, and tried carefully not to violate the Internet specifications.

Implementation and testing always preceded TCP/IP standardization. Writing and testing programs often uncovered ambiguities and omissions in the design or documentation, and forced designers to correct problems early. As a result, considering the complexity of the protocols, TCP/IP standards documents have had few problems.

The Formula For Success

Many people who encounter the Internet project and success of the TCP/IP technology ask, "What lessons were learned?" Some ask more pointedly, "How can I repeat the success with research projects at my organization?"

Even from an insider's perspective the questions are difficult to answer because the project involved many people working together over several years. Here are a few highlights:

---

†Dr. David Clark served as the Internet Architect from *1983* through *1989*.

- TCP/IP protocol software and the Internet were designed by talented, dedicated people.

- The Internet was a dream that inspired and challenged the research team.

- Researchers were allowed to experiment, even when there was no short-term economic payoff. Indeed, Internet research often used new, innovative technologies that were expensive compared to existing technologies.

- Instead of dreaming about a system that solved all problems, researchers built the Internet to operate efficiently.

- Researchers insisted that each part of the Internet work well in practice before they adopted it as a standard.

- Internet technology solves an important, practical problem of connecting multiple networks; the problem occurs because no single network is optimal for all purposes.

Summary

The Internet represents an incredible technical accomplishment. Although careful planning and attention to detail contributed to its success, agreement among researchers to demonstrate a practical, working system forced them to demonstrate ideas and eliminate weaknesses.

How People Use The Internet

Examples of services currently available on the Internet and explanations of a few exciting applications

21

Electronic Mail

Introduction

This chapter begins a discussion of example services available on the Internet. It examines one of the most widely used services: electronic mail. Successive chapters explore other services. In each case, the text describes the service by first summarizing the basic functionality and showing a typical use. It then describes how the underlying mechanism operates. Finally, the chapter summarizes the significance of the service.

Description Of Functionality

Electronic mail was originally designed to allow a pair of individuals to communicate via computer. The first electronic mail software provided only a basic facility: it allowed a person using one computer to type a message and send it across the Internet to a person using another computer.

Current electronic mail systems provide services that permit complex communication and interaction. For example, electronic mail can be used to:

- Send a single message to many recipients
- Send a message that includes text, audio, video, or graphics
- Send a message to which a computer program responds
- Have a computer program to respond to each incoming message

To appreciate the capabilities and significance of electronic mail, one must understand a few basic facts. The next sections consider how electronic mail appears to a user. Later sections describe how electronic mail systems work, and discuss the impact of electronic mail.

The Best Of All Worlds

Researchers working on early computer networks realized that networks can provide a form of communication among individuals that combines the speed of telephone communication with the permanence of postal mail. A computer can transfer small notes or large documents across a network almost instantaneously. The designers called the new form of communication *electronic mail*, usually abbreviated *email*. Email is an extremely popular service on the Internet.

Each User Has A Mailbox For Email

To receive electronic mail, a user must have a *mailbox*, a storage area on disk that holds incoming email messages until the user has time to read them. In addition, the computer on which a mailbox resides must also run email software. When a message arrives, email software automatically stores it in the user's mailbox. An email mailbox is private in the same way that postal mailboxes are private: anyone can send a message to a mailbox, but only the owner can examine mailbox contents or remove messages.

Like a post office mailbox, each email mailbox has a *mailbox address*. To send email to another user, one must know the recipient's mailbox address. To summarize:

> *Each individual who participates in electronic mail exchange has a mailbox identified by a unique address. Any user can send mail across the Internet to another user's mailbox if they know the mailbox address; only the owner can examine the contents of a mailbox and extract messages.*

Sending An Email Message

To send electronic mail across the Internet, an individual runs an email application program on their local computer. The local application operates similar to a word processor — it allows a user to compose and edit a message and to specify a recipient by giving a mailbox address. Once the user finishes entering the message and adds attachments, email software sends it across the Internet to the recipient's mailbox.

Notification That Email Has Arrived

When an incoming email message arrives, system software can be configured to inform the recipient. Some computers print a text message or highlight a small graphic on the user's display (e.g., a small picture of letters in a postal mailbox). Other computers sound a tone or play a recorded message. Still other computers wait for the user to finish using the current application before making an announcement. Most systems allow a user to suppress notification altogether; suppressing notification means a user must periodically check to see if email has arrived.

Reading An Email Message

Once email has arrived, a user can extract messages from his or her mailbox using an application program. The application allows a user to view each message, and optionally, to send a reply. Usually, when an email application begins, it displays a list of messages that are waiting in the mailbox. The initial summary contains one line for each email message that has arrived; the line gives the sender's name, the time the message arrived, and the message subject. After examining the summary, a user can select and view any message on the list. Each time a user selects a message from the summary, the email system displays the message contents. After viewing a message, a user chooses an action. The user can send a reply to whomever sent the message, leave the message in the mailbox so it can be viewed again later, save a copy of the message in a folder†, or discard the message.

To summarize:

A computer connected to the Internet needs application software before users can send or receive electronic mail. email software allows a user to compose and send a message or to read messages that have arrived. A user can send a reply to any message.

A Browser Can Be Used To Send And Receive Email

We said that a user needs application software to read or send email. Early email systems required a user to install a separate application program. That is, a user launched a separate application that could only manipulate email.

Many modern email systems take an alternative approach: instead of using a separate application, the system allows a user to access email through a web browser (explained in Chapter 23). Usually, web email requires a user to enter a URL that corresponds to a service provider. Once the user has entered a login ID and password,

---

†A user might save a copy of a message to create a permanent record of a conversation.

the provider allows the user to click on a link that opens an email account. The point is:

> *To access email, a user must invoke the appropriate software. Some email systems use a dedicated application program, and others use a web browser.*

Email Messages Look Like Interoffice Memos

Each electronic mail message has a form similar to the one used for a conventional interoffice memo. The message begins with a header that specifies the person who sent the message, the person to whom the message was sent, the date and time the message was sent, and the subject of the message. Following usual office conventions, information in the header appears on separate lines that begin with *From*, *To*, *Date*, and *Subject*, with each followed by appropriate information. For example, suppose on April 1, 2007 Jane sends Bob an email message that contains a joke. If Jane's email address is *jane@company1.com* and Bob's email address is *bob@company2.com*, the message will have the following form†:

```
From: jane@company1.com
To: bob@company2.com
Date: 01 Apr 2007  11:20:23 EST
Subject: some bad news
Bob,

    I heard that they've decided to cut personnel
and you will be the first one fired.
    April Fools!

Jane
:-)
```

On the last line of the message, Jane included extra symbols to ensure that the recipient interprets the statement as humorous. The line contains three characters: a colon, minus sign, and right parenthesis. The three symbols are called a *smiley* because they resemble a smiling face turned sideways.

An email header can contain items not shown in the sample message above. For example, it can contain a line labeled *Cc* that lists mailbox addresses of additional people who receive a copy of the message‡.

---

†Many email application hide the exact form of a message from the user.

‡As in standard office memos, *Cc* stands for *carbon copy*; the term originated when typists used carbon paper to create multiple copies of a document.

Email Software Fills In Header Information

Usually, the sender only needs to supply information for the *To* and *Subject* lines in a message header because email software fills in the date and the sender's mailbox address automatically. In a reply, the mail interface program automatically constructs the entire header. It uses the contents of the *From* field in the original message as the contents of the *To* field in the reply. It also copies the *Subject* field from the original message to a reply. Having software fill in header lines is convenient, and also makes it difficult to forge email.

In practice, email systems supply additional header lines that help identify the sending computer, give the full name of the person who sent the message, provide a unique message identifier that can be used for auditing or accounting, and identify the type of message (e.g., text or graphics). Thus, email messages can arrive with dozens of lines in the header†. A lengthy header can be annoying to a recipient who must skip past it to find the body of a message. Software used to read email often makes it easier for the recipient by skipping most header lines. To summarize:

> *Although most email messages contain many lines of header, software generates most of the header automatically. User-friendly software hides unnecessary header lines when displaying an email message.*

How Email Works

Recall from Chapter 17 that computer communication always involves interaction between two programs called a *client* and a *server*. Email systems follow the client-server approach: two programs cooperate to transfer an email message from the sender's computer to the recipient's mailbox (transfer requires two programs because an application running on one computer cannot store data directly in a mailbox on another computer's disk). When a user sends an email message, a program on the sender's computer becomes a client. It contacts an email server program on the recipient's computer and transfers a copy of the message. The server stores the message in the recipient's mailbox. Figure 21.1 illustrates the idea.

---

†While preparing this chapter, the author received an email message with 376 lines of header!

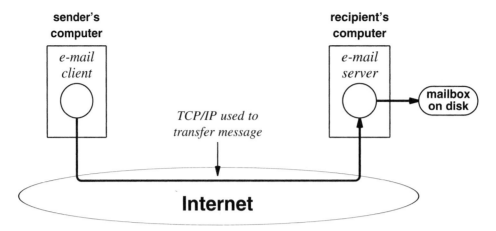

Figure 21.1 An email transfer across the Internet requires two programs: a
client on the sender's computer and a server on the recipient's
computer.

Client software starts automatically as soon as a user finishes composing an email
message. The client uses the recipient's email address to determine which remote computer to contact. The client uses TCP to send a copy of the email message across the
Internet to the server. When the server receives a message, it stores the message in the
recipient's mailbox and informs the recipient that email has arrived.

The interaction between a client and server is complex because at any time computers or the Internet connecting them can fail (e.g., someone can accidentally turn off
one of the computers). To ensure that email will be delivered reliably, the client keeps
a copy of the message during the transfer. After the server informs the client that the
message has been received and stored on disk, the client erases its copy.

Using Email From A Personal Computer

A computer cannot receive email unless it has an email server program running.
On large computers, the system administrator arranges to start the server when the system first begins, and leaves the server running at all times. The server waits for an
email message to arrive, stores the message in the appropriate mailbox on disk, and then
waits for the next message.

A user who has a personal computer that is frequently powered down or disconnected from the Internet cannot receive email while the computer is inactive. Therefore,
most personal computers do not receive email directly. Instead, a user arranges to have
a mailbox on a large computer with a server that always remains ready to accept an

email message and store it in the user's mailbox. For example, most individuals can choose to place their mailbox on a computer run by an ISP. To access email, a user must run a program that contacts the ISP and obtains a copy of their mailbox.

Mailbox Address Format

Mailbox addresses used on the Internet can be quite long, and may seem cumbersome. They consist of a string of characters separated into two parts by the *at sign* character, @. The prefix of the mailbox address identifies the user, and the suffix gives the domain name of the computer on which the user's mailbox resides. On most computers, the email system uses an individual's account or login as their mailbox address. For example, the mailbox address

$$\texttt{jksmith@venus.engineering.somecompany.com}$$

identifies a user who has account *jksmith* on a computer that has domain name *venus.engineering.somecompany.com*. The domain name for a computer can be difficult to remember. For example, a computer in Germany has the domain name:

$$\texttt{i4.informatik.rwth-aachen.de}†$$

while a computer at Purdue University is named:

$$\texttt{angwyshaunce.cs.purdue.edu}$$

The identifier for a user can also be difficult to remember. In practice, the format for a user identifier depends on the computer system and the rules the administrator establishes for assigning identifiers. Some systems use a person's first and last names plus their middle initial, with underscores separating the parts:

$$\texttt{Jane\_K\_Smith@venus.engineering.somecompany.com}$$

To summarize:

> *Mailbox addresses used to send email across the Internet consist of a text string separated into two parts by an at sign (@). The prefix of the address specifies a particular user; the suffix gives the domain name of the computer on which that user's mailbox resides.*

---

†Computers attached to the Internet in Germany have names that end with *de*, the international 2-letter abbreviation for Germany.

Abbreviations Make Email Friendly

Most email systems allow a user to define abbreviations for mailbox addresses. Abbreviations allow a company to establish short names for each of its departments, making it possible for employees in the company to address mail without typing long suffixes. For example, if all the computers in a company understand that *eng* is an abbreviation for computer *venus.engineering.somecompany.com* in the engineering department, it is possible for anyone sending mail from a company computer to address an email message:

```
Jane_K_Smith@eng
```

Aliases Permit Arbitrary Abbreviations

Most commercially available email software also supports an *email alias* facility that allows each user to define a set of abbreviations for the mailbox addresses they use frequently. Usually, alias mechanisms require the user to prepare a short list of aliases, which the mail software stores on disk. When email software runs, it locates the user's list of aliases and honors them. For example, suppose a user sends email to two people frequently: *John Smith* and *Mary Doe*, who have electronic mail addresses *jksmith@computer1.somecompany.com* and *mary_doe@computer2.somecollege.edu*. The user can define two aliases for the mailbox addresses:

```
john = jksmith@computer1.somecompany.com
mary = mary_doe@computer2.somecollege.edu
```

When composing an email message, the user can enter *john* or *mary* in the *To* field. The email software will automatically consult the user's alias list and replace the abbreviation with the full mailbox address. Thus, although the user only types the abbreviation, the outgoing mail message will contain the full mailbox address. To summarize:

> *Most commercial email software permits each user to define a set of abbreviations for frequently used mailbox addresses. If the user types an abbreviation when specifying a recipient, email software substitutes the full mailbox address in place of the abbreviation.*

Aliases Shared By All Users Of A Computer System

Because only a single individual uses a personal computer system, such systems only need one set of email aliases. However, an email system that many users share needs a more complex mechanism. In addition to a private set of abbreviations for each user, a corporate email system usually allows the system administrator to define abbreviations available to all users. When a user specifies a recipient, the mail software first examines the user's private alias list to see if the user has defined an alias for the name. If the user has not, the mail software then examines the system alias list to see if it contains an alias for the name.

Having a system-wide set of mail aliases makes it possible for all users on the system to share abbreviations. For example, suppose a system administrator decides that all reports of problems should be sent to mailbox *william* on computer:

```
computer2.somewhere.com
```

To make it convenient for users, the system administrator can choose an easily remembered abbreviation and create a system-wide mail alias. If the administrator chooses the abbreviation *trouble*, the following alias for *trouble* can be added to the system-wide list of mail aliases:

```
trouble = william@computer2.somewhere.com
```

When any user on the computer wants to report a problem, they send email to *trouble*. The mail system looks up the destination in the alias list, and sends the email message to mailbox *william @ computer2.somewhere.com*.

Sending To Multiple Recipients

Although email was originally designed as a way for two people to communicate, email systems allow a user to send a message to multiple recipients. To do so, the sender specifies multiple mailbox addresses on the *To* line of a message. The system sends one copy of the message to each recipient. For example, the message:

```
To: bob@corp2.com, jim@corp3.com, susan@corp2.com
From: jane@company1.com
Date: 01 Apr 2006  12:34:03 EST
Subject: some bad news

Folks,

    I heard that your corporation is about to cut
personnel and that you will be among the first
ones fired.
    April fools!

Jane
:-)
```

The *To* line in the header specifies three recipients, two at *corp2* and another at *corp3*. Each of the three will receive a copy of the message.

Mailing List: An Alias for Multiple Recipients

One of the most useful features of email arises from a simple extension of the alias mechanism: an alias that specifies multiple recipients. When the mail system expands an alias and finds multiple recipients, it sends a copy of the message to each.

Informally, people refer to an alias that specifies multiple recipients as a *mailing list*. For example, the following definition creates a mailing list named *friends* that contains three email addresses:

```
friends = bob@corp2.com, jim@corp3.com, susan@corp2.com
```

Once such an alias has been created, any message sent to *friends* will be delivered to all three recipients. The concept is straightforward:

> *A mailing list is an email alias that specifies multiple recipients; when a message is sent to the alias, the email system delivers a copy to each recipient on the list.*

Public Mailing Lists And Mail Exploders

System administrators can choose to establish *public mailing lists*. A public list permits a user on any computer attached to the Internet to send a message to a list of recipients. For example, suppose a computer named *comp1.somewhere.com* offers a public mailing list named *sales†*. To send an email message to everyone on the list, an individual mails to address: `sales@comp1.somewhere.com`. The message can originate at any computer. When the email message reaches the destination computer, *comp1.somewhere.com*, a program called a *mail exploder* examines the *To* field, finds the name *sales*, expands the abbreviation, and forwards a copy to each recipient on the list. Figure 21.2 illustrates the concept.

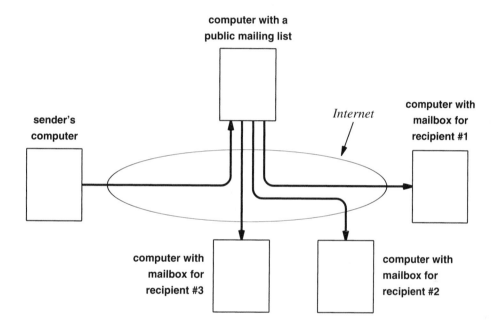

Figure 21.2 The path of a mail message sent to a public mailing list that contains three recipients. A mail exploder receives the message, and forwards a copy to each recipient on the list.

Exchanging Email With Non-Internet Sites

Electronic mail on the Internet is especially useful because it can be forwarded to other networks. In particular, it is possible to arrange email to be forwarded to a cellular telephone or pager that has a messaging capability. Similarly, it is possible to forward messages that are created and sent from a cell phone to an arbitrary Internet email address.

---

†The name of a mailing list can be meaningful or meaningless: *sales* can denote a group of people who work in sales, a group of customers to whom sales have been made, or a group that picked the alias to hide the purpose of the list from others.

To handle forwarding of email, an intermediate computer is used to link the Internet to the cell phone message system. In essence, software on the intermediate computer speaks two languages: it accepts incoming email from either the Internet or the cell phone system, and forwards a copy of each message according to a set of rules. Typically, forwarding is only permitted if a user has paid a fee or has signed a contract that allows the service provider to charge for each forwarded message.

Access To Services Via Email

Because a computer can be programmed to respond to electronic mail automatically, any computer system attached to the Internet can provide access to its services via email. More important, email software on most computers has been designed to make service access easy.

As an example, consider a computer attached to the Internet that has database software running on it. Any user who logs into the computer can access the database software to search the database. Even if both computers have TCP/IP software and both connect to the Internet, a remote user cannot access the database unless both computers have additional software: the user's computer needs a database client program and the computer with the database needs a database server program.

Client and server software can be difficult to create or expensive to purchase. However, once the server is in place, adding software that provides access to the database via electronic mail can be easy. To do so, the system administrator writes a computer program that answers incoming email, passes the message to the database software, and then mails the output back to the original sender. While it sounds complex, an expert can create such a program quickly with a few lines of code. The idea is:

> *Because a computer program can answer and reply to an electronic mail message, email can be used to provide access to a variety of remote services.*

Speed, Reliability, And Expectations

Internet email software is efficient and dependable. An email message usually takes only a few seconds to reach its destination. If the destination computer is powered down or temporarily disconnected from the Internet, email software automatically retries transmission periodically. Furthermore, email service is more reliable than the best postal mail systems; messages are seldom lost because no humans are involved in sorting or delivering email. If an email message cannot be delivered after a fixed time (usually three days), email software automatically informs the sender.

As a consequence of high-quality service, most Internet users view email as a reliable, high-speed delivery mechanism. They send important messages via email without relying on other means of communication. In particular, they do not usually send duplicate copies of messages via postal mail, nor do they use a telephone to verify that important email messages arrive.

Furthermore, because messages arrive quickly, many Internet users view email as an instant communication mechanism that operates more like a telephone service than a postal mail service. Users know that if they send a reply shortly after an email message arrives, their reply may reach the sender while he or she is still working on the computer. Sometimes, a pair of individuals exchange a series of brief email messages that resemble a short conversation. Usually such communication occurs between friends who know each other well enough to send short, abbreviated messages. Often such conversations end after a few exchanges.

However, not everyone views email as an important communication mechanism — some individuals do not respond to an email message for hours, days, or weeks. Some simply do not want to be bothered; others forget to read email. In particular, someone who does not work with a computer does not receive instant notification when email arrives; to read email, they must interrupt normal activities and find an available computer. Furthermore, because many homes do not have a computer permanently connected to the Internet, some people cannot read email easily at home. Differences in expectations and habits among individuals can make email frustrating, users learn that not everyone replies to email quickly.

Impact And Significance Of Electronic Mail

The impact of email is so dramatic that it is difficult to assess. For many Internet users, email has become a necessity. Indeed, email has replaced postal mail as their primary communication mechanism! Email has changed the way they conduct their daily lives — they use email to communicate with friends, colleagues, employees, customers, and family members.

To appreciate electronic mail, one must use it first hand. After extensive use, some of its benefits become apparent:

- Because email provides high-speed transfer while allowing the receiver to choose when to answer, it combines the benefits of instantaneous communication with freedom from interruption.

- Because a mailing list allows an arbitrary group of individuals to exchange memos, it provides a way for a group of people who share a common interest to participate in a discussion.

- Because most computer networks offer an electronic mail service that operates with electronic mail on the Internet, it is possible to communicate with more people using electronic mail than with any other Internet service.

- Because electronic mail can include text, graphics, and voice, it can be used to transfer documents or recorded audio messages.

- Because a computer program can answer electronic mail and send a reply automatically, many services on the Internet have been constructed so a user can submit a request and receive a response using electronic mail.

In summary:

> *Although it was originally designed to provide text communication between a pair of individuals, electronic mail has been extended to allow communication among a group, to include audio and graphics, and to permit a user to communicate with a computer program. As a result, email has become one of the most widely used services on the Internet.*

A Convention For Joining A Mailing List

A user who wants to have their name added to a public mailing list must send an email request. However, the request should not go to the list. Instead, most Internet sites that offer public mailing lists follow the convention of establishing a second mail alias that should be used for requests to join or leave a list.

To understand the problem, assume that a user named *Judy* who has mailbox address *judy @ bluechip.com* hears about a mailing list named:

ballroom @ athena.mit.edu

to which people send memos about ballroom dancing. If Judy sends a message to the list, everyone will receive a copy. To subscribe to a list, one sends an email message to the list name followed by *-request*. Thus, to subscribe to the ballroom dancing list, Judy should send a message to:

ballroom-request @ athena.mit.edu

The message will be delivered to a person who maintains the list (or to a computer program that sends further instructions). After Judy has joined the list, she will receive a copy of all messages and can send replies.

Some sites do not establish a special alias to make requests. In such cases, a user can try sending to *postmaster*. By convention, email sent to *postmaster* will be delivered to the person who maintains the email system.

22

Bulletin Board Service (Newsgroups)

Introduction

The previous chapter explains the Internet electronic mail service and shows how it can be used to exchange messages. This chapter describes an Internet service that extends the use of email to allow an individual to join one or more discussion groups and participate in discussions with other members of the group. Electronic bulletin boards are among the most well-known services available on the Internet, and the discussions encompass a wide variety of topics. After examining how the service appears to an individual and reviewing the underlying mechanisms, the chapter provides hints about how to use bulletin boards and electronic mail.

Description Of Functionality

An electronic bulletin board service allows a person to participate in multiple discussion groups, where each group focuses on a specific topic. The bulletin board service allows an individual to:

- Select one or more discussion groups of interest.

- Periodically check to determine whether new items have appeared in a discussion and, if they have, read some or all of them.

- Post a note to the discussion group for others to read.

- Post a note that responds to an item someone else has written.

Conceptually, the Internet's electronic bulletin board service fills the same role for Internet users that conventional bulletin boards fill in everyday life — it allows individuals to post notices that others can read. In practice, the Internet provides access to thousands of electronic bulletin boards, each of which contains an ongoing discussion about a single topic. For that reason, an electronic bulletin board service is sometimes called a *computer discussion group* or a *computer conference service*.

To enable efficient discussion among an arbitrarily large group of people, an electronic bulletin board service combines features of many communication mechanisms.

- Like a conventional bulletin board, an electronic bulletin board allows anyone to post a message for others to see.

- Like a newspaper, an electronic bulletin board service distributes each message to many subscribers.

- Like a newsletter from a club or social group, the messages posted to a given electronic bulletin board focus on a single topic of interest.

- Like an electronic mail service, an electronic bulletin board service propagates copies of each message quickly.

- Like an informal discussion at a social gathering, an electronic bulletin board permits an individual to listen to a conversation, ask questions, occasionally interject small comments, or contribute lengthy statements.

Many Bulletin Boards With Diverse Topics

Internet electronic bulletin boards cover a widely diverse group of topics. For example, the Internet has bulletin boards about science, humor, politics, cooking, physical fitness, comic books, science fiction, poetry, products or services, movies, stock prices, television shows, popular music, and computers. Although many of the discussions can be understood by an average person, some require highly specialized knowledge, and some are meaningful only to someone who works at a particular company or lives in a particular country†. Consequently a bulletin board can be restricted to a few computers, a single organization, or a small geographic area, or it can be distributed to sites throughout the world. For example, one bulletin board that contains a discussion of politics in Alberta, Canada is distributed only to nearby sites.

Part of the reason for the diversity of electronic bulletin boards arises from the ease with which they can be created. After a group creates an electronic bulletin board and

---

†In addition to text messages, modern newsgroups permit users to share pictures, music, movies, and computer software.

starts a discussion, interesting side discussions inevitably arise. For example, suppose someone mentions a particular brand of cookware in a discussion of cooking. If others who read the message respond by contributing their opinions on cookware, a new discussion results. If the discussion of cookware continues to gain popularity, participants can choose to create a new bulletin board and move the cookware discussion to that bulletin board. Dividing a bulletin board is analogous to the way people form a small discussion group at a party: it allows multiple conversations to proceed without interference. The point is:

> *Because a new electronic bulletin board can be created easily and dividing discussions by topic helps focus the discussion on each bulletin board, many bulletin boards have been created.*

Network News

The original electronic bulletin board service available on the Internet is called *Network News*, often abbreviated *NetNews*. The NetNews system uses the term *newsgroup* to refer to each individual bulletin board (i.e., each discussion group), and *article* to refer to a message that has been sent to the newsgroup for everyone to see. Each article submitted to a newsgroup takes the form of an electronic mail message — it can be as short as a single line of text or can contain many pages. Like an email message, an article has a header that includes a *From* line to identify the sender.

NetNews originated as part of an early computer network that used dial-up modems to place telephone calls between computers and exchange information. Originally, sites exchanging network news over dial-up connections used the term *USENET* to refer to their "network" of computers. As networks began to grow, USENET participants invented ways to communicate network news over other technologies. As USENET sites acquired Internet access, many changed their NetNews communication from the dial-up telephone system to the Internet. Although most sites that participate in network news now receive information over the Internet, those sites that do not have Internet access continue to participate in NetNews using other communication networks, including BitNet and the dial-up telephone system.

Categories

The original NetNews system assigned each newsgroup a unique name. The first part of a newsgroup name identified the type of the group, while successive parts of the name identified the subject and a particular topic within that subject. For example, consider the newsgroup:

rec.sport.baseball

The newsgroup focuses on a discussion of baseball. The type of the group is *recreation*, the general topic is *sports*, and the specific subject is *baseball*†.

More recent bulletin board services have devised new categories. For example, Figure 22.1 lists a few of the major newsgroup categories available on the Internet.

General Category

Arts and Entertainment
Business and Finance
Computers and The Internet
Cultures
Family and Home
Games and Gaming
Health and Fitness
Music
News and Current Events
Politics and Government
Regions and Places
Religions
Romance and Relationships
Schools and Education
Science and Technology
Society and Humanities
Sports and Recreation

Figure 22.1 Examples of newsgroup classifications in use on the Internet.

Obtaining Network News And The Software To Read Articles

Originally, network news required users to run a separate application program that read or posted news articles. However, modern newsgroups are accessible via the web. For example, the sites:

www.groups.google.com

www.groups.yahoo.com

www.usenet.com‡

each list major categories of newsgroups; Google also provides access to USENET archives. In addition, other sites provide web access to bulletin board services.

---

† Although they resemble computer names described in Chapter 18 and IP addresses described in Chapter 15, newsgroup names are completely unrelated to either.

‡Usenet.com is a paid subscription service.

How Network News Appears To A User

Selection of a category is only the first step in exploring newsgroups. In most cases, each category is subdivided into a set of *topics*. Thus, once a user selects a category, the system presents the user with a set of broad topics within the category. For example, if a user selects a category such as *Computers and The Internet*, the user will be shown a set of topics such as:

> Computer Hardware
> Computer Software
> Data Networking
> Internet
> Computer Education
> Social Effects Of Computers

Some topics are so large that the topic area is further divided into specific topics. Under *Computer Software*, for example, one might find one subtopic devoted to *Microsoft Windows*, another devoted to *Linux*, and so on. Thus, once a user selects a topic, the user is shown a list of subtopics from which to choose. Once a user navigates through the topics, the system presents a list of newsgroups and allows the user to choose a specific newsgroup†. Of course, once a user has found a newsgroup of interest, the user can save a reference to the group; using a direct reference avoids the need to navigate through pages of categories, topics, and subtopics for subsequent visits.

Checking For News Articles

Once a user has joined a newsgroup, how can he or she know whether new articles have appeared? One approach consists of checking the newsgroup manually. For example, a user can choose to visit the newsgroup every other day to check for new articles. As an alternative, many news interfaces allow a user to arrange for an *alert* to be sent whenever new articles appear. To summarize:

> *A user who participates in network news can choose to receive alerts automatically or regularly check for new activity in the newsgroup.*

---

†Although some newsgroups are available to the public; others require a user to enroll as a member before reading articles.

Reading Network News

Reading network news is straightforward. Once a user selects a newsgroup, the display changes to show a list of new articles in the newsgroup. Each entry in the list includes summary information that identifies the author of the article (usually an email address) and the content (a one-line *subject* for the article). To view an individual article, a user clicks on the article, which causes the contents of the article to appear in a window.

A news article appears in the same general form as an electronic mail message. That is, each article consists of a message that has two parts: a header and a body. Like the header on an email message, the header on a news article contains a *From* line that supplies the email address of the person who posted the article, a *Date* line that gives the date and time the article was sent, and a *Subject* line that lists the topic of the article. It can also contain other lines such as a *Distribution* line that restricts dissemination of the article. For example, an article may appear in the following form:

```
Article 530 in rec.motorcycles.harley:

From: rick@company1.somewhere.com
Newsgroups: rec.motorcycles.harley, soc.culture.japan
Subject: Harley-Davidson in Japan
Date: 8 Dec 2007 15:35:56
Organization: Somewhere Incorporated, Fresno, California
Distribution: world

Folks,
    A friend of mine told me that Harley-Davidson went to Japan to
sell motorcycles in 1930.  He says that H-D started the Japanese
motorcycle industry, and that the Japanese bikes eventually outsold
Harley-Davidson.  Is there any truth to the rumor?  Does anyone know
of a book that tells the story?
```

Submission Of An Article

Submitting an article to a network newsgroup is as easy as sending electronic mail. A user composes and edits a message, and then requests that the message be *posted* to one or more newsgroups. If an article is posted to more than one newsgroup, a line in the header mentions each.

In addition to composing a message from scratch, a user can form a reply to an existing article. As with email, a news reader forms a header for the reply by extracting necessary information from the article to which the user is replying. The user can then compose and edit the reply before posting the article.

Moderated Newsgroups

Some newsgroups permit anyone to submit an article. In such groups, people who submit articles range from novices to experts. More important, they range from scholars seriously interested in a topic to jokers who merely poke fun at a discussion.

To limit disruptions and compensate for differences in background, some newsgroups are *moderated*. In essence, a moderator agrees to preview all articles submitted to the newsgroup. The moderator determines whether each article is appropriate, and can choose to submit the article as received, edit the article, select and submit parts of the article, or summarize several articles. If a moderator does the job well, a newsgroup does not contain irrelevant, misleading, or disruptive comments.

Size Of Network News

Newsgroups are extremely popular. In 2006, one commercial site advertised over *120,000* separate newsgroups with more than two million articles available each day. In addition, many companies use newsgroup software for internal newsgroups that are only visible to employees of the company.

An accurate count of newsgroup size is impossible to obtain for two reasons. First, instead of one worldwide service for network news, many providers offer bulletin board services. Second, as the Internet has spread around the world, organizations in other counties have formed newsgroups that are specific to a region or country. Although the total size cannot be estimated, we can draw the following conclusion:

> *Because network news contains thousands of newsgroups with articles being submitted each day, no individual can participate in all newsgroups.*

Impact And Significance Of Newsgroups And Mailing Lists

The impact of bulletin boards and public mailing lists is difficult to appreciate. Internet technologies enable millions of people to participate in an electronic discussion. With that many people involved, it is difficult to imagine the diversity of topics that arise. More important, new discussions begin rapidly; a group discussing one topic can quickly shift interest to another. Many people complain that public mailing lists and newsgroups appear so quickly that they cannot possibly participate in all discussions that interest them.

Internet electronic mailing lists and bulletin board services have an interesting social effect: they provide an opportunity for people around the world to offer opinions to a large group. In the past, such interactions have been limited either to people who live close enough so they can meet and talk face-to-face (e.g., a backyard discussion among neighbors), or to a few individuals who write opinions columns and editorials that appear in newspapers and magazines. Interestingly, because the Internet crosses geographic and political boundaries, it can extend discussion to a diverse set of people from many countries.

Identifiable communities develop on the Internet in exactly the same way social groups form among people in a geographic area. People discover others with common interests. Sometimes, they find others who agree with their views. Often, when a discussion diverges or strong opinions form, a newsgroup or mailing list splits in two, allowing the readership of each to form a community that shares an outlook.

Of course, interactions using network news or electronic mail differ from usual interactions. First, because most memos and articles are text, a contributor cannot use tone of voice or gestures to express emotion. Second, because network systems disseminate each message or article to many people, almost any statement causes someone to respond. Third, because articles can expire after a few days, newcomers may be unable to obtain context and history.

Hints And Conventions For Participating In Discussions

Members of a society follow rules of etiquette to keep social interactions civil and to distinguish normal behavior from insults. Learning proper etiquette for Internet communication can be difficult for two reasons. First, because the Internet spans many cultures, economic backgrounds, and levels of education, it is much more likely that two people who communicate will not share a common background. Second, because the Internet is a recent communication medium, some people mistakenly assume that no rules of etiquette apply. Indeed, it seems that some subscribers do not adhere to the normal rules of courteous discussion.

Differences in background often become apparent in subtle ways. In some cultures, one is taught to trust what others say; in others exaggeration is accepted. Similarly, cultures do not all share the same amount of respect for a given position, rank, or title. In fact, a title in one culture or field of expertise may not be meaningful in another. A few simple guidelines help compensate for such differences†:

- When reading an electronic memo or news article, do not make assumptions about the person who wrote it. The writer may have more or less experience than you. The writer may have more or less expertise on a given topic than you. In short, assume neither that the writer is an expert nor a fool.

- Suspect any message that appears to have been submitted by a famous person or well-known authority — header information can be forged, and some people seem to derive pleasure from forging them.

---

†The author compiled this particular list of suggestions from experience; similar lists of suggestions entitled *Netiquette* exist on the web.

- When composing a submission, remember that it will be read by people whose backgrounds differ from yours. Choose words that accurately express your opinion. Provide evidence for your opinions if you have some available (e.g., a reference to a book or magazine article).

- As in any social interaction, use constraint. For example, before responding to a provocative or outrageous statement, take time to think.

- Do not take insults personally, especially when they respond to an article you wrote. Remember that the writer does not know you and may not respect your title or position.

- Use the symbol for a smiley face, :-), to inform the reader that you mean something in a humorous way.

- Many Internet users follow the convention regarding upper and lower case: anything written in all uppercase is assumed to express screaming.

- If you are a novice, start by asking for help. In particular, some public mailing lists and newsgroups maintain a file of *Frequently Asked Questions* (*FAQ*) and answers; others maintain a summary of past discussion topics. You can submit a message that asks whether a FAQ or summary of the discussion is available online.

Summary

The Internet offers bulletin board services that allow a user to post articles related to a given topic. Thousands of individual newsgroups exist on topics as diverse as education, hobbies, politics, science, entertainment, and employment opportunities. Although many newsgroups are distributed worldwide, some are restricted to a particular organization, city, country, or continent.

Most users employ a browser to access newsgroups. The interface allows a user to find out about newsgroups that exist, read messages that have been posted to a given newsgroup, reply to a message, or post a new message. Both newsgroups and electronic mail use the same general format: a header identifies the sender and a body contains the content of the article.

23

Browsing The World Wide Web

Introduction

The previous chapter discusses a basic Internet service used to transfer messages from one user to another. This chapter explores a dynamic service that allows a user to browse information that resides on remote computers. The chapter describes how a browsing service operates, and explains the concept of hypermedia that has made the World Wide Web so popular. Later chapters explore browsing in more detail.

Description Of Functionality

An *information browsing service* allows an individual to conveniently obtain and display information that is stored on a remote computer. Most information browsing services operate interactively — a user enters a request, and the browsing system responds by obtaining a copy of the specified item. If a retrieved item contains information in a form suitable for a human, the browsing system automatically displays the information on the user's screen. We will see, however, that a browsing service can perform other tasks. In general, a browser can:

- Obtain textual information, recorded sounds, graphic images, or video from a variety of sources on remote computers as requested

- Display the retrieved information automatically

- Store a copy of retrieved information on disk

- Print a copy of retrieved information on paper

- Follow a reference found in a document to related documents, possibly on different computers

Browsing Vs. Information Retrieval

In the broadest sense, both information retrieval and browsing provide mechanisms that one can use to obtain information from a remote computer. Early Internet services used the retrieval paradigm — a user specified an item to retrieve, and the retrieval service arranged to place a copy of the item on the user's computer. The chief difference between information retrieval services and browsing services arises from the way they present information to a user. In particular, although an information retrieval service allows a user to obtain a copy of a remote file, the service gives the user no clues about the format or contents of the file. The point is:

> *Although they transfer data efficiently, information retrieval services do not display the contents of documents for users.*

By contrast, browsing services display the information contained on remote computers without requiring a user to learn the names of computers, files, or directories in which the information is stored. In fact, most browsing services use a simple point-and-click interface, making them easy to use. The idea can be summarized:

> *A browsing service permits users to view information from remote computers without knowing the names of individual files. After obtaining a copy of a document from a remote computer, the browsing service automatically displays the contents, and allows the user to select related documents.*

Early Browsing Services Used Menus

Several browsing services have been invented for use on the Internet. One of the earliest services was known as *gopher†*. Because it was one of the first widespread browsing services, many early Internet sites ran gopher servers. Thus, gopher provided access to a large quantity of information. Gopher was especially popular among novice and nontechnical Internet users because the interface was intuitive and easy to use — one did not need to learn commands to use gopher.

---

†The name was chosen because the system was designed at the University of Minnesota, home of the *golden gophers*, and as a pun because the system was designed to "go for" information.

Early Internet services popularized a menu-driven approach to information browsing. The interface for such services displayed a menu of choices for a user, and allowed the user to select an item of interest. Because early services focused on text, each menu item consisted of a short, self-explanatory phrase. To make the system easy to use, the number of items in a given menu was limited to allow the entire menu to fit on a user's screen. In practical terms, a menu was usually limited to approximately a dozen items.

The popularity of menu-driven systems arose because they permit a user to move from an item on one menu to a related item easily. Conceptually, each item on a menu contains a hidden reference to additional information. The additional information can correspond to data in a file or to another menu.

After it displayed a menu, the browser software waited for the user to read the menu and select one of the items. If the hidden reference in the selected item pointed to a data file, the browsing software obtained a copy of the file and displayed its contents. If the hidden reference in the selected item pointed to another menu, the browsing software obtained the new menu, displayed it, and waited for the user to make another selection. The point is:

> *A menu-driven browsing system displays a menu of choices for a user. By selecting an item from the menu, the user requests the browsing service to retrieve information from a file or retrieve another menu.*

A Menu Item Can Point To Another Computer

The power of an Internet browsing system arises from its ability to span multiple computer systems: an item in a menu on one computer can refer to a menu on another computer. Because the references are hidden, a user does not need to take any special actions to follow a link to another computer. In fact, a user can view a series of menus without knowing whether the menus all come from one computer or many computers. More important, because browsing software can obtain a new menu quickly, a user does not experience long delays. From the perspective of a user:

> *A browsing system hides computer boundaries completely, and makes information on a large set of computers appear to be part of a single, integrated system. A browser can jump from one computer to another without a user knowing or caring about which computers are being accessed.*

How A Browser Works

Like other Internet services, browsing services use client-server interaction as described in Chapter 17. Figure 23.1 illustrates how a browsing service operates.

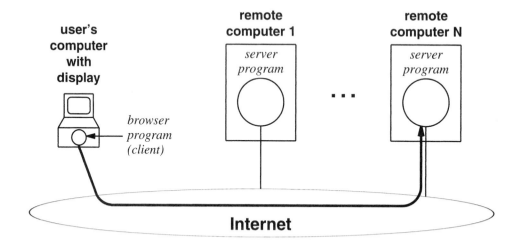

Figure 23.1 A browsing service using client-server interaction. Multiple servers run continuously; the browser is a client that contacts one server at a time.

As the figure illustrates, a *browser* program runs on the user's local computer. A user interacts with the browser to control the selection and display of information. For example, a user specifies an initial menu and then selects an item that the browser should follow. The browser acts as a client to obtain information. Each time the user specifies an item, the browser extracts the hidden reference information associated with the item, and uses the reference to determine which remote server should be contacted and which item should be requested from that server. A new selection can come from the same computer as the current menu or from another computer. A browser only contacts one server at a time — the browser establishes a connection, retrieves the needed information, closes the connection, and displays the information for the user. To make the system useful, servers must remain ready to be contacted at all times, and must agree to provide information to any client that requests it.

An Example Point-And-Click Interface

To understand how information can be stored in simple menu items, consider a *point-and-click* style of interaction that uses textual menus. That is, the software permits a user to navigate through menus using only the mouse; one does not need to type on the keyboard. The mouse is used, for example, to choose an item from a menu, return to the previous menu, or quit using the browsing application.

Figure 23.2 illustrates how a screen might appear to someone using a point-and-click interface. The screen is divided into three main areas. The center area contains the most important information — a title for the menu and a list of items that the user can select. The example contains thirteen menu items. Each item corresponds to another menu, a data file, or a computer program. To select one of the items, a user slides the mouse across the desktop until the cursor, shown as an arrow in the diagram, is positioned over the desired item. When the user clicks the mouse button, the browser highlights the item under the cursor and fetches the selected item. For example, Figure 23.2 shows the display after a user has moved the cursor to item number *8*.

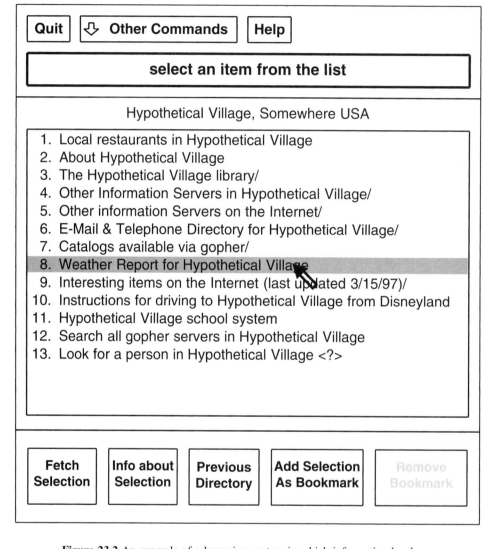

Figure 23.2 An example of a browsing system in which information has been organized into menus. The cursor is an arrow that moves as the user moves the mouse.

Combining Menu Items With Text

Early browsing systems kept menus separate from data files. The display either contained a menu of items that the user could select or it contained a document that the user could read. In essence, a user browsed through menus until discovering information of interest. Once a user selected information, the menu disappeared from the screen and was replaced by a document. Similarly, when a user finished viewing a document and chose to browse again, the last menu reappeared and replaced the document.

A browsing service that keeps menu items separate from other information makes it easy to recognize the type of display; there is no ambiguity about whether the screen contains a menu or other information. However, such browsing services often limit a menu item to a short phrase that can fit on a single line of text. Thus, because it does not provide much detail, an individual menu item can be difficult to understand. For example, a short menu item does not include descriptive prose, pictures, or other information.

Current browsing services take a fundamentally different approach. Instead of separating menus from other information, they embed menu items directly in the text. Embedded menu items can make selection easier because the surrounding prose can add context. To understand integration, consider the following example paragraph which is shown as it might appear when displayed by a browsing system that provides embedded menu items.

> The New York Stock Exchange is a world-renown center of business activity. Located on <u>Wall Street</u> in downtown New York City, the stock exchange allows <u>stock brokers</u> to buy or sell <u>shares of stock.</u> At the end of each day, the <u>average price per share</u> of stock as well as the total <u>number of shares traded</u> are computed and used as a measure of activity. Many newspapers list the <u>closing stock prices</u> each day in their business section.

The example contains a short narrative about the stock exchange in New York City. It provides facts such as the location of the exchange, and has been written to inform the reader. In addition to the narrative, the paragraph contains several terms that have been highlighted with an underscore. The highlighted terms correspond to links that a reader can select, analogous to menu items in a menu-oriented browser.

When the browsing service displays a paragraph, the user can choose to read all the information or scan for highlighted terms. A user who already knows basic information about the topic and is searching for details can choose to look at highlighted terms; he or she only needs to read the surrounding text when the meaning of a term is unclear.

Because highlighted terms catch a reader's eye, looking at embedded terms can be as fast and easy as looking through a menu. For example, one can scan the sample paragraph above and locate the highlighted terms in a few seconds; it is not necessary to read the entire text.

As in a menu-driven browsing system, each selectable item contains a hidden reference to another item. Once a user selects a highlighted term, the browser responds by following the hidden link, obtaining a copy of the item, and displaying the new information. The user can then select a link from the new display to obtain more information. For example, if a user selects the item *average price per share* from the paragraph above, the browser will follow a link to a document that describes the average cost of stock shares. If a user selects the item labeled *Wall Street*, the browser will displays details about Wall Street in New York City.

The Importance Of Integrated Links

Although the example paragraph is brief, it illustrates how links can be embedded in other information. An integrated system helps a user in two ways.

- First, displaying information and selectable links on the screen simultaneously explains a topic in more detail and makes it easier to understand highlighted items. Often, for example, the context around an item helps clarify its purpose and eliminates ambiguities.

- Second, having links embedded in information encourages a user to explore items as they are encountered. A browsing service can help further by remembering where a user was reading when an item was selected, and can return to the same place after the user finishes reading about the item.

One way to think about using an integrated browsing service is to imagine reading a book. A reader who reaches an unknown word or phrase can stop reading and consult a dictionary. If the dictionary's definition contains additional terms that the reader does not understand, the search may continue further. Eventually, after mastering the terminology, the reader returns to the book and continues reading. An information browsing service that embeds selections in information encourages the same behavior — a user can begin to examine a document, pause to obtain information about an embedded link, and then return to the original document.

In summary,

> *Current browsing services embed selectable links in other information, eliminating ambiguities and making it easier to understand each item. Combining links with other information encourages a user to explore items as they are encountered.*

Embedded Links In Text Are Called Hypertext

The concept of embedding selectable items in text is called *hypertext*. Hypertext did not originate with Internet browsing services — it has been used with conventional computer programs for many years. For example, one computer manufacturer uses a hypertext system to display documents that describe how to use the computer and the programs it contains. A user begins by asking the system to display a document that describes the computer. The user can read the display like an ordinary piece of prose, or can select any term in the document. When a user selects a word or phrase, the hypertext software looks up the term and displays information related to it.

To understand hypertext documents stored in a computer system, imagine a set of paper documents laid on a desktop with the items in each document that refer to other documents highlighted. The diagram in Figure 23.3 shows an example of six documents with references to other documents indicated by arrows.

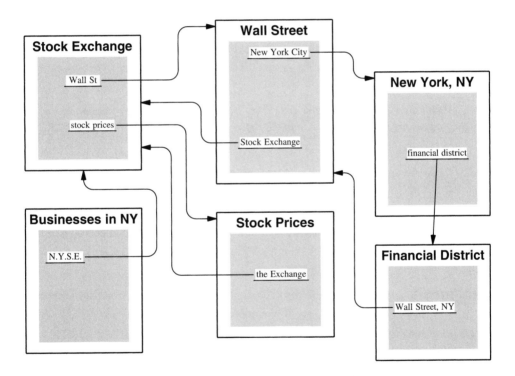

Figure 23.3 An illustration of six documents with text obscured except for the title and references to other documents. An arrow has been drawn between a word or phrase and the document it references.

In the figure, the document labeled *Wall Street* contains two references: one to *New York City* and another to *Stock Exchange.* The reference labeled *New York City* points to a document titled *New York, NY,* which contains a reference to the *financial district.*

When hypertext is viewed as a collection of documents, two points become clear:

- A highlighted phrase does not need to be the same as the title of the document to which it refers. For example, the document that has title *Stock Prices* contains the highlighted phrase *the Exchange.* However, the hidden reference points to a document that has the title *Stock Exchange.* The designers of a hypertext document specify the phrases that should be highlighted as well as the location of the exact item to which each phrase refers.

- Not all documents contain the same number of highlighted references. A given document can contain no references, many references, or only a few.

Of course, when using a hypertext system, a user does not see a graphic illustration of the links among documents. Instead, one document appears on the screen at a time, and the user must click on a highlighted phrase to determine where it leads.

In summary,

> *Although documents in a hypertext system can contain a complex maze of references, the complexity may not be obvious to a user who is viewing only one document at a time.*

The power of hypertext arises from its combination of generality and instant reference — each document can contain text or embedded menu items that point to other documents. A user can choose to read an entire document or merely scan for highlighted phrases. At any time, the user can return to the previous document or select a highlighted phrase that leads to a new document.

Multimedia

To understand how Internet browsing services extend hypertext, it is necessary to understand the capabilities of modern computer systems. Although early computers could only display text in a typewriter font, modern computer systems have sophisticated hardware that can display graphic images, video, and play sounds. Such computers use the graphics hardware to display text using proportional spacing — the space allocated for each character is proportional to the character's width†. Modern computer systems can also display multiple colors, geometric shapes and diagrams, as well as still or moving pictures along with high-quality audio. Because a computer system capable

---

†Because this book is typeset using proportional text, the letter *i* occupies less width than the letter *w.*

of playing audio and displaying video has *multiple media* available for output; such computers are called *multimedia* computers.

Video And Audio References Can Be Embedded In Text

Multimedia computers make it possible to access additional forms of information. For example, consider the following paragraph.

> Several <u>city tours</u> include visits to the New York Stock Exchange. During a typical working day, many people crowd onto the floor of the exchange. Visitors can <u>hear the sounds</u> of traders bidding and <u>view the sights</u> of trading activity recorded by cameras that look down on the scene.

The paragraph describes a day at the New York Stock Exchange and the activity that a visitor can encounter. As in the earlier examples, phrases that can be selected are highlighted by an underscore. Unlike earlier examples, however, some highlighted phrases do not correspond to textual information. Instead ''view the sights'' and ''hear the sounds'' refer to available video and audio information.

When a hypertext system contains references to nontextual information, it is called a *hypermedia* system. Figure 23.4 illustrates the conceptual organization of a hypermedia document that contains references to nontextual information.

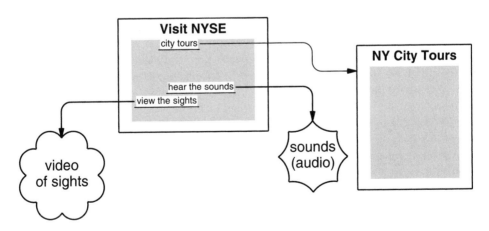

Figure 23.4 The conceptual organization of a hypermedia document. When a user selects *hear the sounds*, the computer plays stored audio. When a user selects *view the sights*, the computer displays the stored images.

Inside a computer, nontextual data must be stored in digital form. For example, a computer stores sound as a sequence of numbers, similar to the way music is stored on a compact disc or an MP3 player. A computer also uses numbers to store pictures or video clips. Of course, a user who plays audio or displays video never sees the underlying sequence of numbers.

To summarize:

> *A hypermedia system can embed references to nontextual information as well as references to textual information in a document. If the user selects a reference to a document, the hypermedia system displays the document; if the user selects a nontextual reference, the hypermedia system plays the audio and displays the images.*

The World Wide Web

The most popular Internet browsing service uses hypermedia. Known as the *World Wide Web*† or simply *the Web*, the service is a mechanism that links together information stored on many computers. In essence, the Web allows the references in a document on one computer to refer to textual or nontextual information stored on other computers. For example, a World Wide Web document on a computer in the United States can contain a reference to a stored video image on a computer in Switzerland.

A user browses the World Wide Web in the same way that one browses hypermedia documents on a single computer. At any time, the user's display shows a document that contains highlighted references. When the user selects an item, the system follows the reference, obtains the referenced item, and either plays the sound or displays the document. Thus, a user can browse through the World Wide Web without knowing where information resides.

Although it can be difficult to understand how a hypermedia service works, its ability to present information visually makes it appealing. As a result, the World Wide Web is the most popular Internet service‡. That is:

> *In addition to containing textual information, web documents can contain sounds, graphical images, and video. To display nontextual information, a computer must have multimedia hardware.*

---

†The World Wide Web was initially developed to allow physicists around the world to share information.
‡Between the summers of 1994 and 1995, web browsing surpassed file transfer as the major use of the Internet, and has remained the number one service since.

Browser Software Used To Access The Web

Software used to access the World Wide Web is known as a *web browser*. The first web browser was developed at the National Center for Supercomputer Applications (NCSA). Called *Mosaic*, the browser controlled the user's display and permitted the user to navigate through hypermedia documents using a mouse. Currently, companies such as Microsoft offer commercial browsers. In addition, the Mozilla project has created a popular open source browser.

When a web browser displays a document, some of the items contain a link to another document. For text that corresponds to a link, the browser highlights the text by underlining and displaying it in a different color than the surrounding text (e.g., if the browser displays normal text in black, highlighted text might appear in blue). To select an item, a user moves the mouse until the cursor has been positioned over the desired item, and then clicks the mouse button. In response to a selection, the browser follows the hidden reference, obtains the specified item, and displays it for the user. If the selected link points to a prerecorded sound, the web browser plays the sound. If the selected link points to a drawing or a photograph, the web browser displays the image on the user's screen. If the selected link points to a video clip, the browser can retrieve the video and display it like a television picture.

Although most highlighted items consist of text, web documents allow non-text items to be highlighted as well. For example, if a graphic image represents a link, the entire image will be highlighted; clicking on the image will cause the browser to follow the hidden reference. Indeed, it is possible to associate separate references with different parts of an image. Thus, it is possible for a web document to contain a set of pictures, each of which contains a link to another web document. In short,

A web browser consists of a program that provides access to hypermedia documents on the World Wide Web. A web browser displays a given document, and allows the user to select among highlighted items, which can consist of either text, graphics, video, or audio.

An Example Hypermedia Display

A simple example will illustrate how a web browser appears to a user. Of course, when a browser displays information on a computer screen, the display appears bright and in color; the effect cannot be reproduced easily in a textbook. Commercially available browser software also displays graphic icons on the buttons used to control the browser as well as a colorful logo that advertises the browser maker. Rather than showing the exact details of a commercially available browser, we will use a sketch that resembles a widely used browser interface, and concentrate on examining the functionality the browser provides.

As an example, consider how the browser might display a web document that belongs to a hypothetical company. Assume that a user is exploring the World Wide Web, and reaches the information for a company called the *Hypothetical Rocker Company*. Figure 23.5 illustrates how a web page for such a company might appear when displayed by a browser†.

†In reality, no such company or web site exists.

Figure 23.5 A hypothetical example of information can be displayed by a
web browser. Any highlighted item, whether text or a graphic
image, can be selected.

Control Of A Browser

Conceptually, browsers interact with a user in two ways. The browser's primary form of interaction occurs after the browser obtains an item that the user has requested; the browser automatically displays the information for the user to view. The second form of interaction occurs when a user communicates with the browser. For example, the user may enter the location of a document, or may request the browser to print a copy of the current document, return to a previous document, or abort a request†.

Most browsers divide the display window into two conceptual regions, and associate each region with one of the two forms of interaction. The main region contains the document that the user is currently browsing, while surrounding regions contain controls that allow the user to interact with the browser. Figure 23.5 illustrates the idea. In the example, the browser places the document being viewed in a large region that occupies most of the window. To mark the boundary, the browser places a border around the document. Thus, a user can tell immediately which part of the window corresponds to the document.

In the example, the browser uses the upper part of the window for interaction with the user. In that region, the browser displays items that permit the user to control the browser's operation. For example, the topmost area consists of a horizontal bar that contains a series of terms: *File*, *Edit*, *View...*, *Help*. Each term corresponds to a *pull-down menu* of commands that the browser honors. To select one of the items from the list, one must use the mouse to position the cursor over the item and then hold the mouse button. A menu of options appears, allowing the user to make a further selection with the mouse.

Because many control operations occur frequently, a single button exists to invoke the operation. The buttons are usually located near the top of the screen. The first two buttons are the most frequently used: a button with a left-pointing arrow labeled *Back* moves to the previous document; a button with a right-pointing arrow labeled *Forward* moves in the opposite direction. For example, suppose a user has viewed four documents in the order: *A*, *B*, *C*, and *D*. If document *D* is currently on the screen, selecting the *Back* button will return to document *C*. Selecting the *Back* button again will return to document *B*. Moving back in a sequence can be especially useful when browsing is interrupted (e.g., by a phone call), because it helps one reestablish the context in which a given document is being viewed.

External References

The example illustrates another concept — an embedded menu item can refer to information outside the company. In the example, the highlighted phrase, *The Bakery*, refers to an establishment located across the street from the Hypothetical Rocker Com-

---

†Aborting a request is unusual; it usually occurs when a user becomes impatient while waiting for the browser to transfer a large document.

pany. Presumably, The Bakery has either agreed to provide a reference to the Hypothetical Rocker Company in its web page or has paid the Hypothetical Rocker Company a fee for advertising.

The example in Figure 23.5 shows one possible visual effect produced by a web page that intermixes text sizes and styles as well as graphics. The variety of presentation and lack of uniformity gives the information a cluttered appearance and makes it difficult to read.

Web pages do not need to be complicated or cluttered. Indeed, the best entries organize information and present it simply. For example, consider the item labeled *Types of rocking chairs*. The Hypothetical Rocker Company has stored information describing its rockers. For each rocker, the information could be a picture or a document similar to the one shown, accompanied by a jingle or background music. When a user selects *Types of rocking chairs*, the browser retrieves and displays the associated information. Figure 23.6 shows one possible way to organize the available information as a simple list.

Recording The Location Of Information

Suppose you have been using the browser to wander through the World Wide Web, and reach a page of information that you find particularly interesting. You might want to tell a friend about the page or record its location so that you could return to it later. Because a path through a set of hypermedia documents can be long and complex, it is difficult to remember the entire series of selections that led to a given page. Furthermore, because web documents do not remain static, the sequence of selections that you made to reach a given page may not work the next time you try.

To make it possible for an individual to record the location of a document, the World Wide Web assigns each page of information a unique identifier. The identifier consists of a string of characters that can be recorded in a computer file, written on a piece of paper, or sent to another person. Given the identifier, a browser can return to the page of information instantly — the user does not need to search through menus or select items.

An identifier used to specify a particular page of web information is called a *Uniform Resource Locator* (*URL*). When a browser displays a page of information, it also displays the URL for the page. Think of a URL as analogous to a telephone number — the URL is a short string that one can remember to avoid searching for a page. Many companies now put their URLs in advertisements (e.g., television commercials) or on labels attached to products.

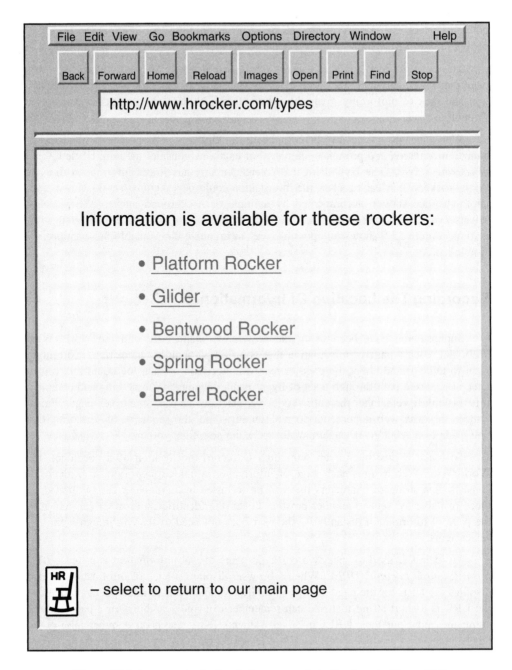

Figure 23.6 An example display that corresponds to the item in Figure 23.5 labeled *Types of rocking chairs.*

For example, the box near the top of the screen in Figure 23.6 contains the URL†:

http://www.hrocker.com/types

A URL may seem like a nonsensical collection of letters and punctuation. However, the precise syntax conveys meaning that a browser can use to retrieve information.

A Uniform Resource Locator *consists of a short character string that identifies a particular multimedia document. Given a valid URL, a browser can go directly to the page without passing through other documents.*

Bookmarks Or Favorites

To make it convenient for a user to move directly to a frequently-accessed page, browsers include a special mechanism. Known formally as *bookmarks* (sometimes called a *hot list* or list of *favorites*), the mechanism allows each user to maintain a list of frequently accessed URLs. For example, suppose an office worker frequently needs to access web pages for three other companies (e.g., three suppliers). The worker can construct a bookmark for each of the three pages.

The chief advantage of bookmarks arises because they are both convenient and fast. Once a bookmark list has been constructed, a user can select any of the bookmarks by using a pull-down menu (the menu labeled *Bookmarks* in Figure 23.6). When the user clicks on the *Bookmarks* label, the list of the user's bookmarks appears in the menu. If the user clicks on one of the entries in the list, the browser obtains and displays the web page for that entry.

Bookmarks are permanent. Bookmarks do not disappear when the user quits running a browser or shuts off the computer. Permanence is achieved by storing the list in a file on a disk in the user's computer. The browser writes a copy of the list to disk whenever the list is changed, and the browser reads a copy of the list from disk whenever it begins execution. Thus, a bookmark saved one day will be available later.

Maintaining a list of bookmarks is as easy as using the list. Updating the list can be performed by making a selection with the mouse — a user does not need to enter a URL manually. That is, once a user has found an interesting page, the user selects a pull-down menu, and chooses the entry *Bookmark This Page* or *Add New Bookmark*. The browser adds the current URL to the bookmark list, making it possible to return to the page quickly. Similarly, a user can select an entry labeled *Edit Bookmarks* or *Manage Bookmarks* to remove an existing bookmark or change the way a bookmark is displayed in the pull-down menu.

---

†This URL, like the company in the example, is hypothetical.

How The World Wide Web Works

Like earlier browsing services, the World Wide Web uses client-server interaction. A web browser acts as a client that uses the Internet to contact a remote web server for a copy of a requested page. A server on the remote system returns a copy of the page along with additional information.

The additional information a web server returns tells the browser two important things. First, it describes how to display the information. Second it gives a URL for each selectable item on the page.

After it has retrieved a page from a remote server, a web browser displays the page, and then waits for the user to select one of the highlighted items. Once a user makes a selection, the browser consults the hidden information that arrived with the page to find the URL that corresponds to the selection. The browser then uses the Internet to obtain the newly selected page of information.

A URL Tells A Browser Which Computer To Contact

How does a browser determine which remote computer contains a given page of information? The URL tells it. Each URL contains, among other information, the domain name of a remote computer. A URL is like a telephone number — it is a short string that identifies a specific point of contact. When given a URL, a browser extracts the computer's name, and then uses the Internet to contact a server on that computer.

A URL Tells A Browser Which Server To Contact

In addition to the name of a remote computer, a URL describes a particular server and a page of information available from that server. After contacting the server on the remote computer, a browser asks the server for a copy of the specified page of information. To summarize:

> *Each URL uniquely identifies a page of information by giving the name of a remote computer, a server on that computer, and a specific page of information available from the server.*

Figure 23.7 illustrates how the URL encodes the information. The initial part of the URL specifies an *access protocol* that tells the browser how to contact the remote server. The domain name of the computer on which the server runs follows the colon and two slashes. Finally, a slash is used to separate the computer name from the suffix that identifies a specific item.

Figure 23.7 The meaning assigned to each part of a URL. Not all URLs require all parts.

Although the example URL in Figure 23.7 explains the meaning of each part found in a typical URL, not all URLs follow the same form. First, many browsers allow users to omit the protocol prefix; if no prefix is given, the browser adds *http://* to the URL. Second, many URLs omit the suffix. Each web server has a *default* item that the server returns if no item is specified. The default item for a given server is usually a page that provides an overview and summary of all available information, with links pointing to other pages. Thus, some browsers allow a URL to consist only of the domain name for a server.

Use Of The Name www In URLs

The domain name in a URL does not need to begin with *www* because a web server can run on an arbitrary computer in the Internet. Why does the domain name in most URLs begin with *www*? The answer is that most organizations choose the name *www* for the computer that runs the organization's web server to make URLs simple and uniform so they will be easier to remember.

Giving the name *www* to the computer on which a web server operates is surprisingly easy. The ease arises from the domain name system, which permits a site to assign multiple names to the same computer. For example, when the Computer Science Department at Purdue University installed a web server, the department chose one of its existing computers to run the server. The computer had the name *lucan.cs.purdue.edu* and IP address *128.10.19.20*. To make it convenient for humans to know which computer ran the server, the department registered an additional entry in the domain name system for the name *www.cs.purdue.edu*. Thus, if a user enters the URL:

$$http://www.cs.purdue.edu$$

a browser will contact exactly the same server as if the user entered the URL:

$$http://lucan.cs.purdue.edu$$

A Browser Provides Access To Multiple Services

In addition to providing access to multimedia documents, the World Wide Web extends earlier browsing services in another significant way: it provides access to multiple services. For example, a web browser understands how to access information from a local file on disk or from the FTP file transfer service described in Chapter 29. Furthermore, references to information from other services can be associated with a selectable item in a web document just like references to other web documents.

The key to understanding the Web's generality lies in realizing that the URL mechanism contains an identifier for a service as well as the name of a computer on which the service operates. A URL that begins with the string *http* refers to the web service that clients use when they retrieve a standard web document. A URL that begins with the string *ftp* refers to a file accessible through the FTP file transfer service.

People often employ the same technique as the Web to encode a type of service. For example, a business card often contains strings such as:

Telephone:	315-555-7895
Cell:	315-555-9537
Fax:	315-555-7802

The initial string specifies whether the number can be used to place a voice telephone call or to send a fax. That is, a prefix like *Fax:* tells one the exact access mechanism to use.

Inside A Browser Program

Because a URL can specify the service to use as well as the location of the item to retrieve, a browser must be prepared to handle multiple services. That is, a browser program must contain all the software needed to access a variety of services. Conceptually, one can think of a browser as a giant program that has several other client programs built in. The interface piece of a browser handles interaction with a user by receiving input and controlling the operations the browser performs. When a user enters a URL or uses the mouse to make a selection from a document, the interface extracts the prefix of the URL that specifies a service, and uses the prefix to choose the appropriate client. The interface then invokes the client to obtain the specified item, and displays the results for the user. Figure 23.8 illustrates the concept.

User

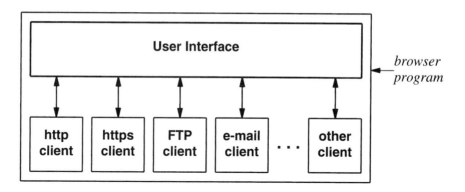

browser program

Internet

Figure 23.8 Conceptual organization of a browser. A user interacts with a single, uniform interface that uses information in the URL to choose one of the built-in client programs to access information on the Internet.

For example, browsers understand how to send email and allow a user to examine their incoming email. They also understand how to use the FTP file transfer service to download a file onto the user's computer. From the user's point of view, the selection of an appropriate mechanism is automatic — the user browses through the World Wide Web making selections to request information; the browser uses the URL to determine how to proceed.

A browser's novelty and power arise because it integrates access to multiple Internet services into a single, seamless browsing system. The browser uses information in the URL to automatically select an access mechanism from among such services as email and file transfer.

Summary

Internet browsing services enhance information access in two significant ways. First, such services use an interactive paradigm that allows a user to view documents from remote computers without performing tedious file transfers. More important, browsing services integrate selectable items, text, audio, video, and graphic images into documents. The result is known as a hypermedia system in which a given multimedia document can contain references to other multimedia documents. To display output from a multimedia document, a computer must have hardware that can display images and reproduce sounds.

The World Wide Web has become the most widely-used information service on the Internet. One can think of the Web as a large set of hypermedia documents stored on computers throughout the Internet. A given web document can contain embedded menu items that refer to web documents stored on other computers. A user can follow a link from a document on one computer to a document on another as easily as a user can follow a link between documents on the same computer.

A browser is a computer program used to access the World Wide Web. Browsers offer a point-and-click interface that allows a user to access information using a mouse. After the browser displays a particular multimedia document, the user clicks on one of the embedded menu items to request the browser to obtain and display a new document. Thus, from a user's point of view, the location of information is irrelevant — the World Wide Web appears to be a seamless interconnection of documents, each of which can be accessed directly.

To make it possible to record the location of a particular piece of information, each web document is assigned a unique name known as a Uniform Resource Locator (URL) that contains the information a browser needs to obtain the document. A URL can be entered manually by a user or obtained from an embedded link. Given the URL, a browser determines the service used to access the document, the computer on which the document resides, and the location of the specified item on that computer. Because it includes software for a variety of access mechanisms, a browser can access items stored in a menu system, files available for download, or hypermedia documents stored on a web server. Thus, a browser provides a uniform, seamless way to access most information on the Internet.

An Observation About Hypermedia Browsing

Most people find the World Wide Web fascinating. In only a few minutes, one can learn how to make a selection and move from one page of information to another. In a short time, novices find that they have examined documents on a myriad of topics located on a variety of computers at Internet sites around the world. For example, one professor at a midwest university found pictures of a resort in Hawaii that he was about to visit, while a colleague viewed a foreign movie trailer from a site in Europe.

The maze of interconnected web documents is continually evolving. Because the World Wide Web is growing at an incredible rate, the information available on the Web keeps changing, enticing one to browse again. As a result, web browsing can become addictive and time-consuming.

24

World Wide Web Documents (HTML)

Introduction

The previous chapter describes the World Wide Web, and discusses how an information browsing service appears to a user. This chapter examines the internal representation used in web pages. It shows the language one must use to create a web page, and explains how a multimedia document can be created that contains items such as text and graphic images and how a link in one web page can point to another page.

Why should one learn about the internal representation used for web pages? After all, a browser completely hides the internal details from a user. There are two reasons. First, learning a few basic concepts can help explain the idea of hypermedia and remove much of the mystery from web pages. Second, learning about the internal language will show how much detail is needed to represent a web page.

Display Hardware Varies

The display hardware used with computers varies widely. A few computers have low-resolution monitors that are limited to a set of two hundred fifty-six colors, while others can display millions of colors. Some display systems limit fonts to a few possibilities, while others can display text in arbitrary sizes and a wide variety of fonts.

More important, the popularity of the Internet means that users around the world employ all types and models of computers to access and display web pages.

It may seem that a person who designs a page of multimedia information for the World Wide Web would need to understand the details of many types of computers. After all, the author of a web page needs to specify how a page is presented as well as the contents. That is, an author must specify the text of each message that will appear on a page, whether the messages should be highlighted (e.g., displayed in a larger size than surrounding text), which pictures should be included, and the general arrangement of items on the page.

A Browser Translates And Displays A Web Document

Interestingly, a person who creates a web page does not need to understand the details of computer display hardware, nor does an author need to prepare a separate copy of the page for each type of computer display screen. Instead, a web page is created in a general-purpose manner that can be used with any display hardware. Thus, an author only needs to prepare a single copy of each web page — instead of including all details in the specification about how to display the page on various types of computer hardware, the author uses a computer language that specifies the contents of the page. The language contains general guidelines for display without giving details. For example, an author can specify that a group of sentences form a paragraph, but the author cannot specify details such as the exact length of a line or whether to indent the beginning of the paragraph.

How do general guidelines in a web page result in output on the display hardware of a given computer? Software in a web browser performs the necessary translation. When it obtains a page from the Web, a browser receives a copy of the specifications for the page exactly as the author wrote them, and translates the author's general guidelines into detailed commands suitable for the local computer's display hardware.

For example, a browser understands the size of the window in which text must be displayed, and uses the size to determine how many words can fit on each line. Similarly, if a computer has color capability and the web page specifies that a given word should be displayed in red, a browser on the computer will instruct the hardware to show the word in red. If a given computer does not have color capability, a browser on the computer will display the page in black and white, using shades of gray in place of colors. In essence, a browser attempts to create a representation that provides the best display possible on the available hardware.

A Consequence Of The Web Approach

Allowing a browser to choose display details has an interesting consequence: the same web page may appear differently when viewed through two browsers or on two computers that have dissimilar hardware. In addition to the difference between color and black-and-white, the screens on some computers are wider than the screens on others. Thus, the length of a line of text or the size of images that can be displayed on a single line varies from computer to computer. The browser must compensate by wrapping a long line of text onto multiple physical lines or by only showing part of a page at a time and allowing the user to move the part that is visible. To summarize:

> *Web pages are written in a computer language that gives general guidelines about the desired presentation; a browser translates the specification into commands suitable for specific display hardware when rendering a web page on a given computer display. As a result, the same web page can appear slightly different when displayed on two different computers or by different browsers.*

HTML, The Language Used For Web Documents

Although the language used for web pages is high-level, it is not a natural language such as English. Instead, each web page is written in a language called the *HyperText Markup Language* or *HTML*.

Like other languages used with computers, HTML has its own rules of grammar, and uses conventional punctuation symbols in unusual ways. Unfortunately, HTML is designed to make it easy for a computer to process. Consequently, the grammar rules can make it difficult for a person to compose an HTML document. In fact, it can even be difficult for a person to read or understand HTML†.

People accustomed to using word processors are often surprised to learn that a web page specification does not appear the same to its author as when it is translated and displayed by a browser. Indeed, the HTML language used to compose a web page differs dramatically from the resulting page a browser displays. For example, the arrangement of words on lines in an HTML document may not have any relationship to the arrangement of words and lines that a browser shows when displaying the document. Figure 24.1 illustrates the idea by showing part of a web page an author created in HTML and the resulting output when a browser displays the document.

---

†To see the HTML for a web page, use a browser to display the page and then select *Page Source* under *View*.

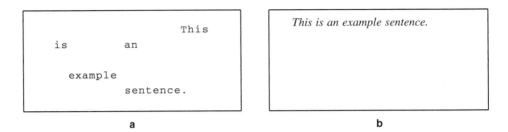

a   b

Figure 24.1 (a) Part of a web page in HTML, and (b) the result when a
browser displays the page. Spacing in HTML does not affect
the spacing when a page is displayed.

In the example, the author has chosen to split words from a single sentence over
several lines and add random amounts of extra spaces between words. When it displays
the document, a browser places the words together on a single line, with no unnecessary
spacing between the words.

The concept of allowing HTML to contain arbitrary spaces and extra lines is
known as *free format input*. The motivation for free format input should be clear: because HTML does not specify exactly how to display the output, a browser has the freedom to choose a form that is appropriate for a given computer.

Instructions In A Web Page Control The Output

Although HTML uses free-format input, a web page can contain instructions that
tell a browser how to interpret or display the page. For example, an author can include
instructions that tell a browser when to begin a new line of output, when to center a line
of text, and whether to display items in a list or in paragraph form.

To separate HTML instructions from text to be displayed, each instruction consists
of characters surrounded by less-than and greater-than symbols. The result is known as
a *tag*. For example, the HTML tag <BR> instructs a browser to begin a new line†.
The convention of using less-than and greater-than symbols to distinguish tags from ordinary text works well because common English syntax does not place these symbols
around words.

---

†The characters *BR* were chosen because the printing industry uses the technical term *line break* to refer
to the beginning of a new line.

A Web Page Is Divided Into Two Main Sections

Each HTML document is divided into two main parts a *heading* and a *body*. The heading contains information to identify the page, while the body contains the actual information to be displayed. For example, the heading contains a title for the page. A browser can choose whether and how to display items from the heading; most browsers place heading information in a separate area of the screen, reserving the main browser window for items found in the document body.

An author uses tags to tell the browser which part of the page corresponds to the heading and which part corresponds to the body. Like many tags in HTML, the tags used to bracket the heading and body come in pairs, with one of the pair used to start a section and another used to close it. Both tags in a pair have the same name except the closing tag includes a slash before the name. For example, the pair of tags <HEAD> and </HEAD> bracket the heading. Similarly, the pair of tags <BODY> and </BODY> bracket the body. Another example of paired tags occurs inside the heading, where the pair of tags <TITLE and </TITLE> bracket the document title.

Figure 24.2 illustrates the arrangement of paired tags in a typical web page. Of course, a browser does not display the tags for a user to see. Instead, the tags merely control the way the browser displays the output.

```
<HTML>
<HEAD>
   <TITLE>
        ...Formal Document Title Goes Here
   </TITLE>
   ...additional heading information, if needed
</HEAD>

<BODY>
   ...actual information to be displayed on the page
</BODY>
```

Figure 24.2 The basic tags used to divide a web page into a heading and body†. A browser displays the heading separate from the body.

Indentation Can Make HTML Readable

We said that HTML uses free-format input, which allows arbitrary spaces to be inserted. However, the illustration in Figure 24.2 is neatly-formed. Each tag has been placed on a separate line, and information in both the heading and body are indented. Furthermore, pairs of tags such as <HEAD> and </HEAD> are indented exactly the same amount.

---

†Although the examples in this text show tags in uppercase, HTML is not case sensitive. Thus, <head> is equivalent to <HEAD>.

Why should an author bother to place HTML tags on separate lines and indent each section? Certainly not for benefit of a browser — when it reads a page, a browser will ignore all extra spacing. The answer is that web page specifications are arranged neatly to make it easier for humans to understand them. In addition to composing the document, a human may need to manually edit a web document that contains a problem or update the document if information changes. Placing HTML tags on separate lines and indenting text makes it easy for a human to understand the document structure and locate individual items.

It may seem that humans infrequently examine the internal form of a web page. Indeed, many automated tools are available that allow a human to create a web document without entering or viewing the internal HTML. However, professional web programmers sometimes need to manually change HTML to enhance the code generated by an automated program. We can summarize:

> *Although a browser ignores indentation when displaying an HTML document, placing tags on separate lines and indenting items can make it easier for a human to read a document.*

The Body Of A Web Page Can Contain Text

If a web page contains text organized into paragraphs, a browser places a blank line between paragraphs when displaying the text. However, the browser does not expect a blank line to separate paragraphs in the HTML version of the page. Instead, the author must use a paragraph tag to tell the browser where one paragraph ends and another begins. A paragraph tag consists of the three characters <P>, with the *P* chosen to make it easy to remember.

Figure 24.3 illustrates part of an HTML document that contains three paragraphs along with the resulting output when a browser displays the document.

Indentation Can Make Paragraphs Easier To Find

The example HTML in Figure 24.3a has been formatted to make it easy for a human to read. The author carefully placed each paragraph tag on a line by itself and indented the text. Recall that careful formatting of HTML is intended for humans — it will not affect how a browser displays the page. For example, Figure 24.4 illustrates two possible alternatives for the HTML found in Figure 24.3a. Although a browser displays all three versions exactly the same, the version in Figure 24.3a is much easier for a person to read or modify because spacing in the HTML version corresponds to spacing a browser uses to display the document.

```
     This is an example of text on a Web page arranged in
     paragraphs. The first paragraph is quite short; the
     paragraph contains only two sentences.
<P>
     The second paragraph contains two sentences.
     A sentence can span multiple input lines and can
     contain additional      spaces; a browser ignores such
     spacing when displaying the paragraph.
<P>
     This is the final paragraph.
     In HTML, a tag separates each pair of paragraphs.
     On the screen, however, vertical blank space
     separates paragraphs as in a textbook.
```

a

This is an example of text on a Web page arranged in paragraphs. The first paragraph is quite short; the paragraph contains only two sentences.

The second paragraph contains two sentences. A sentence can span multiple input lines and can contain additional spaces; a browser ignores such spacing when displaying the paragraph.

This is the final paragraph. In HTML, a tag separates each pair of paragraphs. On the screen, however, vertical blank space separates paragraphs as in a textbook.

b

Figure 24.3 (a) Part of an HTML document that contains three paragraphs of text, and (b) the result when the example section is displayed by a browser. The browser uses tags in the HTML document to determine how to group sentences into paragraphs.

```
This is an example of text on a Web page arranged in
paragraphs. The first paragraph is quite short; the
paragraph contains only two sentences. <P> The second
paragraph contains two sentences. A sentence can span
multiple input lines and can contain additional spaces;
a browser ignores such spacing when displaying the
paragraph.<P> This is the final paragraph. In HTML, a tag
separates each pair of paragraphs. On the screen, however,
vertical blank space separates paragraphs as in a
textbook.
```

a

```
      This  is  an  example  of  text  on  a  Web
page arranged in paragraphs.

      The first paragraph is quite short; the paragraph
contains only two sentences.<P>The second paragraph
contains two sentences.

      A sentence can span multiple input lines and can
contain additional spaces; a browser ignores such spacing
spacing when displaying the paragraph.<P>This is the
final paragraph. In HTML, a tag separates each pair of
paragraphs. On the screen, however, vertical blank space
separates paragraphs as in a textbook.
```

b

Figure 24.4 Two alternative versions of the HTML document in Figure 24.3a.
A browser displays all three versions as shown in Figure 24.3b.

A Web Page Can Link To Another Page

The previous chapter illustrates that a web page can contain selectable links that allow a user to move from one web page to another by using a mouse to select an item. How does an author of a web page indicate that an item corresponds to a selectable link? HTML uses a pair of tags: when creating a web page, the author places one pair of such tags around each group of items that form a selectable link. The tags can be placed around a single word, two words, a phrase, or an entire paragraph. When a browser finds the tags, it marks the items as a selectable link. Typically, the browser underlines the marked items and displays them in color.

In HTML terminology, items on a page that correspond to a link are said to be *anchored*. Consequently, the character A was adopted for use in the pair of tags that mark a link. A link begins with the tag <A>, and ends with the tag </A>.

To specify the page to which a given link points, the initial tag contains the keyword *HREF*, followed by an equal sign and a URL enclosed in double quotes. For example, Figure 24.5 shows part of an HTML page and the corresponding output that a browser produces on the user's screen. In the example, the phrase *William Shakespeare* is anchored to the URL:

$$http://the\text{-}tech.mit.edu/Shakespeare$$

When a browser displays anchored text, the browser changes the color and underlines the anchored items, indicating to the user that the text corresponds to a selectable link. When a user clicks on a selectable item, the browser loads the new page specified by the URL.

```
On the Web, you can find some of the classic
works of English literature.  For example, the
works of
<A HREF="http://the-tech.mit.edu/Shakespeare">
                William Shakespeare
</A>
are available.
```

a

On the Web, you can find some of the classic works of English literature. For example, the works of <u>William Shakespeare</u> are available.

b

Figure 24.5 (a) HTML for part of a web page that contains a link to another page, and (b) the result when displayed by a browser. Most browsers show links in a different color or in gray.

HTML Allows Numbered And Unnumbered Lists

HTML includes mechanisms that can be used to format items. For example, Figure 24.6 illustrates the HTML used to create an *ordered list*, which is sometimes called a *numbered list*. The pair of tags <OL> and </OL> surrounds the entire list, while the tag <LI> precedes each list item.

```
<OL>
    <LI> breakfast
    <LI> lunch
    <LI> dinner
</OL>
```

a

```
1. breakfast
2. lunch
3. dinner
```

b

Figure 24.6 (a) An example of the HTML needed to create an ordered list,
and (b) the result when displayed by a browser.

As an alternative to an ordered list, HTML allows an *unordered list*, which is
sometimes called a *bulleted list*. As Figure 24.7 illustrates, an unordered list also uses
the tag <LI> before each item, but is surrounded by the pair of tags <UL> and </UL>.

```
<UL>
    <LI> cars
    <LI> trucks
    <LI> buses
</UL>
```

a

```
● cars
● trucks
● buses
```

b

Figure 24.7 (a) An example of the HTML needed to create an unordered list,
and (b) the result when displayed by a browser.

Images On A Web Page Are Digital

So far, we have described facilities that allow a web page to include text. One of
the most interesting aspects of HTML, however, is its ability to include images such as
pictures or graphics as well as text. Before an image can be included on a web page,

the image must be *digitized*. That is, the image must be converted into a sequence of numbers and stored in a data file on disk.

Each number in a digital image represents information about one small piece of the picture. The pieces are microscopically small; a typical digital image has hundreds of pieces per inch. When a browser displays the image on a computer screen, the browser uses the sequence of numbers in the file to determine the color and intensity of small dots on the computer's screen.

Digital images on a computer screen work for the same reason that television pictures work: human eyes have limited ability to focus on small items. When a screen contains hundreds of dots per inch, a human eye cannot distinguish an individual dot. Instead, humans use larger patterns of color and shading to determine what an image shows. When a human sees a digital image displayed on a computer screen or a picture on a television screen, the human is able to focus on the picture and not the individual dots.

How are digital images produced? There are two general methods. The first method uses a *digital camera*, while the second method uses a *digital scanner*. In a digital camera, the lens focuses light on an electronic device that converts the image into digital form. The digital image is sent to a computer, where it is stored in a file on the computer's disk.

The second method uses a digital scanner, a device that is attached to a computer. The user places a picture or document in the scanner and starts the scan. The scanner moves along the picture, produces a digital version, and sends the result to the computer. As with a digital camera, the result is stored in a file on the computer's disk. Figure 24.8 illustrates the two methods used to produce a digital image.

Just as a conventional photograph can be stored as a negative, a color slide, or a color print, a digital image can be stored in several forms. In essence, all forms convey the same information, but the details differ. Furthermore, computer software is built to understand specific image formats — trying to use one format with a program that was designed for another is like trying to use a photographic negative in a slide projector.

One of the most popular forms for representing a digital image is known as the *Graphics Interchange Format*. The format is often referred to by its acronym, *GIF*†. Another format is known as the *Joint Photographic Experts Group* (*JPEG*) format. Although computer software exists that can convert an image from one format to another, some scanners produce one form exclusively.

---

†Most professionals pronounce *GIF* with the same sound the three letters have in the word *gift*.

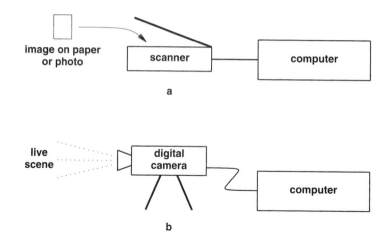

Figure 24.8 Illustration of (a) a digital scanner, and (b) a digital camera. Either produces a file stored on the computer's disk.

HTML Allows A Web Page To Include An Image

Once a GIF image has been stored on a computer's disk, a web page on that computer can include the image by referencing the file. In HTML, an image reference consists of the *IMG* tag, which includes the keyword *SRC* followed by the name of the file on disk. For example, suppose someone has used a digital scanner to produce a GIF image. Further suppose the digital image has been placed in a file named *xxx.gif* on the computer's disk. The tag used to include the image in a web page is:

```
<IMG SRC="xxx.gif">
```

Note that all references to images use the keywords *IMG* and *SRC*; only the name of the file is different for each image.

The name given to a file depends on the computer operating system used. In some systems, file names begin with a slash and contain multiple words separated by slashes. In other systems, file names begin with a single letter, followed by a colon. For example, if a file that contains a digitized image has the name *c:stickman.gif*, a web page on the computer where the file resides can use the following tag to include the image:

```
<IMG SRC="c:stickman.gif">
```

Text Can Appear Adjacent To An Image

An image on a web page can appear by itself or adjacent to text. In fact, when a browser displays a web page, the browser treats an image like an oversized "word" that appears in the middle of a line of text. For example, Figure 24.9 illustrates how a browser displays a page that specifies an image in a line of text.

```
This example shows
<BR>
a line of text <IMG SRC="stickfig.gif"> with an image in it
<BR>
and other lines around it.
```

a

b

Figure 24.9 (a) Part of a web page that includes an image along with text, and (b) the result when a browser displays the page. A browser treats an image like a giant word.

HTML provides a way to control the details of how an image is aligned with surrounding text. Alignment information is provided in an *IMG* tag. If no alignment is specified, the bottom of the image is placed on the same line as illustrated in Figure 24.9. If the *IMG* tag specifies *ALIGN=TOP*, the browser will place the image so the top aligns with the surrounding text, and *ALIGN=CENTER* will center the image. Figure 24.10 illustrates alignment specifications in *IMG* tags and the display that results.

```
This example shows how text can be aligned in the
<BR>
middle <IMG SRC="stickfig.gif" ALIGN=CENTER> of an image
<BR>
or along the <IMG SRC="stickfig.gif" ALIGN=TOP> top.
<BR>
Succeeding lines are back to normal spacing.
```

a

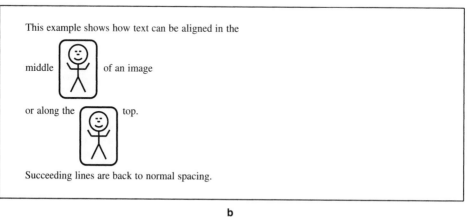

b

Figure 24.10 (a) Part of a web page that combines images with text, and (b) an illustration of how a browser interprets the alignment requests.

Images Can Link To Another Web Page

We have seen that placing the pair of tags `<A>` and `</A>` around text makes the text a selectable link that refers to another web page. HTML uses the same pair of tags to make an image correspond to a selectable link. For example, suppose a digitized image has been placed in file *yyy.jpeg*. The following HTML includes the image in a web page, and makes the image a selectable link:

```
<A HREF="http://www.hrocker.com/index.html">
    <IMG SRC="yyy.jpeg">
</A>
```

If a user clicks on the image, the browser will follow the link to URL:

http://www.hrocker.com/index.html

Some Browsers Can Stretch Or Shrink Images

A digital image can be enlarged or reduced. More important, changing the size of a digital image does not require a significant amount of processing. Thus, it is possible to build a browser that can change the size of digital images as the images are being displayed. To make resizing images easy, HTML allows an *IMG* tag to include additional information that specifies the desired height and width of an image.

Unfortunately, not all browsers can resize images. Some browsers ignore the height and width specifications, and display images in the size used when the image was created. Thus, to ensure that images in a web page appear the same on all browsers, instead of depending on a browser to resize images, web pages are often generated with images in the desired size.

The Background Can Be Controlled

In addition to the text and images that appear on a web page, HTML allows an author to specify the background of a web page. There are two possible approaches: either the author specifies a color for the background, or the author specifies an image to use. If a background color or image is specified, the browser begins by painting the entire page with the color or the image, and then proceeds to add the text and graphics.

It may seem that a background image would detract from the display and make it difficult to read information. However, background images are usually chosen to enhance the page. Thus, instead of a picture with intricate detail and vivid colors, background images usually use soft, muted colors. Often, for example, a background image consists of a pattern that makes the page appear on a textured background similar to a document printed on textured paper.

Recall that each browser can choose a window size and shape in which to display pages. What happens if a background image does not cover the entire window? The browser simply makes extra copies of the image. Using an analogy to ceramic tiles, the technique is known as *tiling* the window. Thus, to make the entire background appear to have texture, one only needs to create a small rectangular image that contains the desired texture, and allow the browser to tile the entire screen with copies.

Other Features Of HTML

HTML contains many facilities not described in this chapter. For example, HTML allows a web page to contain two-dimensional "tables" of information. When a browser displays a table, the browser aligns rows and columns. HTML also provides a way to associate multiple selectable links with a single image, making it possible for the link that is followed to correspond to an item in the picture. For example, the web page for a department store might include a picture of the store that has large signs to identify each department. If a user moves the mouse to the area of the picture that shows a given department and makes a selection, the browser will display information about that department. Finally, a web document can specify that a video clip should be shown or an audio clip played when a web page is displayed.

Of course, the HTML needed to use advanced facilities is more complex than the examples shown in the chapter. However, advanced features use the same general scheme: tags are embedded in the input to specify how to display items.

Importance Of HTML

Before HTML became available, displaying combinations of text and graphics on a computer screen required complex computer programs. Consequently, only someone with an extensive background in computer programming could make graphic images appear on a screen.

Although HTML may seem to require advanced technical skills, it does not. Most people who design web pages have training in graphic arts and design, not in computer science. Few are computer programmers.

GUI Tools Help With Web Page Creation

Although HTML is the language of the Web, tools are available that hide the internal details and make it possible to compose a web page without learning HTML. Known as *web authoring tools*, the programs have a Graphical User Interface (*GUI*) much like a conventional word processor. As the user creates a page, the tool shows how the page will appear when displayed by a browser. For example, if the user chooses to use a background color, the tool changes the background to the specified color. As the user enters text, the tool breaks the input into lines, and displays the lines in approximately the same position as a browser. Finally, when the user specifies an image, the tool displays the image in approximately the same way a browser will display the image. Authoring tools permit a user to edit a page by moving, deleting, or changing items. Once the page has been arranged on the screen, the user requests the tool to save a copy in a file.

Web authoring tools differ from applications like word processors in a significant way — the saved version of a page is written in HTML. Thus, the output is ready for a browser to read. Of course, because HTML only gives guidelines for display, slight differences my arise between the display the author sees when creating a page and the display produced by a browser. The point is:

Although HTML is the ultimate underlying language, web authoring tools are available that allow a user to compose a Web page without learning HTML.

Summary

Web pages are written in a computer language known as the *HyperText Markup Language, HTML*. Because a browser hides the specification completely when displaying a web page, most users never encounter HTML. Instead, when a user gives a browser a URL, the browser contacts the specified server, obtains a copy of the web page, interprets the HTML, and displays the result.

HTML is significant for two reasons. First, the language is sufficiently general to allow it to be used with a variety of browsers and computers. In particular, the language does not specify all the display details, but allows a browser freedom to choose. Second, HTML is significant because it allows people to create web pages without a background in computer programming. Much of the popularity of the World Wide Web can be credited to HTML and web authoring tools which have made it easy for individuals and businesses to create web pages.

25

Advanced Web Technologies (Forms, Frames, Plugins, Java, JavaScript, Flash)

Introduction

The previous chapters discuss the World Wide Web and describe the internal language used for conventional web documents. This chapter describes advanced web technologies that make it possible for a web document to interact with a person who views it. In particular, advanced technologies allow a web document to contain animation and audio, and to provide for direct dialogue with a user. The chapter begins by describing how a browser loads a conventional web page, and goes on to explain how advanced services operate.

Conventional Web Pages Are Static

Many web pages follow the scheme described in the previous chapters. Such pages are called *static* or *passive* because they do not change. That is, like a page in a book, the content of a static web page is fixed by its author, and remains unchanged until the author revises it.

Static documents behave exactly as one would expect. If two people, who are using the same brand of browser on identical computer systems, specify the URL for a static web page, both will see exactly the same output on their screen. The text and the graphic images will be identical on both screens, and the links to other web pages will operate exactly the same.

Static web documents have another useful property: if an individual visits a web page repeatedly, the content remains the same. Thus, if a user records the URL for a page one day and then uses the URL to return to the page the next day, the user will see exactly the same information. Of course, an author might choose to revise a web page, in which case a user would see the revised version. For example, users who visit a page after an author corrects a typo will see the corrected version. Once a change has been made, however, the page will remain unchanged until the author makes another revision.

To summarize

> *Most web pages are* static, *meaning that all users who visit the page see exactly the same contents.*

How A Server Stores Static Web Pages

Corporations or individuals can make information available on the World Wide Web. Doing so requires three basic items:

- A conventional computer with a disk
- A permanent connection from the computer to the Internet
- Web server software

Although any computer can provide the necessary service, most web sites use a relatively fast computer that can respond to requests quickly. In addition, the computers used at most web sites have a large disk because digital images can be quite large.

Because the Internet is global, at any time, people somewhere in the world can be using the Internet. Thus, a web site that is available to the general public must be available continuously (i.e., it needs a permanent Internet connection that is accessible 24 hours a day). In short, to be accessible on the global Internet a web site must remain available and ready for access at all times.

The third item is a computer program that turns a conventional computer into a machine that sends web pages on demand. Called a *web server*, the program must run continuously so it will be available when needed. Unlike a conventional program, a web server does not display information on the computer's screen, nor does it use the computer's keyboard or mouse. Instead, a web server uses the Internet to communicate, speaking a language only browsers understand. A browser can contact the server to request a web page.

Figure 25.1 illustrates the communication between a browser and a server.

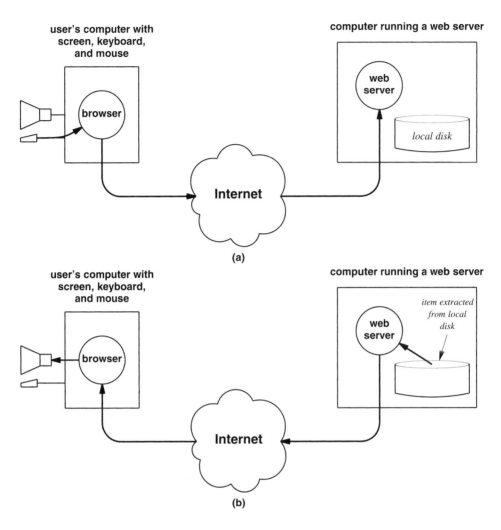

Figure 25.1 (a) A user enters a URL, causing a browser to contact a web
server and request the item, and (b) the server extracts the specified item from its local disk and sends a copy to the browser.

A browser uses information in a URL to determine which computer to contact.
Recall that each URL contains the name of a computer and the name of an item stored
on that computer. Given a URL, a browser extracts the name of the computer and uses
the Internet to contact the web server on that computer. The browser then sends a request to the server that contains the name of the item it needs.

A web server does not take any action until a browser contacts it. That is, the server patiently waits for the next request to arrive. If no browser requests a page from a given server, the server will wait forever. Fortunately, a computer operating system can run other programs while a web server waits for requests. Thus, a computer that runs a web server does not need to be completely idle while the server waits. In fact, companies often run servers for multiple services on a single computer. Thus, it is not uncommon to find a file transfer server using the same physical computer as a web server. Although the servers ''share'' the computer, modern computer systems are so fast that the sharing usually does not delay response — a user cannot tell whether a server is running alone or is sharing the computer.

After a browser makes a connection to a web server and sends a request, the server responds. The server extracts the name of the requested item, finds the specified item on its local disk, and sends a copy back to the browser.

Fetching Items One At A Time

After the server sends a requested item to a browser, the browser and server usually terminate communication. If the browser needs another item from the same server, the browser must contact the server again. Most browsers display messages that tell the user what the browser is doing. For example, one message might say, *contacting computer*, while another might say, *fetching document*. Messages that give an estimate of the time remaining while a browser fetches a large document (e.g., a file download) are especially helpful.

Fetching one item per contact can be inefficient because most web pages contain multiple items. In particular, recall that if a page contains graphic images, each image corresponds to an item that is stored in a separate file on the server. Thus, if a browser fetches a page that contains three images, the browser will pass four separate requests to the server. During the first contact, the browser will obtain the main page. Before the browser can display the page, however, it must request each of the three images. To overcome the disadvantage, newer browsers can choose to remain in contact with the server until all parts of a page have been fetched.

Conventional Web Pages Use The Entire Screen

A conventional web page occupies the entire viewing area in a browser. That is, when a user moves from one page to another, the new page completely replaces information on the screen. If the user wants to see information on the previous page, the user must invoke the browser's *Back* function. Only one page can be seen at any time; when a user moves back to the previous page, the current page contents are replaced.

Although viewing one page at a time works well in most cases, it can be inconvenient. Suppose, for example, that a company has six main products and that a user wants to view information about all of them. The company's web page lists all six products with selectable links that lead to information about each. The user selects one of the links to find out about a particular product. The disadvantage of the scheme is that a user must return to the original list to view additional products. Furthermore, once a user begins reading about one product, he or she may become distracted and forget about the others because the list of products disappears when the user follows a link.

To help users remember, companies often place a set of selectable links at the bottom of a page. For example, each page describing a product might end with two selections:

<u>return to company homepage</u>
<u>return to list of products</u>

A Web Page Can Change Part Of the Screen

To allow users to browse through a list of items easily, web pages use *frame* technology. Frames allows an author to divide the viewing area in a browser into multiple rectangular regions, and to change the display in one region without affecting another. For example, Figure 25.2 illustrates how a browser might display a page that uses frame technology.

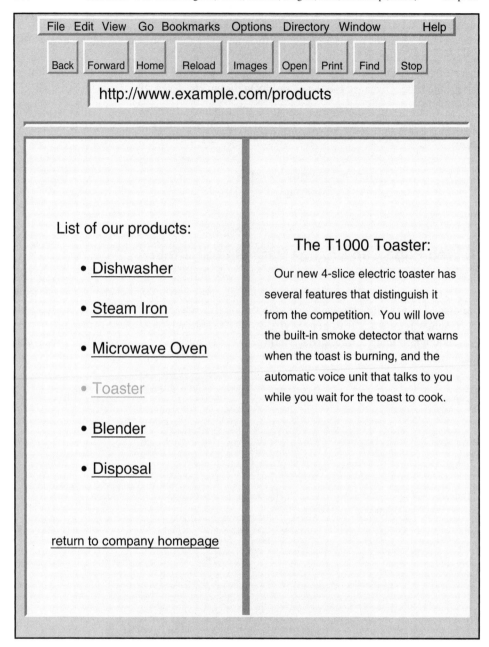

Figure 25.2 Illustration of a web page that uses frame technology. In the example, the left half of the page remains constant while the right half changes as items are selected.

As the figure illustrates, frame technology makes it easy to browse through a list of items. In the example, the left half of the page contains a list of the company's products. The list remains on the screen, allowing a user to select an item, view information, and then select another item. For example, the figure illustrates how the screen appears after a user selects the item *Toaster*. We can summarize:

> *Frame technology divides the browser's screen into multiple regions that can be controlled independently. The contents of one region can remain fixed while another changes.*

The Web, Advertising, And Frames

Most companies that operate web sites do not provide information as a public service. Instead, a company runs a web site for an important commercial reason: to promote the company and its products or services. In a nutshell, the primary motivation for corporate web sites can be summed up in a single word: advertising. If the company provides general information, it does so to lure potential customers or to educate them about uses of the company's commercial offerings.

Because advertising is an important part of corporate web sites, companies have developed ways to exploit web technologies for advertising. Some corporations place advertisements on each web page at their site, meaning that anyone who browses the pages will see the ads. Others add intermediate pages that contain ads. When a user clicks on a link to obtain information, the user is not shown the information he or she expects. Instead, the user sees an advertisement that contains a link to the desired information; the user must make an additional selection to move past the advertisement.

Many companies use frame technology for advertising. The company's web pages are each designed to use frames. Unlike the example above, however, the frames do not contain related information. Instead, the company uses one frame to hold an advertisement, while the other is used for general browsing. Often, the frame containing the ad has a brightly colored background as well as graphics to attract the user's attention.

Using a separate frame for an advertisement has both advantages and disadvantages. For example, an advertisement placed in a frame will stay on the screen longer than one placed in an individual page. The potential advantage is that longer exposure means the user is more likely to notice the ad. The potential disadvantage is that the company cannot display ads for as many different products or services. In addition, using a frame restricts advertising to a separate area of the screen. The potential advantage is that a user will not become irritated by advertisements interspersed with other information. The potential disadvantage is that a user might find it easier to ignore the ad.

Of course, a company does not need to use one style of advertising exclusively because frame technology can be combined with other advertising schemes. For example, a company can place its most important ads in a frame, but allow individual web pages to mention other products. Or the company can choose to restrict an advertisement to a small frame that invites the user to find out more about the company's products. Thus, the frame reserved for advertisement might contain a simple message such as:

Click here to view this month's featured product.

Placing a simple message in a frame instead of a full advertisement leaves more space on the screen for other frames.

Pop-Ups And Pop-Up Blockers

In addition to using frames for advertising, some web sites use a technology known as *pop-ups*. As the name describes, a pop-up consists of a new window that appears automatically without any user request. Although pop-ups can be used to prompt a user (e.g., to suggest a related web page), most pop-ups carry advertising. Often, a pop-up window will obscure part of the main window, which interrupts browsing, and requires a user to close the pop-up before continuing.

Because pop-up advertisements are annoying, some browsers have an option that allows a user to disable pop-ups. In addition, third-party software known as a *pop-up blocker* is also available.

The point is:

> *A web page can include* pop-ups *that cause a browser to create a separate window automatically. Because pop-ups carry advertising that disrupts a user, browsers and other software allow a user to block pop-ups.*

Static Documents Have Disadvantages

Web technologies were originally designed to store information that remains stable over long periods of time in the same way a library stores books that do not change quickly. Indeed, researchers working on electronic retrieval mechanisms often use the term *digital library* to characterize their work. As a result, the original web design focused on providing access to documents that did not change.

Although technologies have been added to the Web that provide more sophisticated display, static web documents remain popular for three reasons. First, static documents are easy to create. Second, static documents are inexpensive to maintain. Third, static documents can be retrieved quickly. These advantages have had a significant impact: many documents on the Web are static.

Despite their popularity, static web pages have several disadvantages. First, although they can include text and graphic images, static pages cannot include additional forms of data such as sounds. Second, the contents of a page cannot include an instantaneous snapshot of information (e.g., the current weather or a current stock price). Instead, the contents of the page must be stored on the server before a request arrives. Thus, a short time usually elapses between the time the page is composed and the first time a user can view the page. Third, because the information travels in only one direction (from a web server to a user's browser), static web pages cannot be used to interact with a user. In particular, although they can present a list of items and allow a user to make a selection, static pages cannot ask a user to type a word or name on the keyboard and then use the name to search for information. Fourth, once loaded, the page does not change — a user must take action (i.e., by typing a URL on the keyboard or selecting an item with the mouse) before a browser moves to a new page of information. Thus, static pages cannot present continuous changes to the information on the screen. The lack of rapid update means that static pages cannot contain animation; they never appear to move.

Controlling How A Browser Processes Data

Several technologies have been developed to overcome the disadvantages of static web pages. One of the earliest extensions was developed to permit a web page to contain audio clips in addition to text and images. An audio clip is sound that has been recorded with a microphone. The clip might contain a spoken message, music, or a conversation — any sound can be used. Furthermore, the clip can be as short as a single tone or a musical note, or as long as a complete speech.

Because users do not interact with audio the same way they interact with images, browsers must treat the two differently. In particular, when a browser retrieves a web page that contains multiple images, the page specifies exactly which images should appear and exactly where they should be placed on the page. The browser automatically obtains a copy of each image, which it displays at the appropriate point in the page. A user can then scan the page and see each image in its correct context. The audio analog of displaying an image is playing a sound. Unfortunately, if a browser automatically obtained and played a copy of all the audio clips on a page, the result would be meaningless — the user would have no idea why the sounds were being played or where on the page the sounds belonged.

To ensure that sounds make sense, audio clips are not merely embedded in the text of a web page. Instead, each clip is associated with a selectable link. When the user wants to hear the clip, the user clicks on the link. At that point, the browser accesses the audio and plays it though the computer's speaker or earphones. For a small amount of audio (e.g., a few words), the browser retrieves a copy of the *audio clip* and stores it locally. Thus, if the user clicks on the link again, the browser can play the stored version without delay. To summarize:

> *A web page can contain stored audio. When a user selects an item that corresponds to an audio clip, the user's browser plays the audio through speakers or earphones attached to the computer.*

From the above description, it might seem that adding audio to web pages is straightforward. However, two problems made it difficult. The major problem arose because there was no single standard for storing digitized audio clips. Various organizations developed digitizing schemes, but none was best in all situations. For example, the digital audio format that has been developed for music CDs could have been chosen. Unfortunately, to make CDs high quality, the format creates many bytes of information for each second of recorded sound. If all audio on the Web used the music CD system, the files used to store audio would be large and require excessive time to download. As an alternative, several formats were developed to store audio using fewer bytes. Although the formats work well for human voice, they tend to distort music.

Engineers designing audio for the Web faced a minor problem as well: although many types of computers were used to access the Web, no standard audio hardware was available. When audio facilities were added to computers, each vendor chose a technology. Some chose hardware that produced high-quality stereo sound, while others used less expensive mechanisms. More important, each vendor chose specific computers and operating systems with which their hardware would operate; there was no guarantee that a particular brand of audio hardware would be available on all computers.

Plugins Allow Variety

It became obvious that not all audio clips on the Web would use the same format. Similarly, engineers were busy developing alternative formats for graphic information and other data files. Browser vendors realized that new formats were being developed rapidly. Instead of trying to make each browser handle all possible data formats, the vendors took a different approach by building browsers that understand basic data formats, and then developing a technology that allows each user to extend their browser as needed.

Known as *plugins*, the system solves the problem of having multiple formats nicely. A plugin is a small computer program that understands how to interpret one specific data format. When a company or individual invents a new data format, the inventor must also write a plugin program that handles the format. For example, the plugin for an audio clip must know how to use audio hardware to convert the digitized information into sounds. Before someone can use the company's new format, they must download the plugin and use it to extend their browser.

Many new browsers come with common plugins; users can add additional plugins easily. More important, a web page can be designed to test whether the user's browser contains a given plugin, inform the user, and download the plugin from another web site. Thus, from a user's point of view, the plugin scheme seems automatic. The user browses the Web as usual until selecting an item that requires a plugin. If it already contains the required plugin, the browser uses the plugin to process the item (e.g., to convert an audio clip into sound). If the user's browser does not contain the plugin that is needed to process the item, the user is informed. Typically, a message appears on the user's screen that specifies which plugin is needed, gives a URL from which the plugin can be obtained, and asks the user whether to retrieve and install a copy or skip the page†. If the user requests that the plugin be installed, a copy is placed on the user's local disk as well as loaded into the running browser. Each time a browser starts, it loads all plugins from the local disk, meaning that a user will always have the plugin capability and will not need to download the plugin again.

A Server Can Compute A Web Page On Demand

Although plugins solve the problem of having multiple data formats, they do not overcome all the disadvantages of static web pages. A set of mechanisms known collectively as *server-side scripting technologies* were invented to allow web pages to have *dynamic content*‡. That is, instead of placing a single, fixed copy of a page on a web server, server scripting allows the contents of a page to be composed each time someone requests a copy of the page. The idea is straightforward: server scripting allows a web server to associate a given URL with a computer program instead of a static document on disk. When a browser requests such a URL, the server does not fetch a page from a file on disk. Instead, the server runs the associated computer program and sends the output from the program back to the user. A server can have an arbitrary number of scripting programs that each perform a different computation; the server uses the URL in the incoming request to determine which program to run.

Why is the output of a computer program more interesting than a static document? Because a computer program can access data and perform computations. For example, a web server running on a computer that has a digital thermometer attached can use a program to produce a web page that reports the current temperature at the server site. Or a server running on a computer that has access to stock information can return current stock prices (not the price at the beginning of the day, but the price at the exact time the page is referenced). Similarly, a store with an online catalog can use a scripting program to display the exact inventory at the instant the web page is created rather than the inventory count from the previous night's summary. Or a server, running on a computer that has a video camera attached, can capture an image from the camera and include the image on a web page whenever the page is requested. Thus, server-side scripting allows a web server to operate as a surveillance system.

---

†Unfortunately, the plugin needed to view a given item may not be available for all brands of browsers or for all computer systems.

‡The initial server scripting technology was known by the obscure name of *Common Gateway Interface* (usually abbreviated *CGI* or *CGI-bin*); additional technologies have also appeared.

Instantaneous computation is not the only reason for using server-side scripting. A program can store information on disk, and can keep a history. One of the simplest scripting programs keeps a count of how many times a given web page has been accessed. With scripting technology, counting access is easy: a site associates a web page with a program that stores a counter on disk along with an HTML file that contains the data for the web page. Each time the page is accessed, the web server runs the program. The program increments the counter on disk, replaces the count in the document and returns the document to the browser. Although it may sound complicated, a professional programmer can create such a program in a few minutes (i.e., only a few lines of code are required). The result is an automatic counter — the corporation's web page can contain a sentence such as:

This page has been accessed N times.

where N is the number of times the page has been requested. Each time a user accesses the page, the value of N increases. In fact, merely asking the browser to reload the page will increase the count!

How Server-Side Scripting Works

How do server-script programs operate? The easiest way to envision a script is to imagine that it is part of a web server. A browser sends a request to the server. If the requested URL corresponds to a script, the server starts the appropriate program and passes the program a copy of the URL. The server waits for the program to produce output, and returns the output to the browser in the form of a reply. Figure 25.3 illustrates the concept.

Interestingly, from a browser's point of view, there is no difference between a URL that corresponds to a static document and one that corresponds to a script. Requests for both static documents and script programs have the same syntactic form. Similarly, all replies that a browser receives from a server have the same form — there is nothing to tell the browser whether the server is returning a copy of a static document or the output from a script.

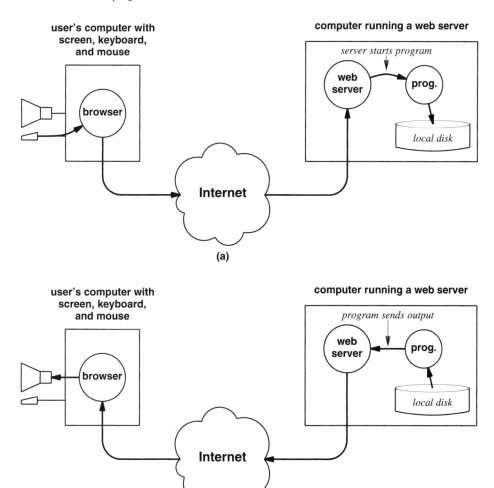

Figure 25.3 (a) A browser requests a URL that corresponds to a program, causing the server to start the program, and (b) the program computes a response, which the server returns to the browser.

Professional Programmers Build Server Scripts

Who builds scripts? Only someone who knows how to write a computer program can create a server-side program. Thus, the technology is beyond the capabilities of most users. More important, script programs are somewhat unusual because they interact directly with a web server. The script must be written to follow the server's guidelines. For example, unlike a conventional computer program, a script cannot accept input from a keyboard or display output on a user's screen. Instead, a web server captures the output from the script, and transmits the output back to the browser.

Interestingly, the interaction between a web server and a script also depends on the computer's operating system. Therefore, like conventional programs, each script is written for one brand of web server and for one brand of computer operating system. Before the script can be used on a different computer system, it may need to be rewritten.

Personalized Web Pages

Corporations quickly realized that dynamic content technologies can be used to enhance the Web by making web pages *personalized*. That is, instead of creating a series of pages with static content and allowing the customer to choose among them, the server can compose the content of a page to suit the customer who requests it. For example, a server can rearrange the order in which items are displayed on the page (e.g., to place items of interest to the person who requested the page near the top). The server can even use information about the requester to choose the set of items that appear on the page.

To understand the benefits and disadvantages of personalized web pages, consider a personalized web page that lists songs. Assume the server has a way of approximating the age of the person sending in a request. If a teenager accesses the page, the server might choose to display songs that are currently popular. If a middle-aged person accesses the same page, the server might choose to display rock and roll songs from the 1970's. Finally, if someone over the age of 70 accesses the page, the server might display songs from the 1950's. Thus, the content of the page can be chosen to suit the individual.

Personalized content has a severe disadvantage because it can eliminate *reproducibility* — two users who view the same page may not obtain the same information. The problem can become significant. For example, suppose that a middle-aged mother wants to purchase music as a gift for her teenage son. Further suppose that the son browses the Web, chooses a list of songs, and passes his mother the URLs. He might tell her that he likes the song listed on a specific page. If the server personalizes pages, a different song might appear in the list when the boy's mother accesses the page. The point is:

> *Dynamic content technologies allow a server to personalize pages by choosing items to display and the order in which to display them. Although it helps focus on items that interest a particular user, personalized content can make pages irreproducible.*

Personalized Advertisements

Recall that frame technology makes it possible to separate advertisements from the web pages themselves. A script can store information about previous contacts from a given user, and then use the information to select advertisements. That is, whenever it receives a request for a page, the script can select an ad to place in one frame, while sending the requested page in another. As a result, the server can display a different ad each time a user visits the site.

Server scripts can also keep a record of which corporate web pages a user visits, and choose advertisements that suit the user. If the user has browsed pages about furniture and appliances, the script might choose to include ads appropriate for furnishing a home. If a user browses pages of popular music, the script might choose to include advertisements about events such as upcoming rock concerts.

Web Pages Can Interact

Although the scripting technology discussed above can be used to create web pages that change, such scripts run only at the server. Thus, a server script cannot interact directly with a user. To make it possible for a user to enter data, another technology was invented. Known as *forms*, the technology permits a web page to contain blank areas in which the user must enter information. After a user fills in the required information, the browser sends the information to the server when requesting another page.

The advantage of forms technology should be clear: instead of merely selecting items from a list, forms make it possible to enter data directly. For example, suppose a user wishes to purchase an item over the Web. The user must supply a credit card number and a postal address to which the item should be mailed. Without forms technology, entering such information is almost impossible. With forms technology, a single web page can be displayed for the user that contains a form for the credit card number and another form for the mailing address. Once the user has filled in the forms and clicked on a selectable item (e.g., an item labeled *purchase*), the browser sends the information to the server.

Shopping Carts

One particularly useful type of personalized web page is known as a *shopping cart*. As the name implies, the technology is analogous to a conventional shopping cart. Shopping carts are used by commercial web sites that sell products. At any time while visiting the site, a user can create a shopping cart. When the user sees an item they want to purchase, the user clicks on a selection that says *add to shopping cart*. The server keeps a list of all items the user has added to his or her shopping cart. At any time, the user can request the server to show the contents of the shopping cart.

Shopping carts do not persist forever. Typically, a store will only guarantee to keep a cart and its contents for a few hours or days. If a user waits longer than the guaranteed time, the shopping cart will expire, and the user must begin shopping with a new cart. Of course, most users ''check out'' (i.e., place the order) before their cart becomes invalid.

Cookies

How can a server remember a shopping cart, know about a user, or tell whether the user has visited before? Most systems assign a number to each user or each order. The number can be visible to a user or hidden. For example, a user can be told to print a page that contains an order number, and the site can ask a user to re-enter the number during a subsequent visit. In most cases, however, the internal number used to identify an order is kept hidden from the user — a clever scheme is used to embed the number in each page that the server sends, which means that every response from the user contains the hidden number.

Note that an order number does not specify the contents of the cart. Instead, it merely provides the server with an identifier that the server uses to look up the cart; the server must store the list of items in the cart. The idea of using a short identifier is a powerful technique — because only a small amount of information travels between a browser and server, communication can proceed quickly.

Although a shopping cart number suffices for a single order, it does not tell a server about multiple orders. If an individual visits a site twice in a month and places two separate orders, he or she will be assigned two separate shopping cart numbers.

How can a server automatically identify a single individual who visits many times? The most common identification technology extends the shopping cart idea so there is an identification number *for each user*. To keep the scheme invisible to users, browsers must cooperate with servers. When a user first visits a web site, the server assigns the user an identification number and passes the number to the browser. The browser stores the identification number on the disk of the user's computer. Later, when the user revisits, the browser passes the identification number back to the server.

The numbers that a browser and server use to identify a user have an odd name — they are called *cookies*. Like a shopping cart identifier, each cookie is relatively small, and does not include all the information about a user. Instead, the server keeps the information on its disk, and merely uses a cookie to find the information in its database. Thus, although a cookie is small, a server can keep arbitrary amounts of information about the user (e.g., what pages the user has viewed, what ads the user has been shown, and what the user has purchased during each visit).

Should You Accept Cookies?

A server can pass a cookie to a browser at any time. Before it accepts the cookie, however, the browser asks the user what to do. Many browsers allow a user to configure their browser to reject all cookies, accept all cookies, or prompt the user for each cookie. Thus, a user must decide how to handle cookies.

The advantage of accepting cookies is that they allow servers to keep a history of your visits. The server can use dynamic content technologies to personalize web pages. The disadvantage is that the server finds out about your browsing and shopping habits. To summarize:

> A cookie *is a value that a browser and server exchange to identify you. Accepting cookies allows servers to tailor content and advertising to your tastes; rejecting cookies enforces anonymity.*

A Web Page Can Display Simple Animations

When the Web first appeared, many users wondered why web pages did not display continuous motion like a television picture. The reason was that both web technologies and the Internet were initially designed to work with static documents, not to deliver video. To provide the illusion of motion, a computer must display a sequence of images quickly. But even server scripting does not deliver a continuous stream of images — the output of script is a fixed document that the server sends back to the browser.

Several technologies have been developed to allow web pages to include animation. One of the first animation technologies was given the awkward name *client-pull.* The name arises because the technology requires a browser to repeatedly send requests to a server. Thus, the browser ''pulls'' a sequence of images from the server, and displays them one after another.

How does a browser know that it should employ client-pull? The information is stored in the web page. When an author creates a page that is part of a client-pull sequence, the author adds a tag that specifies that a browser should obtain another page and includes the delay that the browser should wait before requesting the new page. Thus, an author can arrange to display a sequence of pages: the first page instructs the browser to load the second, the second instructs the browser to load the third, and so on. To make the set of pages run continuously, the last page in the sequence must instruct the browser to start over by loading the first page again.

In theory, client-pull technology can be used to produce a moving image on the user's screen. After all, a television picture merely consists of a sequence of images that flash in rapid succession. If an author creates a sequence of web pages similar to a sequence of television images and specifies zero time delay in each page, the browser will load the pages one after another without waiting. A human observer will perceive the web page as moving.

Unfortunately, although it works in theory, the scheme does not work well in practice. The display that results from client-pull is poor even for simple animations. The chief problem with client-pull is delay. To convince human eyes that items are moving smoothly, a browser must display at least twenty-four images per second. Even using a high-speed computer with a high-speed Internet connection, a browser takes too long to obtain and display an image; a browser cannot load pages quickly enough to show smooth motion. Furthermore, because the Internet does not deliver data at a constant rate — the motion may speed up for a few frames and then pause or slow down. As a result, client-pull provides jumpy motion that is only suitable for primitive animations (e.g., a stick-figure of a person waving a hand back and forth). In fact, the picture often freezes for seconds at a time while the browser fetches the next image.

Active Documents Are More Powerful

Newer, more powerful web technologies have been developed to help solve the problems of providing smooth motion and animation. The new technologies take an entirely different approach by making documents *active*. An active document is a computer program that paints an image on a screen. Active documents are stored on web servers, and each active document is associated with a URL just like conventional web pages. Furthermore, retrieval works as usual: a browser receives a copy of an active document when it requests the document's URL just like it receives a copy of a conventional web page. Once a browser receives a copy of an active document, however, the browser does not follow the conventional display procedure. Instead, the browser runs the program on the local computer. The running program then paints an image on the browser's screen. Figure 25.4 illustrates the concept.

Why is active document technology so powerful? There are two reasons. First, because active document technology performs computation on the user's computer, there is no delay between the time an image is produced and the time the image appears on the user's display. Thus, it does not matter if the browser is located arbitrarily far from the web server or delays change on the Internet — output does not start until the active document has been loaded, and then the document can control the screen without using the Internet. Second, active document technology scales well because it does not depend on a web server to perform computation. To understand what can go wrong with a centralized system, consider what happens if a thousand users simultaneously try to access a URL that corresponds to a server-side script. The web server responsible for the URL must run the script one thousand times! Even if a script only takes five seconds each time it runs, servicing all one thousand requests will take over an hour. Now consider what happens with active document technology. Each request to the server results in a copy of the active program being sent to a browser. Once the active document has been retrieved, each browser runs it locally. Thus, instead of one server running a script repeatedly, one thousand copies of the active document program can run on one thousand computers at the same time!

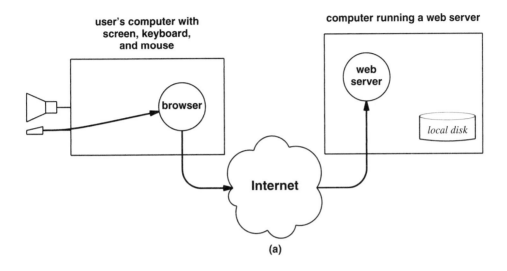

(a)

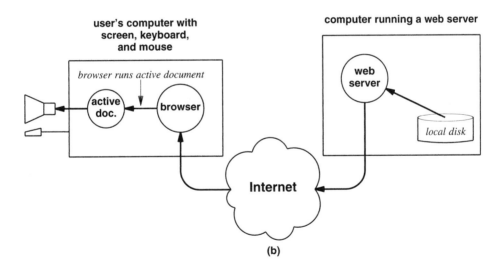

(b)

Figure 25.4 (a) A browser requests a URL that corresponds to an active document, and (b) the browser runs a copy of the active document, which then controls the screen.

Java Is An Active Document Technology

Sun Microsystems, Incorporated has developed a popular active document technology. Called *Java*, the technology can be used to create animated web pages that interact with the user or pages that use the screen in unexpected ways. Java calls an active web page an *applet*; the terminology is so widespread that most other vendors either have adopted the term or chosen to use a minor variation.

Java became popular for four reasons. First, the designers chose to make the Java language similar to a widely-used programming language, meaning that professional programmers could learn to write Java applets easily. Second, no other active document technology was available. Third, because the Java system includes software to handle common tasks such as controlling the screen, a programmer can use predefined pieces to create a Java applet quickly. Fourth, Java is so powerful that it provides more functionality than most other technologies. For example, Java can handle direct user interaction better than forms, can fetch a sequence of pages better than client-pull, can control multiple areas of the screen better than frames, and can manipulate a variety of data formats better than plugins. Thus, Java can subsume these other technologies.

Despite its many advantages over existing technologies, the strongest motivation for Java came from its ability to provide functionality that other technologies could not: high quality animations. Because they use a computer's processing power to compute new images instead of trying to download them from a web server, active document technologies like Java can change the display fast enough to present the illusion of smooth motion. Because none of the older web technologies can provide the same functionality, many web sites are eager to use Java.

JavaScript Is An Active Document Technology

Although Java is among the most powerful active document technologies, it is also among the most complex. Creating a Java program that can control the display requires extensive background and training; the language is designed for professional programmers.

Several technologies have been designed as alternatives to Java. One of the most popular alternatives incorporates a few of the basic features of Java, while omitting many of the more complex features. Known as *JavaScript*, the language can be embedded in a standard HTML file. When it encounters a JavaScript section in an HTML document, a browser performs the specified computation, and then displays the results. Thus, although it is not as complex as Java, JavaScript offers much of the same functionality to users.

Flash And Real Technologies

Two technologies have become popular for creating active web pages with animations and other visual effects. Macromedia Corporation, now owned by Adobe, created a technology specifically designed for use with web pages known as *Flash*. RealNetwork, Inc. created technologies for playing audio and displaying video under the names *RealAudio* and *RealVideo*; although the technologies can be used separately, each has been integrated with web browsers to permit a browser to display audio and video. The chief difference between the programming technologies such as Java or Javascript and multimedia technologies such as Flash or RealVideo lies in the way they coordinate moving pictures and sounds. Multimedia technologies include facilities that allow a designer to specify all details of the audio and video independent of any particular computer. For example, instead of allowing the speed of a video clip to depend on the speed of the computer, a multimedia technology allows a designer to specify the time that should elapse when the clip is displayed. Similarly, a designer can coordinate audio and video to specify exactly where during the video a given sound should occur.

The point is:

> *Many technologies are now available that allow a browser to display active web pages. In addition to programming languages like Java and Javascript, companies have produced multimedia technologies that can provide visual effects or coordinate audio and video.*

The Importance Of Advanced Web Technologies

Many web pages consist of static documents, which means that browsing the Web is similar to examining information in a library. The information remains stable; change is slow. With advanced web technologies, however, web pages can be dynamic. The contents displayed can depend on the interests of the person browsing, the page can be divided into parts that change independently, and the page can contain dialog boxes that provide users with the opportunity for direct interaction.

Active document technologies like Java, JavaScript, Flash, and RealVideo have gained popularity and have displaced older server-based technologies. There are two reasons. The first is economic: the owner of a server cannot afford to purchase a server that is sufficiently fast to perform computation for all users. The second is functional: only an active document can make objects on a screen appear to move smoothly. The availability of smooth animation and video has dramatically changed web pages.

26

Group And Personal Web Pages (Wikis And Blogs)

Introduction

The previous chapters explain how email, bulletin board, and web technologies use the Internet. This chapter continues the discussion by exploring two services that allow a group or an individual to create web pages for others to view.

The Disadvantage Of A Bulletin Board System

Chapter 22 discusses Internet newsgroups, a bulletin board application that allows subscribers to post articles that can be viewed by others. It may seem that newsgroups provide a way for everyone to express their opinion on almost any topic. After all, newsgroups exist on virtually any topic, and if a new topic arises, a new group can be created.

Although a newsgroup does indeed permit many users to submit articles that express their opinions, a newsgroup has drawbacks similar to a physical bulletin board. On a physical bulletin board, for example, care must be taken to avoid a situation in which new notices are posted on top of old notices until a jumble exists and the bulletin board is completely unusable. A newsgroup can have an analogous problem: if the newsgroup is flooded with articles, it may be difficult to separate the most relevant from others.

The analogy with a physical bulletin board is especially pertinent in two ways. First, because most newsgroups permit arbitrary users to subscribe and post articles, some articles stray from the main topic. Second, articles are ordered by the date they were posted. To understand how postings can stray from the main topic, consider an example. Suppose a newsgroup has been created to discuss football. The purpose is to focus on teams, games, strategies, and plays. However, an innocuous comment or poorly chosen phrase can generate an entire side discussion. For example, a political phrase such as *republican team owners* or a complaint about *insane ticket prices* can generate a flurry of responses that are only semi-relevant to the topic at hand.

The linear order of messages creates a problem for two reasons. First, minor side discussions are integrated into the sequence of postings, meaning that a subscriber is forced to skip by irrelevant postings. Second, because articles are ordered by the time they are received, the discussion can become confused and repetitious. For example, suppose a recent discussion on a newsgroup resulted in six messages:

$$A, \; B, \; C, \; D, \; E, \; F$$

Then suppose that a subscriber, Joe, returns from vacation and reads the first message in the series. If Joe generates and posts a reply, other subscribers will see it as a new message, *G*, even though Joe has only read *A*. Later, when Joe discovers that the discussion in *B* through *F* makes his point invalid, he sends another message to apologize and ask everyone to ignore his previous post. Thus, the newsgroup contains eight messages, the last two of which are irrelevant:

$$A, \; B, \; C, \; D, \; E, \; F, \; G, \; H$$

The sequence of messages becomes much more convoluted in a newsgroup that has thousands of subscribers because out-of-order messages from multiple subscribers are interleaved. If a new subscriber, Nancy, joins the newsgroup, she will need to spend time to untangle and understand the message sequence.

Shared Pages

The chief alternative to a bulletin board service is a *page sharing service*. Unlike a bulletin board service, a shared page service does not permit postings to pile up, nor does it store a history of all submissions. Instead, the service creates a single web page that many users share. Any of the subscribers can change the page, and changes are visible to all users. Thus, if a user replaces a string of text, other users see the change and the original string is lost.

Although the details of page sharing systems vary, many shared pages are *anonymous*. That is, the software does not store *attribution* or information about the identity of the user who entered the item. Thus, when a user views a shared page, it is impossible to know who entered each item.

Shared Pages Are Called Wikis

Page sharing technology was pioneered by the *Wikimedia Foundation*. A shared web page is called a *wiki*, and the software to share a page is known as *wiki software*. The name is derived from the phrase *wiki wiki*, which means *rapidly* in native Hawaiian.

The name is appropriate because wiki software does not wait to incorporate changes. Instead, each change is exported quickly, making it visible to other users almost instantly.

To summarize:

> A wiki *is a web page that is shared by multiple users; each user can change the page, and other users see the changes quickly.*

Sharing And Consensus Building

The primary motivation for shared web pages is rapid *consensus building* — a group of individuals can work toward general agreement, and can then refine and polish the details. To understand how wiki technology can help consensus, compare a wiki page to a newsgroup. If a group of six individuals attempt to reach consensus with a newsgroup or email list, messages appear in chronological order without context. If the group uses a wiki, however, suggestions and changes can appear rapidly enough to allow everyone to understand the context of each suggestion. Thus, a group that is working together can reach consensus more rapidly and with fewer misunderstandings.

The Disadvantage Of Wikis

Although it allows a cooperative group to reach consensus easily, wiki technology can have the opposite effect in a disagreement: instead of encouraging consensus, a wiki allows dissenting opinions to flourish. To understand why, consider the interactions among a group that is using wiki technology to build a shared web page. If one member of the group adds a statement with which other members disagree, the other members are free to change the page. Even if only one person dissents, the person can reverse or negate the statement merely by inserting the word *not*. If the original author notices the change and removes *not*, the dissenter can reinsert it.

The point is:

Although shared web page technologies work well when a group is striving to reach consensus, allowing an arbitrary group member to change a shared page means a single dissenter can make changes that disrupt progress.

Wikipedia Is An Experiment

The Wikimedia Foundation is running a large-scale experiment in the use of shared web page technology. Called *Wikipedia*, the experiment consists of an encyclopedia to which anyone can post an article (or edit an existing article). The encyclopedia is free — anyone can use Wikipedia to look up information.

Entries in Wikipedia are anonymous in the sense that the authors are unknown. Of course, encyclopedias do not generally list the name of the individual who writes each article†. However, Wikipedia differs from a conventional encyclopedia because authors are essentially untraceable, even to the owners of Wikipedia. To summarize:

Wikipedia is a free online encyclopedia created using wiki technology. Anyone can submit an article or edit an existing article; the authors remain anonymous.

Should You Trust Wikipedia?

Many of the entries in Wikipedia have been submitted by reasonable individuals, who have made an honest attempt to provide correct facts and useful information. However, anonymity invites trouble. Some of the submissions are inadvertently incorrect; others are downright malicious. Because the owners do not exert editorial control, do not select authors, do not check submissions, and do not require authors to reveal their identity, a reader cannot easily assess the accuracy of articles. Indeed, some submissions might be written by experts, and others might be created by amateurs or beginners.

The openness, egalitarian nature, and lack of authoritative control for newsgroups and wikis causes some Internet users to avoid trusting the information obtained from such sources. A prime example of an error arising from Wikipedia was published in the newspaper *USA Today* in November, 2005. According to the story, an apocryphal biography of John Seigenthaler appeared that claimed Mr. Seigenthaler was linked to the assassinations of John and Robert Kennedy. Unfortunately, other sources picked up the false story, and propagated it to other web sites.

---

†The author of this text has written articles for well-known encyclopedias.

Dealing with problems on the Internet is difficult. Current U.S. privacy law prohibits the owners of web sites from revealing the identity of an author unless the author has given permission or a court has issued a subpoena. In addition, current law exempts electronic media companies from being sued for libel. Although Mr. Seigenthaler was eventually successful in having the false biography removed from Wikipedia, the case serves as a warning:

> *Because Wikipedia allows anonymous submissions and does not enforce high standards for correctness and accuracy, misleading and malicious articles can appear.*

Publication Of A Personal Diary

An Internet service exists that provides an alternative to anonymously authored pages: the service allows an individual to publish an ongoing *diary* of personal observations, opinions, and comments. Known as a *web log* and abbreviated *blog*, the service makes it easy for an individual to create a web page that contains a series of informal essays.

Many blogs exist. Some contain intimate, personal diaries that are of interest only to the author's closest friends and family members. Others have broader appeal. For example, some blogs provide commentary on current news, social issues, or political situations.

A blog differs from a wiki in two ways. First, a blog is an individual effort. Second, blogs are not anonymous — an author usually takes credit for the information in a blog. In short, although they often contain opinion, blogs tend to identify a person as the source of the information, making it possible to find out about the author and use the author's background to help judge the value of the blog.

A Personal Note

Years before the Internet became popular, I wrote a few humorous essays about Computer Science, and shared them with students. When I set up an experimental FTP site, I placed the essays on the site along with computer programs I had written. Once the World Wide Web was in place, I moved the essays to my web page.

A few years ago while I was visiting another university, a graduate student came running up to me and excitedly asked if I had seen his blog before creating mine. At first, I denied even having a ''blog'', but he eventually explained that he was talking about the essays on my web page. It seems that a phrase of one of my essays is similar to the title of an essay in his blog, and he hoped that the similarity might be more than coincidence. I assured him that most of my essays were written while he was in elementary school, long before he had enrolled in college. He became dejected, and explained that he had created a blog six months earlier, but no one seemed to be reading it. I tried to reassure him, but what could I say? The fact is that Internet technologies make it possible for many people to make information available, but do not guarantee that others will read it.

27

Automated Web Search
(Search Engines)

Introduction

Previous chapters describe how the World Wide Web permits one to explore information interactively. The process of *browsing* or *navigating* requires a user to specify a web site at each step. To begin exploration, a user must enter a URL that specifies an initial starting point. At each successive step of the process, the user must select a link or enter a URL manually.

This chapter considers an alternative to finding information by specifying known links: automated search services that allow a human to find web pages without knowing the URLs. Such services allow users to go directly to a page on a remote computer without requiring the user to step through a sequence of web pages. More important, such services help a user browse by providing a list of the sites that contain information related to a specified topic. The chapter describes how search services operate as well as how they appear to a user.

Description Of Functionality

An *automated search service*, also known as a *search engine*, allows an individual to find web pages that reside on remote computers. Automated searching differs from browsing or file retrieval because it does not require a human to specify a remote computer or to follow multiple links. Instead, automated search systems use computer programs to find web pages that contain information related to a given topic. In particular, search services allow one to locate the following automatically:

- Web pages that contain information about a particular topic
- Web pages associated with a particular company or individual
- Web pages that contain information about a particular product or brand

To make retrieval convenient and quick, the results of a search are returned in the form of a web page that has a link to each of the items that was found. Thus, the results can be retrieved easily with a standard browser.

Browsing Vs. Automated Searching

Although browsing can be enjoyable, the size of the Internet makes it impossible to find specific information by searching one computer at a time. In fact, the continual growth of the Internet makes such searches futile — new web pages appear faster than a human can browse through the information stored in them.

To keep up with growth, automated searching is required. That is, one needs a computer program that can automatically contact other computers on the Internet, search for specified information, and report the results. Such a program is called a *search tool*, an *indexing tool*, or a *search engine*, and the service it provides is called an *automated index*.

A Search Engine Helps Users Get Started

Automated searching is especially helpful when a user begins to explore a new topic. To understand why, consider how a browser operates and how the Web is organized. Before the browser can display information, a user must enter a URL. That is, a user must find one or more starting points. Because information on the Internet is not organized by topic, however, a user cannot easily guess where to begin. For example, suppose a user wants to find information on automobiles. A user might know the names of a few companies that build cars, and might even guess the correct URL for one company's web page. Few users could name more than a handful of companies; fewer still could guess the correct URLs.

For more general topics, guessing URLs is hopeless. Furthermore, the size and growth rate of the Internet make it impossible to search through all web pages manually. Consequently, the question "where does one begin to look for information?" becomes "how can one find a small set of starting points for a given topic?" In essence, the Internet is so vast that browsing must be limited to be useful.

A search engine provides the assistance needed. When a user first seeks information, the user can invoke an automated search for the topic. The search engine produces a list of pages that may contain information of interest. The user reviews each page in the list to see whether the contents are pertinent and interesting. If so, the user records the location; if not, the user moves on to another page in the list. The point is:

> Because the Internet is vast, finding information on a given topic can be difficult. Automated search tools help users by finding a set of pages that contain information related to the topic.

A Search Tool Can Help Recover From Loss

In addition to helping users find initial starting points for browsing, automated search tools help users recover quickly when the location of information is lost. To understand how loss can occur and how search tools help in recovery, imagine a user who spends many hours searching to find a web page that discusses a particular item (a new video game, perhaps). Further suppose that just after the user discovers the location of the page, a thunderstorm interrupts power to the user's computer, causing the computer to restart†. After the computer restarts and the user runs the browser again, the browser will not return to the last page automatically. Instead, the browser starts with the initial page that the user has selected. To return to the page that was being displayed when the power failed, the user must either specify the URL, repeat the same sequence of selections used to find the page, or use a search tool to find the page automatically. In summary:

> Automated search tools can help users by automatically recovering the location of an item after loss.

How An Automated Search Service Operates

In theory, when a user enters a request, a search engine must examine all computers on the Internet to find documents that satisfy the request. That is, a search engine must first determine whether a given computer runs a web server that makes information available, and must then examine each web page that the server offers. In practice, however, searching through the entire Internet takes much longer than one is willing to wait (e.g., weeks). Fortunately, search engines do not require weeks — a search produces an answer after a few seconds. How can a search engine answer requests quickly if searching the entire Internet takes a long time?

To understand how search services respond quickly to a request, think of a telephone book. To make telephone number lookup efficient, the phone company collects a

---

†Loss can also occur when a user accidentally erases information or exits a browser without recording the location of a page.

list of each customer's name and number, sorts the list into alphabetical order, and prints a telephone book. When someone wants to find all people named *Jones* in a given city, they do not need to search all locations that have a telephone. Instead, they look under *J* in the city's telephone book.

The Internet's automated search mechanisms use a similar trick to enable them to reply quickly. Before any users place search requests, the computer that runs a search engine contacts other computers on the Internet, gathers a list of available information, sorts the list, and then stores the result on a local disk. To request a search, a user runs a browser, contacts a search engine, and enters a specific search string. The browser sends the request to the search engine. When a request arrives, the search engine does not need to contact all computers on the Internet. Instead it consults the list that has been compiled on the local disk (similar to looking up the answer in a telephone book).

Gathering Information In Advance

Gathering information before it is needed makes lookup fast, but has a disadvantage — the information can become incorrect if changes occur. Telephone companies solve the problem of change by producing a new telephone book periodically, usually once each year. Automated search systems use a similar technique. Periodically, automated search services run a program that contacts all computers on the Internet to obtain a new list of available items. For example, the best search engines run *spider* programs that probe the Web continuously†. After obtaining a new item, the spider software adds it to the database on the search engine disk, where the search server can access the item to answer requests. Figure 27.1 illustrates the process.

In the figure, computer *A* is owned by the search engine company. It runs a spider to contact other computers one at a time (e.g., computer *B*) and compile a list of all items on web pages. The spider program stores the list on *A*'s local disk.

Later, when a user makes a request, the browser on the user's computer becomes a client, contacts the server on computer *A*, and sends the string the user entered. The server compares the string to the items stored on its local disk and returns any that match. In the example, the search server on computer *A* can tell the user about items on any computer (including computer *B*). Because it extracts the information from its local disk instead of contacting other computers, the server can respond quickly. The important idea is:

> *Because each search server gathers information and stores it on a local disk, the server does not need to search computers on the Internet when responding to a user's request.*

---

†The name *spider* was chosen to be humorous: as it gathers information, a spider crawls around the Web!

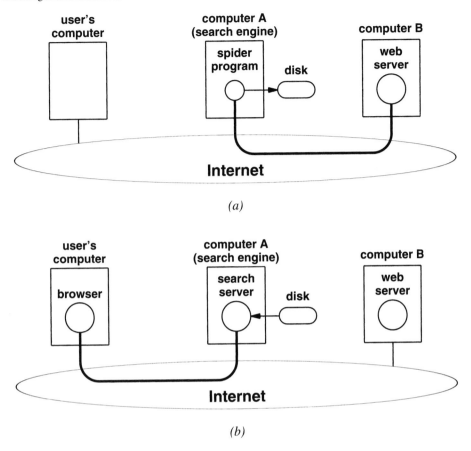

Figure 27.1 An illustration of the two-step process an automated search service uses. (a) A spider program automatically contacts web sites and obtains a list of available items. (b) When a user runs a browser to contact the search engine, the search server consults the database on its local disk.

Modern Systems Search Web Page Contents

Early Internet search services concentrated on matching file names — a user supplied a name and the search service produced a list of all files of that name available for download. Modern automated search systems concentrate on web page contents. When a user requests a topic, the search service identifies pages that contain the specified topic. Content search is now the norm:

A search engine will find a set of web pages where the content matches the topic a user specifies.

How A Web Search Appears To A User

To a user, web search mechanisms appear straightforward. A user enters a topic, and after a short delay, the search engine responds with a list of web pages that contain information about the topic. The user can then explore each page on the list.

A user does not need a separate application program to perform a search. Instead, search services are accessed through a browser. Each automated search service has a web site; a user who wants to perform a search begins by invoking a browser and specifying the URL of a search engine. The user's browser contacts the search site.

The web page for a search service usually contains three pieces of information. First, the page identifies the company and the service being offered. Second, the page contains instructions that specify how to use the service. Third, the page provides a way for the user to enter a topic for the search. Figure 27.2 illustrates how the main section of such a page might appear†.

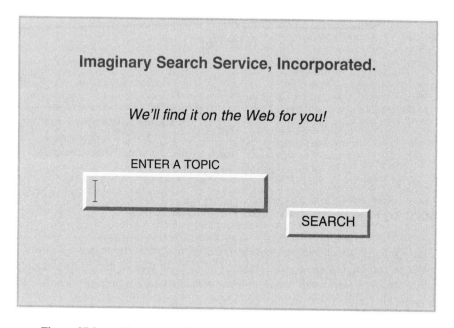

Figure 27.2 An illustration of how the web page for a search service might appear.

---

†In practice, a search engine page also includes ads as a later section discusses.

Because the web page for an automated search service needs to allow a user to interact, the page often uses forms technology. For example, the figure above shows a web page with two functional areas. The first consists of a dialog box, and the second is a button that the user can click. To use the search service, a user enters a topic in the dialog box and then clicks the button to request a search.

How A Search Engine Returns Results

We said that after an automated search engine finds a list of pages that match a user's request, it creates a web page that has a link to each of the pages. The search engine returns the web page to the user's browser, which displays the results. The web page that results from a search is not a static document. Instead, the search engine creates the page dynamically. Thus, the page returned to a user contains only the results of that user's search. Figure 27.3 illustrates how the output might appear to a user.

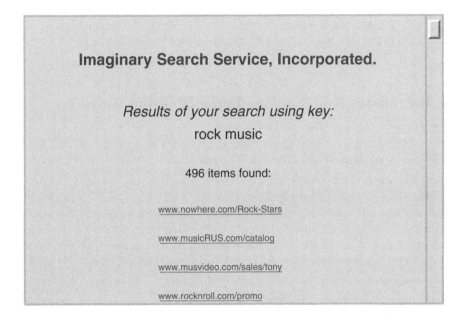

Figure 27.3 Illustration of the main section of the user's screen after a search engine returns the results of a search. These examples do not refer to actual web pages.

The figure illustrates how a browser displays a page that contains more information than can appear on the screen at one time. The right-hand edge of the browser window contains a scroll bar that allows a user to select which part of the page appears at any time. In the example, the search found sixteen items, only four of which currently appear on the screen. Instead of generating a long page that a user scrolls through, some search engines generate individual pages with twenty items on each page; a user must select a *Next* button to view each successive page of items.

Automated Search Services Use String Matching

Some automated search services employ conventional *string matching* when selecting web pages. That is, the service looks for pages that contain the specified search term in text on the page. That is, the service looks for an exact match between the characters in the user's topic string and the characters that appear on a web page. For example, if the user enters the string *automobile*, the search service looks for web pages that contain the same ten-character string. The point is:

> *When a user enters a topic in the dialog box of an automated search engine, the user is requesting the search engine to find web pages that contain the topic string.*

The Advantages And Disadvantages Of String Matching

The chief advantages of string searching lie in simplicity and ease of use. Specifying a search by giving a string makes sense to most users. Furthermore, the mechanism is convenient.

From the perspective of programmers who must build search tools, string matching is also easy and efficient. Building computer programs for string matching has been studied extensively; many Computer Science textbooks explain how to create programs that match strings. More important, because researchers have found mathematical tricks that make string comparison efficient, computer programs can perform string searching quickly.

The chief disadvantage of string matching arises from the lack of semantics — although it works with individual letters in a word, a string matching program does not understand the meaning of words or phrases. That is, a string matching program finds exact matches letter-by-letter, but is unable to tell what a user means. For example, if a user enters the topic *automobile*, a string matching program cannot report pages that contain synonyms or related terms such as *car* or *vehicle*. Furthermore, if a user misspells a term, a string matching program may report that no matches were found.

For example, an automated search service is unlikely to find any pages for a misspelled term such as *auotmobile*.

Another disadvantage of string matches becomes apparent when one considers entire sentences. For example, consider the following sentence:

> *This sentence does not contain any information about biol-*
> *ogy, money, or foods like butter and milk, and certainly is*
> *not about automobile pictures, airline fares, lawyer jokes,*
> *opera singers, or library books.*

Although the sentence is truthful, it would confuse string matching programs because such programs do not understand the meaning of the word *not*. Therefore, a string matching program would match this sentence to requests for information about such diverse topics as *money*, *automobile*, *jokes*, *opera*, or *law*.

Automated Search Programs That Use Multiple Keys

Although they begin with simple string matching, most search engines offer more sophisticated lookup mechanisms as well. For example, one service allows a user to enter two or more words in a search string. The search program finds web pages that contain any of the specified terms.

Each word given to a search service is known as a *lookup key* or simply a *key*. Consequently, a service that accepts more than one key is called a *multi-key search service*. The advantage of a multikey search lies in its ability to group synonyms together. For example, a user might enter the two-key search term:

> *car automobile*

to find pages that mentioned either *automobile* or *car*. Similarly, groups of related words can be specified to include pages that may have a common theme. For example, a user interested in all aspects of health care might specify the multi-key search:

> *health doctor physician hospital medical nurse ambulance*

to find pages that contain any of the terms†.

---

†A multi-key search is especially useful if the search service does not recognize plurals because a user can enter both the singular and plural form of each search term.

Advanced Services Offer More Sophisticated Matching

Some automated search services go beyond multi-key searching. Such services offer the opportunity to give more detailed specifications. For example, some services allow a user to give an exact phrase that must appear on a page. To understand why such facilities are necessary, consider a user interested in rock music. It might seem natural for the user to enter the following when asked for a search term:

rock music

Unfortunately, the search may not have the desired effect. Instead of finding pages about a popular type of music, the search identifies any page that contains the term *music* or the term *rock*. Consider the following sentence:

> *Before you listen to Wagner on a 2500 watt stereo, be sure to*
> *warn everyone that the music will be so loud that it will*
> *make the entire house rock.*

Clearly the sentence is not about rock music. However, because it contains the word *rock* as well as the word *music*, a search engine might select the page. Besides the above page, a search engine might return pages about other types of music, a page that contains music for the hymn *Rock Of Ages*, or even pages about topics in geology! The point is that, in addition to pages relevant to a user's request, a typical search can include many pages that a user does not expect.

Why does a search service handle seemingly reasonable requests so poorly? The answer lies in how we use language. Basically, our language is ambiguous — we assume recognition of common phrases (i.e., sequences of words that belong together). For example, the phrase ''rock music'' identifies a type of music, not two independent words. Indeed, search engines do attempt to identify and understand common phrases. However, because they are automated, search engines cannot resolve all ambiguities and recognize all synonyms. Therefore, search engines can misinterpret terms and context. The point is:

> *Although it attempts to understand language, an automated search engine does not recognize all phrases. Consequently, a user must remember that, unless otherwise specified, each word will be treated as an independent search term.*

To avoid ambiguous search requests, most search engines provide an *advanced search* feature that permits a user to specify search terms more precisely. For example, an advanced search mechanism allows the user to specify that a set of terms must *all* appear on a page, *at least one* must appear, *none* should appear, or that an *exact phrase* must appear. In addition, some advanced searches allow a user to limit the search to a specific natural language (e.g., English) or a specific type of file (e.g., web page in HTML). Thus, much of the ambiguity can be eliminated. In our example about rock music, once a user can tell the search service that the two words are part of a phrase, the search service will not return a page unless it contains the exact phrase *rock music*.

Personalized Search Results

The previous chapter discussed how dynamic content technologies can be used to provide personalized web pages. Interestingly, major search engines use the same strategy — they gather as much information about an individual as possible, and then use the information to control search results. The ultimate goal is to create a search engine that can match responses to the individual who made the request. For example, consider a user who enters the search term *jaguar*. If the user had previously viewed information about automobiles, the search engine might place pages about Jaguar automobiles higher on the list of results than other sites. In contrast, if the user had previously viewed information about cats, the search engine might place pages about animals higher on the list.

How can a search engine learn about an individual? One easy way involves a small deception — when returning search results, the engine does not include the correct URL for each page. Instead, each URL hidden in the search list refers to a special program on the search engine itself. If the user clicks on a link, the user's browser sends the request back to a search engine script. The script records the user's selection, and then forwards the request to the actual web site automatically, which means the user receives the page as expected. Thus, the search engine merely acts as a middle man by gathering information about the user's selection before forwarding the request. If the user performs another search, the search engine can use the information that has been gathered to help control which pages are matched.

To summarize:

> *Search engines keep information about users and use the information to select and order search results. As a consequence, the personalized search results that a user obtains may differ from the results another user obtains for the same request.*

More Details About How Content Searching Works

Recall that the size and growth rate of the Internet makes it impossible to search the entire web quickly, and that a search engine uses a *spider* to crawl the Web and compile a list of topics along with web pages that contain the topic. The results are stored on a local disk at the search engine site, making it possible to return an answer quickly.

A spider program must explore all pages on all web sites. How does a spider find all pages? One way is to record and follow all links. For example, once a spider retrieves the main web page, the spider can examine the HTML document and extract all URLs. The spider then adds the new URLs to the set that it must explore.

The size of the Web means that a search engine company cannot keep information about all possible strings in all web pages — the search engine filters the data and only stores the most important items. That is, as it explores web pages, a spider program filters out common words that do not help identify pages. For example, a spider filters articles, and prepositions, such as: *a, an, and, the, for,* and *with.*

Searches Are Restricted

Automated search services use another important optimization that helps limit the amount of information they need to store: instead of indexing all the information on a web page, a spider can search only the beginning of each page. For example, a spider can emphasize keywords from the document title. A program can find the title easily because HTML places the title between the tags <TITLE> and </TITLE>. Authors who create a web page can add keywords to the title to help search services find the document. A travel agent might have a page with the following title:

<TITLE> Holiday Planner (vacation, travel, Thanksgiving,
Valentine) </TITLE>

Some search services also recognize the *META* tag, which allows the page to specify keywords that do not appear when a user views the page in a browser. For example, a travel agent might choose to add the following *META* tag to a page:

```
<META NAME="holiday travel" CONTENT="travel, airplanes,
reservations, tickets, hotels, rental cars, trains,
restaurants, theaters, shows">
```

In addition to keywords in the title and *META* tags, some search services also extract the first two or three hundred words on each page and use them to compile search keys. Thus, authors often try to use keywords early in a document.

Advertising Pays For Searching

How does a search service generate revenue? Most do not charge a user who requests a search. Instead, the service generates revenue from advertising. Typically, when a user invokes a search service, the initial web page contains advertising plus a dialog box in which a user enters a search key. Corporations are willing to pay the service to display advertisements because many people will see the ads. More important, users who invoke a search service are looking for information on the Web — they may also be interested in learning about related products and services. The point is:

> *Web searching appears to be free because automated search services do not charge users for each search. Instead, such services use advertising to generate revenue.*

As expected, some search engine companies also collect revenue by offering to give a company's pages higher visibility. For example, a search engine company might sign a contract with a specific automobile manufacturer, agreeing to place the manufacturer's web site high on the list of results whenever a user searches for *car*. We can summarize:

> *Some search engine companies agree to favor specific web pages in exchange for a fee.*

Examples Of Automated Search Services

Many automated search services exist, and new services appear regularly. Figure 27.4 lists some of the search services that were available when this edition was written.

http://www.100hot.com

http://www.altavista.com

http://www.bigbook.com

http://www.bigfoot.com

http://www.excite.com

http://www.google.com

http://www.hotbot.com

http://www.looksmart.com

http://www.lycos.com

http://www.shareware.com

http://www.worldpages.com

http://www.webcrawler.com

http://www.yahoo.com

Figure 27.4 Examples of automated search services available on the World Wide Web. Although most services provide a general index to web pages, a few are restricted to specific types of information.

Significance Of Automated Web Search

Because the Web is large and growing rapidly, automated search engines have become an essential part of finding information. Without such tools, the task of browsing through pages manually is overwhelming, and the probability of finding information is extremely small. With help from a search engine, a user can narrow the search to a reasonable set of initial pages.

28

Text, Audio, And Video Communication (IM, VoIP)

Introduction

Previous chapters describe a variety of Internet services that allow users to send memos, read messages on a bulletin board, browse web pages, and perform automated searches. In all cases, the information being accessed consists of items that have been stored. This chapter focuses on Internet services that provide interaction among users.

The chapter begins with a discussion of a service that permit two users to exchange text messages. It then considers audio and video communication. After explaining how software plays sounds or displays video segments that have been recorded and stored in a file, the chapter describes services that propagate audio and video across the Internet "live". Finally, the chapter explains a service that makes it possible for people to interact and work together over the Internet.

Instant Messaging Provides Textual Communication

One of the most popular textual communication services on the Internet has become known as *Instant Messaging*, usually abbreviated *IM*. An IM service provides direct communication between a pair of users. Either of the participants can use the keyboard to enter text, and then transmit the text for the other user to see. IM services are usually used to send short comments — the users interact by sending short replies to each others' comments.

To understand IM services, imagine two individuals, Bob and Mary, using laptop computers to communicate during a meeting. Figure 28.1 illustrates items that appear in a window on Mary's screen.

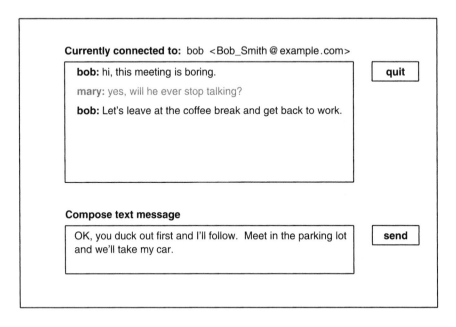

Figure 28.1 Example of the items that appear in a window when using an instant messaging service. The user, Mary, is composing a message to send.

As the figure shows, there are two main text areas: one displays messages that have been sent, and another allows a user to compose a message. After a user enters a message, the user clicks the *send* button to transmit the message and allow the other party to see it. In a typical system, each message is color-coded to indicate which user entered the message.

Audio And Video Functionality

Audio and video services extend IM by making it possible to:

- Send audio to another person or a specific group
- Send video to another person or a specific group
- Broadcast audio or video to anyone on the Internet
- Allow a group to view and edit a document simultaneously

Audio And Video Require Special Facilities

Before a user can participate in audio or video services, he or she needs an Internet connection with sufficient capacity and a computer with special hardware. Technically, the capacity of a network is known as its *bandwidth*; live video or audio requires a *broadband* connection because audio and video packets are generated rapidly. If the network has insufficient capacity, the video and audio are not smooth — playback freezes at times, and then jumps ahead. Furthermore, even with compression, video requires approximately 500 times more bandwidth than audio. Thus, a connection that is sufficient for audio may not be sufficient for video.

In addition to a high-bandwidth Internet connection, audio and video services require a computer to have:

- A *microphone* to capture sounds. A typical microphone is small enough to be mounted on the front of the computer or pinned to a user's clothes.

- A *speaker* to reproduce sounds; two speakers are required to reproduce stereo. Speakers can be integrated inside a computer or can be separate. Most computers provide an inexpensive internal speaker, and permit a user to plug in an external speaker when higher quality sound is desired. As an alternative, a user can wear earphones.

- A *camera* to record images, typically attached to the display and pointed at the user's face; inexpensive cameras are known as a *webcam*.

- A *graphics processor* that can manipulate video and audio without introducing delay.

To understand how computers use such hardware, it is important to understand that the computer controls all the devices electronically. For example, a computer can start or stop a camera and raise or lower the volume of sound without requiring the user to physically turn dials and switches. Software allows a user to control devices with keystrokes or mouse movements.

An Audio Clip Resembles An Audio CD

The easiest form of audio to understand consists of a file that encodes a digitized version of recorded sound. Commonly called an *audio clip*, the file consists of a sequence of numbers that represent audio samples. When a user plays an audio clip that resides on a remote computer, software on the user's computer performs two steps. First, software transfers a copy of the entire clip across the Internet to the user's computer. Second, an application on the user's computer converts the digitized samples to sound, and plays them through the computer's speaker.

Real-Time Means No Delay

Computer scientists and engineers use the technical term *real-time* to describe a system that operates without delay. For example, conventional telephone and television operate in real-time because the transmission is "live" (i.e., almost instantaneous). However, the process of retrieving and playing an audio clip is not real-time. Instead, a significant delay occurs while the clip is copied across the Internet — the user will not hear any output until the entire clip arrives and playback begins.

Internet Audio In Real-Time

Can audio be transferred over the Internet in real-time? Yes, but not easily. The basic TCP/IP technology was not designed to handle real-time applications. It does not guarantee to deliver packets in a timely fashion. Instead, the Internet works more like a highway system. When multiple packets travel at the same time, only one can proceed and the others must wait. If there is no other traffic, a stream of audio packets sent at regular intervals will arrive at regular intervals. Because the Internet consists of millions of computers that can send data at the same time, however, there is little hope of receiving a long audio transmission successfully. If a computer simply plays the audio as the packets arrive over the Internet, the results are disappointing — the output is filled with pops and clicks that result when a packet is delayed as well as garbled sounds that result when the audio from a delayed packet overlaps the audio from a packet that is not delayed.

Surprisingly, the Internet can be used for high-quality, real-time audio. The engineering trick that makes audio possible is analogous to the way a large supermarket handles supplies of food. To understand, imagine that a supermarket is open twenty-four hours a day, and that the store is filled with customers that are each buying milk. If we think about the milk leaving the store, we can imagine milk moving through the checkout at a steady rate. If we think about milk entering the store, however, we can see that large quantities arrive on a truck periodically. When it arrives, new milk is placed in the back of the refrigerator case. As long as the refrigerator in the store is large enough, the delay between shipments does not affect customers — the supply may be low, but the store will not run out.

Software that transfers real-time audio across the Internet uses the same technique. When it first starts, the software on a receiver's computer gathers several seconds of audio which it places in a list in memory (analogous to a supermarket placing an initial shipment of milk in its refrigerator). Then, the software starts playing the audio at a fixed rate. While the playback occurs, additional packets that arrive are added to the back of the list in memory. Packets often arrive in clumps, with a delay between clumps. When arrivals are delayed, the software keeps playing the audio at a fixed rate — the list in memory may dwindle, but does not run out before additional packets arrive. Figure 28.2 illustrates the idea.

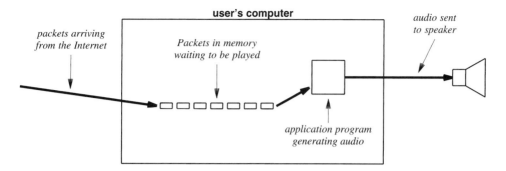

Figure 28.2 The technique that software uses to play real-time audio. Software keeps a list of unplayed audio in memory.

Radio Programs On The Internet

Many Internet services have been created that use the technique described above. For example, music companies make samples of new recordings available using an *MP3* digital encoding. If a user requests a particular song, a server will send a sample that the user can hear. Audio from special events such as concerts and political speeches is also available.

Some services transmit real-time audio continuously. For example, the audio from commercial radio stations is available on the Internet, as is video and audio from some television programs. Usually, a radio station sends the same programs on the Internet that it transmits over radio waves. To do so, the station uses computer equipment that converts the audio signal to digital form, places the result in packets, and sends the packets across the Internet. A user who wants to listen to a radio broadcast over the Internet must run software that contacts the station's server, extracts digitized audio from the packets that the server sends, converts the data back to sound, and plays the sound through a speaker or earphones connected to the computer.

Real-Time Audio Transmission Is Called Webcasting

To make it easy for users to receive real-time transmissions, most services use an encoding that can be received by a web browser. To enable a browser to play real-time audio or video, the browser must be extended with a plugin. The plugin consists of software that can receive a digitized transmission, keep a list of packets in memory, and play them at a steady rate. One audio plugin technology stands out as especially popular. Known as *RealAudio*, the technology offers a plugin for most browsers that enables the browser to receive and play audio encoded in the RealAudio format.

Fortunately, installing a plugin is simple. A user does not need to understand the technology because a browser knows how to download and install plugins automatically. Furthermore, most plugins can be downloaded from the Web for free — a user only needs to visit the appropriate site and click on the desired plugin. Once an audio plugin has been installed, the user can choose an audio source and begin listening analogous to the way one selects a station on a conventional radio.

Because most of the real-time audio and video services use a web browser to receive the transmission of real-time data, radio and television stations refer to transmission over the Internet as *webcasting*. How does a user know what webcasts are available on the Internet at any time? One can find out by visiting the web page of a service that lists available programs. For example, the URL:

http://realguide.real.com

leads to a page that provides a list of audio sources, including: radio and television stations, news, live concerts, and broadcasts of sporting events. The URL:

http://www.audionet.com

provides an alternative list that includes a variety of categories.

Internet Telephone Service Is Possible

Many groups have observed that audio transmission technologies make it possible for the Internet to be used as a telephone system. Software is available that can turn the Internet into a private telephone system. A pair of Internet users must each obtain a copy of the software, which then allows the two computers to communicate. Audio is sent between the two computers similar to the way audio is sent between two telephones; if the computers each have a camera attached, pictures can be transmitted as well. The chief advantage of the Internet as a telephone service lies in its low cost — users each pay a flat fee for service regardless of how many calls they make, how far away they call, or the number of minutes they communicate.

Telephone companies have also realized the economic advantages of using Internet technology. Major long-distance carriers have started to use IP to carry calls internally in their networks; many long-distance telephone calls now use IP.

Internet Telephone Service Is Known As VoIP

Companies such as Skype and Vonnage offer IP telephone service to customers. That is, instead of a conventional telephone line, a customer uses an Internet connection. To communicate, the customer either runs software on a computer that has a microphone and earphones or uses a dedicated device known as an *IP telephone* that connects directly to the Internet. The networking industry uses the phrase *Voice over IP (VoIP)*† to describe the technology used by an IP telephone system.

Of course, if an IP telephone could only place calls to other IP telephone, few customers would pay for the service. To make an IP phone system commercially viable, companies offering the service connect the IP phone system to the conventional phone system. Thus, each IP telephone is assigned a conventional phone number, a customer can use an IP phone to call a conventional phone, and a conventional phone can call an IP phone.

Audio Teleconferencing

Although most telephone calls are made between two people, another Internet service permits a group of users to hold a discussion similar to a "conference call." Each discussion is known as an *audio teleconference*. To create a teleconference, a user runs software that organizes and controls the discussion. The software requests the names of the participants, and then attempts to contact each of them. The software either displays a message on each participant's screen or otherwise notifies them that a teleconference exists. The notification is analogous to a telephone call — a user can choose to answer the request and join the teleconference, or ignore the message and let the teleconference proceed without them.

To join a teleconference, a user must run a program that handles audio reception and transmission. The program monitors the user's microphone, converts the signal to digital form, and sends a copy to other users in the teleconference. The program also receives messages, converts the messages back into sound, and plays the results for the user to hear. All participants hear the conversation similar to a conference telephone call.

Audio teleconferencing is significant because it allows participants to convey and understand emotion. Unlike written communication, voice carries inflection that tells the listener whether the speaker is excited, tired, angry, or joking.

A Cooperative Document Markup Service

While audio can simplify interaction among people, a written document is usually needed to guarantee that all participants agree on details. Imagine, for example, a committee of people trying to write a joint report. Initially, the committee can use audio to hold a general discussion and generate ideas. However, audio communication does not provide an effective way to handle details or edit wording. In such cases, a written document is needed.

---

†Engineers usually pronounce the acronym ''voyp''.

Software exists that permits a group of Internet users to examine and edit a single document. Figure 28.3 shows how the screen might appear when a user creates a shared document session.

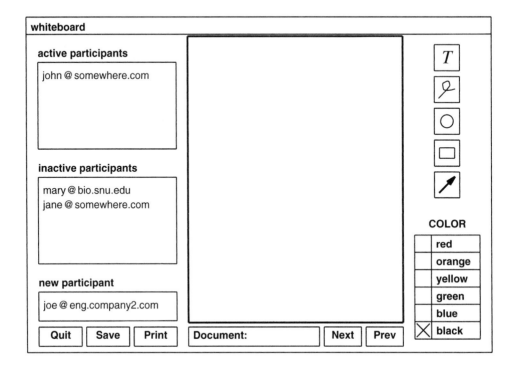

Figure 28.3 An illustration of how the screen might appear as a user creates a shared document session.

A shared document service is called a *whiteboard service*. As Figure 28.3 illustrates, the whiteboard service lists the names of all participants on the left side of the screen. A user named *John* working on computer *somewhere.com* has created the session and is adding participants. To add a participant, John types their login identifier and computer name in the box labeled *new participant*. The system sends a message to each person and moves their name to the *inactive participants* box until they respond. When a person responds and joins the session, their name appears in the *active participants* box.

To display a document, one of the users must move to the box labeled *Document* and enter the name of a document on disk. The whiteboard service obtains a copy of the document, and displays it on all participants' screens. Figure 28.4 illustrates how the session appears when two more participants have joined and a document has been specified. The *inactive participants* box shows that Joe, who has been invited to participate, has not yet responded to the invitation. Recall that a user can only join the session if one of the participants enters their name in the *new participant* box. Any participant can choose to leave the session at any time; when a user leaves, the whiteboard software moves their name to the *inactive participants* box.

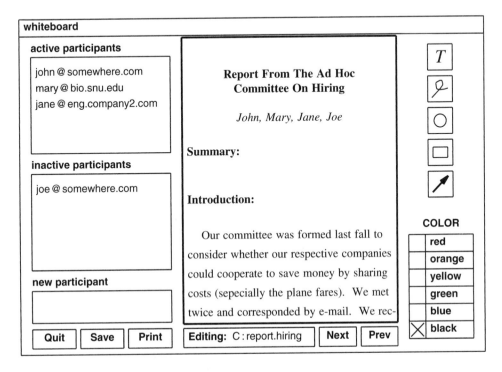

Figure 28.4 Illustration of a document displayed by a whiteboard service. All participants see the same display.

Marking A Document

A participant uses a mouse to control interaction with a whiteboard service. For example, any user can page through the document by selecting the *Next* or *Prev* commands. In addition, a user can draw or type on the document at any time. When a participant moves to the next or previous page or changes the document, all other participants see the change on their screen. In fact,

A whiteboard service is similar to a sheet of paper that all participants can see. Whenever a participant makes a change, all other participants see the change immediately.

Figure 28.4 illustrates how a user controls a whiteboard session. The right side of the display contains a set of boxes that specify a drawing mode. A user selects the box labeled *T* to type *text*, the second box to draw an arbitrary line, the third to draw a circle, the fourth to draw a rectangle, and the last to draw an arrow.

In addition to the drawing mode, a user must select a color from the list on the lower right side of the screen. Modifications a user draws or types on the document appear in the color the user has selected.

The Participants Discuss And Mark A Document

Usually, participants in a whiteboard session also engage in an audio teleconference at the same time. Thus, they can hear each other and see the document on the screen. For example, suppose the participants who view the document shown in Figure 28.4 decide that the committee members' names should be changed to full names. Also assume that in the discussion, Mary agrees to supply a summary and someone notices the misspelling of *especially*. Any of the participants can draw on the document or take notes from the discussion. Jane might notice the misspelling and draw a circle around it, and John might decide to make a note about the names. As the discussion proceeds and the participants add items, the document appears as Figure 28.5 shows. The additions do not become part of the original document — they only appear on the whiteboard. Later, one of the participants will need to use a word processor to change the original document.

Users who have a color display can use colors to enhance their drawings and comments. On a document with black text, for example, red notation stands out. Furthermore, if each participant chooses a different color, the colors show which participant creates a given message. Alternatively, the group may agree to use one color for questions and proposed changes, and reserve another color for final decisions. For example, in Figure 28.5, the circle around the spelling change could be red because the change is mandatory, while the note *USE FULL NAMES* might be in blue until all agree to adopt the change.

Video Teleconferencing

Audio teleconferencing and shared whiteboard services provide a way for people to work together. Such services can be especially helpful when preparing or reviewing a document. However, face-to-face interaction usually works better when a group needs to generate ideas or discuss a topic because facial expressions can show surprise or agreement without requiring words.

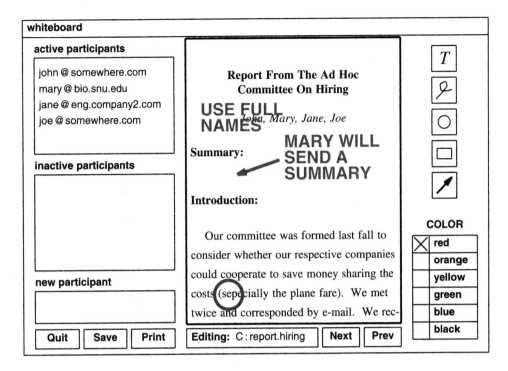

Figure 28.5 A sample whiteboard that illustrates how participants mark a document. The whiteboard service saves the session on disk so it can be reviewed later.

To enable face-to-face interaction, the Internet offers *video teleconferencing* services. A video teleconference begins the same as a whiteboard session: a user runs a program that starts a video session. The software allows the user to enter information about other participants, and contacts each of them. When a new participant joins the teleconference, an image from the camera on their computer appears in a small window on everyone's screen. A picture is similar to an ordinary television picture. When a participant smiles or frowns, everyone sees their expression†.

Of course, video alone does not help people communicate. Therefore, most video teleconferencing services incorporate both video and audio into a single teleconference session. When a participant joins the teleconference, they see and hear all other participants.

---

†The picture produced by an inexpensive camera is not as clear as the picture produced by professional television equipment. The picture may flicker or jump if a user's connection to the Internet does not operate at high speed.

Video Teleconference Among Groups Of People

A video teleconference works well when used with a few people. Each user's display shows the pictures of other participants. However, when more than a few pictures appear on a display, it becomes difficult to watch all of them.

When many people participate in a video teleconference, the screen cannot hold individual images from cameras on the participants' computers. Instead, people must gather in smaller groups in rooms that each have a camera and a large-screen computer display. In essence, the entire room becomes a single participant in the teleconference. The camera sends a picture of the room to all other participants where it is projected on a display large enough for everyone to see. Instead of small rectangles that each contain an individual's face, the display contains rectangles that each show a view of a remote room.

Sending audio for an entire room can be difficult. A single microphone may not be sensitive enough to detect sounds in all parts of the room. Multiple microphones sometimes detect background noise such as papers rustling. To handle the problem, rooms equipped for a video teleconference sometimes have portable microphones that can be passed to whoever needs to speak.

A Combined Audio, Video, Whiteboard, And IM Service

Audio and video teleconferences become more interesting when combined with a whiteboard and IM service. To understand the effect, imagine that each user's computer has a display as large as a typical television screen. Small rectangles around the edge of the screen each display the video image from the camera of one remote participant, usually a close-up of their face. A whiteboard occupies the center of the screen. Finally, IM is available to allow pairs of individuals to communicate privately.

The combination of audio, video, whiteboard, and IM makes it possible for everyone to see and hear one another as well as view a common document. When the participants need to discuss an idea, they can use audio and video communication. When they need to specify a precise document modification, they can rely on whiteboard communication. When privacy is needed, they can use IM. In fact:

> *Because experience has shown that combining a whiteboard service with a video teleconference and IM provides the most flexibility, many teleconference services include all three.*

Summary

The Internet offers several services that permit two or more people to interact. Instant messaging allows a pair of individuals to exchange text messages.

An audio teleconference service works like a multi-way telephone call. Two or more people establish a teleconference, and begin talking to one another. The group can designate other users and allow them to participate in the conversation. A video teleconference service operates like an audio teleconference except that it sends a motion picture from the camera attached to each participant's computer. To display video from other participants, a computer divides the screen into rectangles, and displays the video from one camera in each rectangle. When many people participate in a video teleconference, they gather in rooms that have a camera and microphone. Each room acts as one participant.

A whiteboard service permits a group of people to interactively review and mark a document. One person creates the whiteboard session by designating a list of participants. Each participant receives an invitation to join the session, and can leave at any time. The whiteboard service shows each active participant a copy of the shared document, and allows them to choose a color and then modify the document by drawing or entering text. All other participants see the results.

A Personal Note

Although a video teleconference provides exciting possibilities, it uses more network resources than other services. Unlike data transfers which simply slow down or stop temporarily when the Internet becomes overloaded, video and audio transmission must continue or the picture and sound will be lost. As a result, a teleconference can overload slow Internet connections.

During the time I was writing the first edition of this book, I was engaged in an audio teleconference and whiteboard session in which one of the participants was located at a University that had a low-speed Internet connection. Every so often, our colleague was cut off from the conversation for a short period of time. Eventually, my friend, who is a computer scientist, measured the network traffic and found the problem — our teleconference was completely saturating the connection from the Internet to his university. When the teleconference began again, we discussed ways to reduce the traffic. We decided that if we wanted to stay in contact, we would all have to talk less!

Today, because most universities have high-capacity Internet connections, an audio teleconference will not saturate them. For individual subscribers, however, video teleconferencing can produce a jerky, stop-motion display because even when compressed, video generates a significant amount of traffic. In such cases, fewer frames per second are received, resulting in a noticeable degradation in video quality.

29

Faxes, File Transfer, And File Sharing (FTP)

Introduction

Previous chapters discuss Internet applications that an average user is likely to encounter. This chapter considers three additional services. Although the services may not be as well known to casual users, they demonstrate how general the Internet is and how it supports a variety of uses.

Sending A Fax

Although it was available for decades, the business community did not adopt facsimile (*fax*) transmission until advances in modem technology improved the speed. By the late 1990s, most businesses and many individuals had a fax machine, and fax transmission was in widespread use.

Fax is a simple form of digital transmission that uses the conventional voice telephone system. Each fax machine consists of four main components: a printer, scanner, dial-up modem, and a dedicated computer that operates them. The modem is used for both sending and receiving faxes. When sending, the machine uses the modem to dial a number and wait for another fax modem to answer. Once the two modems synchronize, the sending machine uses its scanner to read and digitize pages of input. It sends the digitized version of each page across the telephone connection to the receiving machine, which uses its printer to recreate a copy of the original page.

Early in the history of the Internet, engineers created software that uses the Internet to communicate from a computer to a fax machine. Although fax services are still available, they are used infrequently because the transmission of documents in email has become common.

To summarize:

> *Although the Internet can be used to send a fax, sending documents via email has become more popular.*

The Internet Can Be Used To Copy Files

Although services such as email and instant messaging can be especially useful for sending short notes, they are not designed for sending large volumes of data. Instead, the Internet includes a service that can transfer an arbitrary-sized file from the disk on one computer to the disk on another efficiently. Someone might use such a service to *download* (i.e., obtain a copy of) a file containing music or a video clip. The next sections explain how a file transfer service appears to a user and how the software works.

Data Stored In Files

Computer systems use storage devices, such as disks, to hold large volumes of data. From a user's point of view, the data on a disk appears to reside in named *files* that are collected together in *folders* or *directories*. In most systems, files are variable size — a file can be large or small, and automatically grows or shrinks as a user adds or removes data. For example, because a word processor usually stores each document in a separate file, a file can hold a few lines or hundreds of pages.

Copying A File

Soon after researchers began using the ARPANET, they realized that a network could be used to transfer a copy of a file from the disk on one computer to the disk on another. They devised software to perform the task, which they called *file transfer*. Later, researchers rewrote the software to work across the Internet. Known as the *File Transfer Protocol*, the service is usually identified by its acronym, *FTP*.

FTP Is Invoked From A Browser

Although FTP was originally designed to run as an independent application, it has been integrated into web browsers. Thus, most users who copy files do so by clicking a link on a web page, rather than by launching a separate application. A browser uses the URL associated with a link to decide whether to run FTP — if the URL begins with the prefix *ftp://*, a browser interprets the rest of the URL as a request for a file transfer. For example, the following URL specifies a file that is available via FTP from a computer at Purdue University:

ftp://ftp.cs.purdue.edu/pub/comer/tib/example.txt

When a user enters the URL, the user's browser contacts an FTP server on a computer named *ftp.cs.purdue.edu*, requests a file named *pub/comer/tib/example.txt*, and displays the file for the user.

To summarize:

> *The File Transfer Protocol can be used to download large files. Although independent applications exist, most users access FTP via a browser; the prefix* ftp:// *on a URL tells a browser to use FTP.*

FTP Allows A User To View Directory Contents

In addition to retrieving a specified file, FTP allows a user to browse a directory (i.e., a folder). When a user enters a URL that corresponds to a directory, the browser will contact the specified site, request a list of the available files, and display the list for the user. The display of an FTP directory does not resemble a normal web page: instead of an aesthetically pleasing layout and colorful images, the page merely contains a heading and a list of file names. Each file name corresponds to a link that the user can click to download the file. Thus, FTP sites are only useful if file names are chosen to make the contents self-explanatory.

An example will clarify the concept. A small FTP directory has been set up that readers of this chapter can explore. To see it, enter the URL:

ftp://ftp.cs.purdue.edu/pub/comer/tib

The directory contains three files:

Crazy_Example.ps
README
example.txt

The example FTP site should make it clear that:

> *Although FTP allows a user to view the contents of a directory, the output merely consists of a list of file names without further explanation.*

FTP Allows A User To Upload Files

The discussion above explains how a user can invoke FTP to obtain a copy of a file from a remote system. Indeed, most people use FTP to do just that — contact a remote computer and obtain a copy of a file. We use the term *download* to describe the process, and say that a user *downloads* a file.

Interestingly, FTP is designed to allow a user to transfer a file in either direction — a user can send a copy of a file to a remote computer as easily as he or she can download a copy of a file. We use the term *upload* to describe the reverse direction of transfer: uploading means moving a copy of a file from a local computer to a remote computer. Of course, FTP on the remote computer must be configured to allow uploading, and a user must be authorized.

FTP Transfers Must Be Authorized

How can an organization allow some users to access files via FTP and not allow others? For example, how can a site that sells music prohibit arbitrary users from downloading copies without paying a fee? FTP solves the problem by requiring an authorization check: whenever an FTP server is contacted, the program that initiates contact must send a valid login ID and password. Without a login and password, no transfer is possible. Furthermore, an administrator at the FTP site can arrange specific permissions for each login. One user might be given permission to download specific files, without having permission to download others. Another user might have permission to upload files, but not to download them.

If each FTP session requires a login and password, how does a browser obtain files without prompting the user for a login? FTP has a convention known as *anonymous login* that permits access to *public* files. Basically, a server that provides public file access honors the special login *anonymous* and password *guest*. Thus, when a user clicks on a link that corresponds to FTP, the user's browser tries anonymous login. If anonymous login fails, the browser prompts the user for a login and password. Of course, if a user employs anonymous login, FTP restricts the user's access to files that have been declared public; even if other files exist, an anonymous user will not be able to access them. To summarize,

*A remote FTP service asks each user for authorization by prompting
for a login identifier and password. To obtain access to public files,
a user enters the login* anonymous *and the password* guest.

How FTP Works

Like most other Internet applications, FTP uses the client-server approach. When
the user enters a URL that specifies FTP, the user's browser becomes an FTP client that
uses TCP to contact an FTP server program on the remote computer. Each time the
user requests a file transfer, the client and server programs cooperate to send a copy of
the data across the Internet. Figure 29.2 illustrates the path data follows when a user requests a copy of a file.

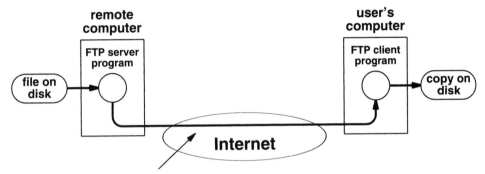

TCP/IP used to transfer data across the Internet

Figure 29.1 The path data takes when a server sends a copy of a remote file
in response to a user's request. The FTP client and FTP server
programs use TCP/IP to communicate.

The FTP server locates the file that the user requested, and uses TCP to send a
copy of the entire contents of the file across the Internet to the client. As the client program receives data, it writes the data into a file on the user's local disk. After the file
transfer completes, the client and server programs terminate the TCP connection used
for the transfer. The client side (i.e., the user's browser) may then choose to invoke an
application to view the file.

Impact And Significance Of FTP

FTP data transfers accounted for a significant portion of traffic on the early Internet. In fact,

> *FTP data transfer caused more traffic on the early Internet than any other application.*

In 1995, the World Wide Web replaced FTP as the leading source of packets on the Internet.

Peer-To-Peer File Sharing

A new use of file transfer became popular in the Internet around 2002. Euphemistically called *file sharing*, the application started from the observation that if two users each had digital music stored on their computer, it would be easy to swap copies. Thus, if user *A* had songs from one artist and user *B* had songs from another artist, it would be trivial to exchange copies of songs so that each user had songs from both artists. However, the system quickly degenerated from a few friends exchanging songs to a way for large groups of individuals to make (illegal) copies of copyrighted material. Soon, complete strangers were participating in file sharing schemes, with digital music and videos being the most popular items exchanged.

How does a file sharing scheme work? Unlike a traditional Internet service that requires an expensive, powerful computer to handle requests, file sharing uses small, slow computers. In essence, an individual participating in the scheme agrees to let their computer act as a duplication device — in exchange for the right to obtain copies of files, the user runs software that can forward copies of files to others. Thus, instead of all users obtaining copies of files from a single server, each user can request files from a nearby computer. The file sharing software keeps track of which files reside on the local disk as well as sites to search for additional files. When a file request arrives, the receiving computer either returns a copy, if the file is available on the local disk, or suggests other computers to contact.

Recall that the Internet was designed as a *peer-to-peer* network in which any computer can communicate with any other computer. Because it relies on communication among arbitrary computers, file sharing is often called a *peer-to-peer application* (abbreviated *P2P*). Peer-to-peer communication is extremely powerful and has allowed the Internet to spawn new applications easily. Unfortunately, as file sharing demonstrates, the power can be exploited for illicit purposes. To summarize:

File sharing is called a peer-to-peer application because arbitrary computers participate in transferring copies of files. Unfortunately, file sharing is often used for the (illegal) transfer of copyrighted materials.

Summary

The Internet can be used to send a copy of a file from one computer to another. The service, which is known as FTP, handles the transfer of large data files. Most users access FTP through a web browser — when the user supplies a URL that begins with the string *ftp://*, the browser becomes an FTP client.

Although most users employ FTP to download a file into their computer, it is also possible to use FTP to upload a file to a remote computer. In addition, a browser can display a list of the files in a remote directory and allow a user to choose a file.

File sharing is classified as a peer-to-peer application because arbitrary pairs of computers interact. In essence, each participating computer agrees to make copies of files available to others in exchange for the right to access the files. Unfortunately, many uses of file sharing involve the illegal exchange of copyrighted materials.

30

Remote Login And Remote Desktops (TELNET)

Introduction

Previous chapters describe a variety of Internet services. This chapter continues the discussion by focusing on services that allow a user to access a remote computer. In addition to describing how the services operate, the chapter explains why such services are useful.

Early Computers Used Textual Interfaces

To understand the basic Internet remote access service, it is necessary to understand textual computer interfaces. When the Internet was being invented, computers consisted of *timesharing* systems. Unlike a small personal computer that is usually dedicated to a single individual, a large timesharing system allows many people to use the computer simultaneously. An individual user interacts with a timesharing computer through a terminal which has a keyboard and display; multiple terminals attach to a given timesharing computer.

From an individual's point of view, a timesharing computer appears to operate the same as a personal computer – the software gives each user the illusion of an independent computer. A user can choose an application program and decide when to run it. The computer is so powerful that it can handle multiple computations concurrently. For example, one user can run a spreadsheet application, while another runs a word processor. In addition, the timesharing system allocates each user disk space that can be used to save files.

Like a personal computer, a timesharing system appears to respond to input instantly. For example, the timesharing system displays characters or moves the cursor as fast as a user presses keys or moves a mouse. In fact, many timesharing systems operate so efficiently that a user usually does not know whether other users are working on the same computer, unless they attempt to use a shared resource simultaneously (e.g., when two users attempt to use a printer at the same time, one of them must wait until the other finishes printing).

A Timesharing System Requires User Identification

Because multiple users can interact with a timesharing computer, the system requires each user to identify themselves when they begin. Each individual is assigned a unique *login identifier* and a *password*. Whenever a user begins interacting with the computer, the user must enter their login identifier and password. Computer professionals refer to the procedure as *logging in* or *login*.

After successfully logging into a timesharing system, a user enters commands to invoke application programs. When a user finishes using a timesharing computer, he or she informs the system by *logging out*.

To summarize:

> *A timesharing computer system permits multiple users to run programs simultaneously. Each user is assigned a login identifier and a secret password; the user enters the login identifier and password whenever they begin to use the computer.*

Remote Login Resembles Conventional Login

The Internet offers a remote login service that allows a user to access a remote timesharing computer system as if the user's keyboard and display attach directly to the remote computer. To use the service, a user launches an application program on the local computer and specifies a remote computer. The local application creates a window and connects to the remote computer. Every keystroke the user enters in the window is sent to the remote computer, and every item displayed in the window is transmitted from the remote computer. In fact, the window appears to be a terminal connected directly to the remote machine.

How Remote Login Works

Like other Internet applications, remote login follows the client-server paradigm. When a user on a local computer decides to log into a remote system, the user launches a local application program. The application becomes a client that uses TCP/IP to connect to a server on the specified remote computer. The server treats the network connection exactly the same as a local terminal (i.e., the server begins by prompting the user for a login and password). Figure 30.1 illustrates the idea.

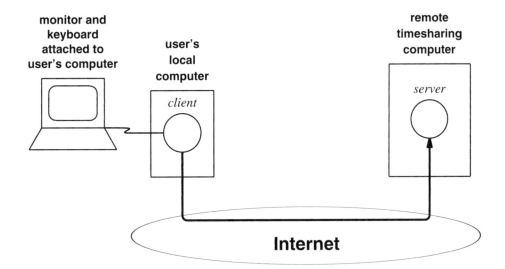

Figure 30.1 A remote login service uses two programs. The user invokes an application on the local computer that becomes a client of a server on the remote computer. Keystrokes are sent to the remote computer, and output from the remote computer is displayed in a window on the user's screen.

Escaping From Remote Login

Although a remote login client usually passes each keystroke to the remote computer, client software provides a way for a user to *escape* and communicate with the local client. To understand why such a facility is needed, one must understand two facts:

- During remote login, two programs run simultaneously – the application on the remote computer and the remote login client on the local computer.

- Most operating systems reserve one combination of keys as a way to control the system (e.g., Windows uses CONTROL-ALT-DELETE).

The question arises: when a user enters the keystroke combination that controls the system, should the client send the combination to the remote computer or should the combination be used to control the local computer? In fact, a user may need to control either the local or remote system. Thus, remote login services offer an *escape sequence*. That is, the service assumes all keystrokes should be sent to the remote machine except a keystroke that immediately follows the escape sequence†. In essence, the escape key means, "Please stop communication with the remote system, and allow communication with the local client program."

The Internet Remote Login Standard Is TELNET

The Internet standard for remote login service consists of a protocol known as *TELNET*; its specification is part of the TCP/IP documentation. The TELNET protocol specifies exactly how a remote login client and a remote login server interact. The standard specifies, for example, how the client contacts the server, how the client encodes keystrokes for transmission to the server, and how the server encodes output for transmission to the client.

Because both the TELNET client and server programs adhere to the same specification, they agree on communication details. For example, although most computers interpret one of the keys on a keyboard as a request to *abort* the running program, not all computer systems use the same key. Some computers use a key labeled *ATTN*, while others use a key labeled *DEL*. TELNET specifies the sequence of bits a client uses to represent an *abort* key. When a user presses the abort key on a local keyboard, the TELNET client program translates the key into the special sequence. The point is:

> *The TELNET standard for remote login allows remote login between computers with dissimilar keyboards because TELNET provides a standard translation.*

Remote Access Can Display A Desktop

Unlike the character-oriented terminals used on early computers, modern computers have a screen capable of displaying multiple windows, graphical images, icons, and pull-down menus. Many modern applications use a mouse to select and manipulate information. Because it has a character-oriented interface, TELNET cannot display such items across the Internet

Fortunately, additional Internet technologies have been invented to handle modern graphical interfaces. We say that new technologies provide a *remote desktop* capability. In essence, remote desktop systems intercept the output that would appear to a user on the display of one computer and transfer a copy to another. That is, software can be

---

†Although the keyboard key labeled *ESC* was originally intended to be used as described here, so many programs use *ESC* for other purposes that Internet remote login programs use *CONTROL-]* for escape.

placed on two computers that makes an exact copy of one computer's screen appear on the display of another computer. When using such software, a user can see exactly the image that would normally appear on the remote computer's screen. Figure 30.2 illustrates the concept, and shows that the underlying mechanism is similar to the one used for remote login.

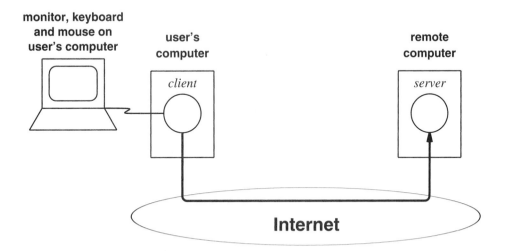

Figure 30.2 Illustration of a remote desktop service. Software permits the display on a user's computer to show the screen image from a remote computer.

How Remote Desktops Operate

A remote desktop service operates similar to a remote login service. To start using the service, the user invokes an application and specifies a remote computer. The application is a client that forms a connection to a server on the specified remote computer. In addition, the application takes over the screen, keyboard, and mouse on the user's computer†. When the user moves the mouse or enters a keystroke, the client sends the information to the server.

The server operates on the remote computer. It intercepts the output that would normally appear on the remote computer's screen and sends it to the client so it can be displayed for the user. At the same time, the server accepts keyboard and mouse input from the client, and processes the input as if it were from the local system.

The most impressive use of a remote desktop service arises from its ability to reproduce all details. For example, when a computer first starts, it usually shows a desktop on the screen. The desktop contains icons that correspond to items such as *My*

---

†Some remote desktop systems restrict the display to a single window, which either makes text and graphics small and difficult to read or requires the user to scroll to see other parts.

Computer. A *remote desktop* service allows the user to view and manipulate the entire desktop from a remote computer. If the user requests the computer to restart, for example, only the remote computer restarts. Similarly, if the user drags a file to the recycle bin, the file is deleted from the remote computer.

Some versions of remote desktop technology are available without charge; others require a user to purchase a license. For example, a company known as *RealVNC* distributes a free version of *Virtual Network Computing* software as well as improved versions that require a license. A description can be found on the following web page:

$$http://www.vnc.com$$

Assessment Of Remote Login And Desktops

Internet remote access services are significant for three reasons. First, remote access makes it possible to have computation remote from the user. Instead of sending a data file or a message from one computer to another, remote access allows a program running on a remote computer to accept input, react to it, and send output back to a user on a distant computer.

Second, remote access is significant because of its generality. After a user contacts a remote computer, the user can execute any application program available on that computer. In particular, although a given program may run on one brand of computer, remote access permits users on other brands of computers to use it.

Third, remote access is significant because many people use it. For example, some users work at a company with many computer systems that each offers specific programs or databases not available on other computers. Without remote access, an individual working in such an environment must continually move from computer to computer. With remote access, however, a user can sit at a desk and access remote computer systems over the network.

Generality Makes Remote Login And Desktops Powerful

Once remote access has been established, a user can invoke an arbitrary application program on the remote computer. In essence, although the computer is remote, it appears to the user to be local — the keyboard and screen react exactly the same way they would if the user had physically moved to the remote computer.

The power of remote login arises because it provides general access to the programs on a computer without requiring modifications to the programs themselves. Once remote login software has been installed, users can run conventional applications from remote locations. An example will help clarify the idea.

Consider a hypothetical company that uses a database to store information about the company's products, prices, and current inventory. Assume that the database software runs on computer X, and that the company's sales personnel use the database to determine product prices and availability.

Suppose the company decides to make the information from the database accessible to potential customers through the Internet. Unfortunately, database software may not be designed to use the Internet or to be accessed from a remote location. More important, because the company invested money acquiring the existing database system and training employees to use it, they cannot afford to replace the database with new software that has been designed to work with the Internet.

Remote access solves the company's problem easily. The company adds remote access software to computer X without changing the database software. The company then issues accounts to remote users so they can connect and access the database. The company can choose, for example, to create a single public account that provides access to the database system. Alternatively, the company can choose to issue each customer a separate account to simplify access control.

Remote Access Accommodates Multiple Types Of Computers

The Internet's remote login service solves an important problem: it permits arbitrary brands of computers to communicate. For example, suppose a company's database software only works on computers manufactured by IBM Corporation, and suppose that sales personnel who need to access the database use computers manufactured by other vendors, including Apple Corporation. Remote access software permits an employee using an Apple computer to contact an IBM computer and run the database software. To summarize:

A remote access service allows a user on one computer to interact with application programs that run on another computer. The power of remote access arises because it does not require any changes to the application programs themselves.

Unexpected Results From Remote Access

Although remote access services are convenient, the results can be confusing to a user. To understand why, remember that the user remains seated at one computer while running an application on another computer. The display does not give the user any visual hints — once a remote desktop begins, the user is unaware that it is running. However, the remote computer provides the environment in which the application runs.

To understand how a remote desktop leads to confusion, consider a user who connects to a remote desktop and then launches a word processor application. After creating a document, the user may choose to save it on disk. Despite appearances, the word processor is actually executing on the remote computer, which causes several unexpected consequences. For example, users expect that if a word processor can display a document on their screen, the word processor will be able to print the document on a printer connected to the local computer. However, the only printers available to the word processor are the printers known to the remote computer. Similarly, if the user requests the word processor to save the document to a file, the word processor will save the file on the remote computer's disk. Thus, although the user sees the document displayed locally, the user will not be able to use all the facilities on the local computer.

The point is:

> *Users must remember that although a remote access service uses the display, keyboard, and mouse on the user's local computer, the application can only interact with the files and printers on the remote computer.*

Summary

A remote access facility permits a user who is using one computer to run an application on another computer. The Internet's first remote access service, *TELNET*, only provides a character-oriented remote login mechanism. More recent services provide a remote desktop capability that provides a user with the illusion of working directly on the remote computer.

Remote access is especially convenient for a user who needs to access many computers. Instead of moving from one computer to another, the user merely invokes a remote access program. When remote access is running, the local keyboard, display, and mouse appear to be connected to the remote computer. Someone using remote access must remember that despite appearances, all files and printers are associated with the remote computer rather than the local computer.

31

Facilities For Secure Communication

Introduction

Previous chapters describe a variety of Internet services and explain how each one works. This chapter and the next two consider the practical matter of how some of the services can be used without risk. The chapter begins by considering a fundamental concept: safeguards are needed to make Internet transactions secure. The chapter explains what security means and why it is needed. It then examines the key technology that provides secure, private communication. The next chapters continue the discussion by explaining a technology that can grant secure network access to employees who are traveling or working at home and the use of secure communication for electronic commerce.

The Internet Is Unsecure

Many of the networks that constitute the Internet are "shared," which means that multiple computers attach. One of the chief disadvantages of shared networks is a lack of security — an arbitrary computer on the network can eavesdrop on other computers' transmissions. We say that such networks are *unsecure*. As a whole, the Internet is unsecure because many of the constituent networks are unsecure.

Chapter 14 describes examples of unsecure Internet access technologies: cable modems and Wi-Fi wireless networks. Recall, for example, that cable modems use cable television wiring to deliver high-speed Internet services to customers. Further recall that each customer is placed in a group of about one hundred customers who share bandwidth. Because it allows customers to share bandwidth, cable modem technology also allows customers to eavesdrop on one another — a customer can install inexpensive software that permits a PC to receive all messages sent from or to other members in the group. To summarize:

> *Because it uses technologies such as cable modems that allow a group member to eavesdrop on other group members' communication, the Internet is unsecure.*

Lack Of Security Can Be Important

In many cases, lack of Internet security is merely annoying, but in others, it can pose a serious risk. For example, suppose a third party obtains a copy of every message you send. If the third party reveals the statements you make in confidence to business associates, business or trade secrets could be revealed. If the third party finds your credit card number or the PIN for your bank account, you risk losing a large amount of money.

Authentication And Privacy Are Primary Problems

The specific security problem described above is known as the *privacy problem*. It can be summarized:

> *The term privacy refers to keeping data confidential. Communication is* private *if only the sender and intended recipient can read the message.*

A second security problem arises when trying to conduct business on the Internet. The problem, which is known as the *authentication problem*, centers on verifying identity. A simple example will help explain why identification can be difficult. Some ISPs allow each customer to choose a name for their email address. As a joke, some customers choose the name of a famous person. Thus, one might receive email that appears to come from the richest man in the world, the chief justice of the Supreme Court, or the president of the United States.

Although a fake email address can be humorous, being able to verify identity is a serious problem. For example, suppose a user who is browsing the Web sees a product advertised by a company. To order the product, the user must supply a credit card number. How can the user know that the ad is authentic? Perhaps a thief has arranged a fake web page that looks exactly like a well-known business, and is hoping users will submit their credit card numbers†. How can a customer know that an advertisement came from the company the ad claims to represent? The problem can be summarized:

> *The term* authentication *refers to verifying the identity of a communi- cating party. A customer needs to be assured that a business is au- thentic before placing an order.*

Data Can Be Changed

In addition to the need for privacy and authentication, other problems can exist. One of the most basic arises because data passes through many networks and routers as it crosses the Internet. How can the receiver know that the data arrived unchanged? For example, suppose someone sends an order to a store's web site. If a third party intercepts the order, they can arrange to steal the shipment by changing the shipping address. How can the store know that the information was not changed in transit?

Although most ISPs are reputable and data is seldom changed as it passes through the Internet, the potential exists. Thus, the Internet includes technologies that can guarantee data remains unchanged.

Encoding Keeps Messages Private

Since ancient times, people have used secret codes to keep messages private. For example, kings often used coded messages to communicate with their armies. Because each message was written in code, only the sender and recipient could understand the contents. Thus, even if the messenger who carried a message was intercepted, the contents of the message remained safe.

Modern computer systems use the same basic approach as kings to keep messages private. Before transmitting a message across a network, software on the sending computer encodes the contents of the message. When it arrives on the receiving computer, software decodes the message. Provided the encoding is complex enough, a third party will not be able to decode a message, even if they obtain a copy.

---

†In fact, to defraud unsuspecting users, thieves have set up web sites using slight misspellings of well- known company names — if a user accidentally misspells a name, the user's browser contacts a thief instead of the intended web site.

Computer Encryption Uses Mathematics

Code breaking in the modern world is completely different than code breaking in ancient times. Instead of humans trying to decode messages, modern codebreakers use computers. A computer can try thousands of combinations per second, and multiple computers can be used at the same time to speed the process. Thus, to keep a message private the Internet does not use the same codes that humans use when encoding messages by hand because such schemes are too easy for computers to decode. Instead, the Internet uses sophisticated, mathematical encodings that cannot be broken, even when the highest-speed computers are used. The process of encoding is known as *encryption*, and the process of decoding is known as *decryption*.

Why does encryption need mathematics? The answer is simple: inside a digital computer, all information is stored in numbers. Even a sequence of characters such as *abcdef* is represented by numbers. Consequently, encrypting information means manipulating numbers, which involves mathematics. For example, a human might generate a coded message by replacing each letter of the alphabet by another (e.g., all occurrences of the letter *e* are replaced by the letter *x*). To a computer, the transformation can be specified as replacing the number that represents the letter *e* by the number that represents the letter *x*. Because the encryption used on a computer network is much more complex than mere substitution, sophisticated mathematics is required.

No Network Is Absolutely Secure

Does mathematical encryption guarantee absolute security? No. Just as a physical lock cannot provide absolute safety, encryption cannot guarantee privacy — if a third party uses enough computers and enough time, they will be able to break the code and read the message. However, by choosing the encryption method carefully, designers can guarantee that the time required to break the code is so long that the security provided is sufficient. We can summarize:

> *Although no computer network is absolutely secure, modern encryption makes the task of decoding messages so difficult that a high-speed computer will require years of computing to break a code.*

Keep this principle in mind when thinking about Internet security. When someone asserts that an encryption scheme guarantees security, they mean that although the code can be broken, the effort and time required is great. Thus, an encryption scheme that requires longer to break than another scheme is said to be "more secure."

Encryption Makes Email Private

Encryption can be used to keep an email message confidential. After composing the message, the sender uses software to encrypt the message, and then transmits the result across the Internet. The sender need not worry about anyone seeing a copy because it has been encrypted — no one other than the designated recipient will be able to decrypt it. Figure 31.1 illustrates the idea.

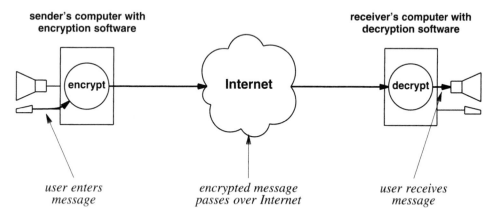

sender's computer with
encryption software

receiver's computer with
decryption software

encrypt   **Internet**   decrypt

user enters
message

encrypted message
passes over Internet

user receives
message

Figure 31.1 Encryption software ensures that the contents of an email message remains private. Only the encrypted version passes across the Internet.

Encryption Software Needs A Key

We said that computer software is used to decrypt messages. Suppose someone buys a copy of the decryption software and then obtains a copy of an encrypted message. Will they be able to decode and understand the contents? No. To understand why, consider an analogous situation in everyday life: although an automobile manufacturer usually makes many copies of each model car, each owner is given a key that only unlocks one vehicle. Therefore, owning a particular car does not mean a person can enter all copies of the model.

Encryption software uses the same basic idea. Each user is assigned a *key* that only "unlocks" messages encrypted for the user. Without the user's key, no one can decrypt messages sent to the user.

Two Keys Means Never Having To Trust Anyone

The earliest computer security schemes assigned each user a single key — the sender used the key to encrypt a message, and the receiver used the same key to decrypt the message. Today, most Internet encryption systems assign each user two keys that are designed to work together. One key is used to encrypt messages, and the other is used to decrypt them. The key used for decryption is called a *private key* because it must be kept secret. The second key, which is used for encryption, is called a *public key* because it can be distributed to anyone. The entire system is known as a *public key encryption* technology.

Why has public key encryption become important? It allows an arbitrary person to send a confidential message to an arbitrary recipient, without requiring either party to trust the other party to keep a secret. To understand why lack of trust is an essential ingredient, think of a business with an online catalog. When a customer orders from the catalog, the customer supplies information that must be kept confidential. If a business used a single key security system, each customer would need a copy of the key before they could encrypt a message. Unfortunately, the business cannot trust arbitrary customers — an unscrupulous person could pose as a customer, obtain a copy of the business's key, and then use the copy to decrypt messages other customers send. In other words, a system that uses a single key requires a business to trust each of its customers. With two keys, however, the business can keep the private key secret and only share the public key with customers. Anyone can use the public key to encrypt messages, but only the business can decrypt them with the private key. Thus, confidentiality is guaranteed without trust. In other words:

Two keys means never having to trust anyone.

To understand how public key encryption is used, suppose that you want to receive confidential email messages. Before anyone can send you a confidential message, you must obtain a pair of keys and the necessary software. Typical encryption keys are between 56 and 256 bits long (17 to 80 decimal digits), but for purposes of this example, let's assume your private key is *98989898* and your public key is *35353535*. Although you must keep your private key secret, you can announce your public key to everyone. You can tell your friends directly. To inform others, you can publish your key in a recognized list†:

John Smith's public key is *35353535*.

The mathematical properties of the keys are such that knowing your public key does not help anyone guess your private key.

When someone wants to send you a confidential message, they use your public key to encrypt the message. They can obtain your public key because you have distributed

---

†Companies exist whose function is to distribute lists of public keys.

it widely. Because you alone hold the corresponding private key, you are the only one who can decrypt the message.

Your public key can only be used to encrypt messages sent to you, and your private key can only be used to decrypt those messages. If you need to send a message to another person, you must use that person's public key to encrypt the message, and they must use their private key to decrypt it. Thus, in a two-way communication, four keys will be used: your two keys will be used for messages sent to you, and the other person's two keys will be used for messages sent to them. Figure 31.2 illustrates encryption and decryption in a two-way conversation.

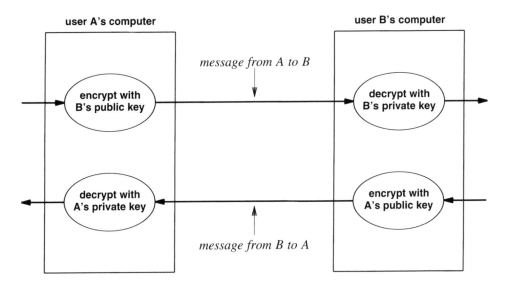

Figure 31.2 An illustration of the keys used when two individuals exchange confidential communication. Messages sent across the Internet between the two computers are always encrypted, but the key used for encryption depends on the destination.

Secure Email In Practice

How do the general ideas described above translate into practice? If a user wants to encrypt messages, what software should they purchase? The answer is that although there are many companies selling encryption software, no single encryption technology has emerged as the universal standard. Two of the most popular systems have captured most of the market. *Secure Multipurpose Internet Mail Extensions* (*SMIME*), adds security to the existing email standard known as MIME. The chief advantage of SMIME is backward compatibility — the general format of an email message is unchanged. Another system that allows users to send confidential email is called *Pretty*

Good Privacy (PGP). PGP was developed by an MIT student who wanted an encryption system when none existed. Although specific vendors have adopted each, PGP has the disadvantage of not being as well integrated with an email standard, such as MIME.

Secure Wireless Networks

As Chapter 19 describes, inexpensive wireless routers are available that use NAT to permit a subscriber to connect multiple computers in a residence or business. Because they do not require physical connections, wireless networks pose special security threats. One security threat arises from violation of privacy: a computer within range of a wireless router can eavesdrop on conversations without being noticed. Thus, a third party may be able to capture copies of all packets sent between a computer and the Internet. Another threat arises from *inadvertent sharing*: a computer within range of a wireless NAT box can obtain access to the Internet without paying a fee. Inadvertent sharing may violate the user's contractual agreement with an ISP. Even if it does not, sharing means that some of the network capacity will be taken by a third party.

Can wireless networks be secure? Fortunately, several mechanisms are available to enforce privacy and restrict access. For example, to guarantee that data is kept confidential, a Wi-Fi network offers an encryption technology known as *Wired Equivalent Privacy*, abbreviated *WEP*. When using WEP, packets traveling between a computer and a wireless router are encrypted to prevent a third party from reading them. In addition, Wi-Fi networks allow a user to set an identifier known as an *SSID*† in the wireless router and in computers that use it; only computers that know the SSID can use the wireless network to send and receive packets.

Each of the security features of a wireless network requires *configuration*. That is, when a wireless network is first installed, the owner must decide whether to use WEP encryption, whether to set an SSID, and whether to broadcast the SSID or keep it secret.

The point is:

> *Although wireless networks include facilities like encryption and SSIDs that keep communication private and prevent others from using the network, an owner must configure the facilities when the network is installed.*

Firewalls Protect Networks From Unwanted Packets

In addition to security problems described above, a computer or an entire network can be subject to attack from unwanted packets. For example, an attacker can probe a computer to see if the computer has services such as a web server, ftp server, or a re-

---

†Although SSID stands for *Service Set IDentifier*, the acronym is seldom expanded.

mote desktop server. Once an attacker finds a server running, the attacker can attempt to exploit the server (e.g., guess a login and password).

The chief mechanism used to protect private networks from outside attack is known as an *Internet firewall*; the term is taken from physical protection systems where a firewall is placed between two areas to prevent a fire from spreading. An Internet firewall is placed between the network to be protected and the rest of the Internet. Figure 31.3 illustrates the placement of a firewall.

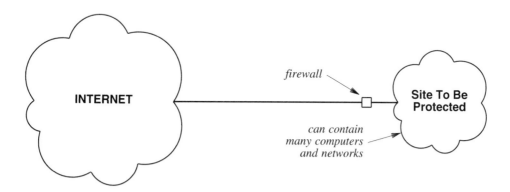

Figure 31.3 Illustration of a firewall that protects a computer or a set of computers from outside attack.

A Firewall Filters Packets

How does a firewall work? When it is installed, a network administrator must configure the firewall according to the desired security policy. Once it has been configured, a firewall examines each packet, and only allows packets to pass through that satisfy the security constraints. For example, if the site does not offer FTP service to outsiders, the firewall is configured to reject all FTP requests. Alternatively, the site can configure its firewall to allow FTP access to a specific computer at the site, but forbid FTP access to all others.

How does a firewall help? A firewall prevents accidental access. For example, if an employee at the company accidentally misconfigures their PC to run an FTP server, the firewall prevents outsiders from accessing files. More important, because a firewall is configured to prohibit packets to ''unknown'' services, the company does not need to worry about a dangerous new Internet service being created — the firewall protects against all access until it is reconfigured to allow access.

Firewalls Guard Against Trojan Horses

Employees are sometimes surprised to learn that their company's firewall does not only restrict incoming packets — it restricts access to the Internet from inside the company as well. Why? If the company did not restrict access in the reverse direction, it would be vulnerable to a *Trojan horse* attack. All that is needed to breach security is an employee who runs an arbitrary computer program. To trick an employee into running such a program, attackers often disguise the program as a game or an animated cartoon. Typically, they are sent to the employee in an email message. When the user runs the program, the display shows an animation. Meanwhile, the program attempts to breach security by contacting a person or computer on the outside and providing access to information in the user's computer. A properly configured firewall can prevent such attacks. To summarize:

> *A firewall is placed between a company and the Internet to restrict access to the company from the outside. To prevent a Trojan horse attack, the firewall also restricts access to the Internet from within the company.*

Residential And Individual Firewalls

Although we have described using it to protect a company's computers and networks, firewall technology can also be applied to networks and computers at a residence. Two forms are available: a hardware device or a software module.

Hardware device. Small, inexpensive firewall devices are available that function exactly as this chapter describes. That is, a user can purchase a separate physical device that is inserted between the user's computer and the user's ISP (e.g., the firewall is inserted on the connection between a user's computer and the local DSL or cable modem). The firewall blocks packets that do not adhere to the rules. For example, the *wireless routers* (i.e., NAT boxes) described in Chapter 19 often include firewall capabilities.

Software module. As an alternative to a separate physical device, software is available that provides the firewall function inside a computer. Firewall software inserts itself in the computer between the network interface and the operating system, which means that all incoming or outgoing packets must travel through the firewall software. In essence, firewall software is kept separate from all other software in the computer, meaning that it can function like an independent hardware device.

Should you use a hardware or software firewall? Because it handles packets from all computers in a residence, a hardware firewall protects all computers that share the connection to an ISP. Furthermore, a firewall may be embedded in a device that is needed for other purposes (e.g., a wireless router that provides NAT functionality). A software firewall has the disadvantage of only protecting one computer, but does have some advantages. Users may be more comfortable installing software. Furthermore, a software firewall can interact with the user (e.g., to report problems or ask whether to change the firewall rules). Consequently, many users have both forms: a firewall in a wireless router that protects all computers and specialized firewalls in each computer that can interact with the user. To summarize:

> *In addition to their use at companies, firewalls can be used to protect residential networks and computers. A user can choose a separate hardware device that protects all computers or a software module that protects one computer. Many users choose both.*

Systems Exist To Detect Intrusion

In addition to firewalls, large organizations often use an *Intrusion Detection System*, abbreviated *IDS*. An IDS monitors networks and computers at a site to watch for unusual or unexpected traffic. Even if a site is protected by a firewall, an IDS can help. The reason is straightforward: users with laptop computers and portable media (e.g., a flashROM) can accidentally import malicious software. An IDS can monitor networks to insure that if such software is introduced, the owner of the computer or the site is informed.

Service Can Be Denied

Another form of attack prevents communication. To describe such attacks, networking professionals use the term *Distributed Denial Of Service* attack, which is abbreviated *DDOS* and pronounced 'd - dos''. DDOS attacks are intended to prevent a site or an organization from using the Internet for legitimate communication. A DDOS attack is analogous to blocking the entrance to a business to keep customers from entering — an attacker arranges many computers on the Internet to send packets to a specific site. If enough computers on the Internet send packets as quickly as possible, the flood of packets can jam a site in the same way that a traffic jam on a highway prevents cars from reaching their destination.

DDOS attacks are more difficult to detect. Most DDOS attacks are aimed at large organizations rather than at individuals. Fortunately, large organizations have a staff of network managers who can work with ISPs to find the sources of an attack and stop the packets. However, no ideal solution exists. To summarize:

> *Although an Intrusion Detection System can help identify unexpected and unwanted traffic inside a site, stopping a Distributed Denial Of Service Attack is more difficult.*

Summary

Although no network is absolutely secure, encryption technologies exist that provide high levels of assurance against third parties being able to intercept and decode or change data as it passes across the Internet. The fundamental technology used to make communication secure is known as public key encryption. Each user obtains a pair of keys; one is kept private and the other made public. A sender uses the recipient's public key to encrypt each message before transmission; a recipient uses their private key to decrypt the message.

Wireless routers that support NAT and other wireless networks pose special security threats. Mechanisms are available for wireless networks that insure privacy and prevent outsiders from using the network; but security must be configured when the wireless equipment is installed.

A firewall checks packets and prevents unwanted traffic from entering a site or a computer. A firewall can also prevent a Trojan Horse program from transmitting outgoing data without the user's knowledge. An Intrusion Detection System further helps identify unexpected traffic on internal networks. Neither firewalls nor Intrusion Detection Systems can prevent a Distributed Denial Of Service attack.

32

Secure Access From A Distance (VPNs)

Introduction

The previous chapter initiates a discussion of technologies and mechanisms that make a network secure. This chapter continues the topic of secure communication by explaining a security technology that allows an individual located at a remote location to access an organization's network as if the computer were physically located inside the organization without risk. The chapter explains how such facilities are used and how they work.

Organizations Grant Employees Special Privileges

To understand why secure remote access is needed, it is necessary to understand how organizations operate a secure network. The aspect that is pertinent to our discussion concerns the distinction most organizations make between networks and computers *inside* the organization and those that are *outside*. Typically, insiders correspond to employees. Outsiders can correspond to suppliers, customers, or people who have no connection with the organization whatsoever.

The organization establishes policies that specify what insiders and outsiders are permitted to do and what each group is prohibited from doing, and then deploys technologies that enforce the policies. Typically, insiders are granted many privileges, such as access to the company's employee data (i.e., an insider is permitted to look up the email address, phone number, and office location of any employee). In contrast, outsiders are prohibited from accessing company resources and information.

Chapter 31 explains one of the technologies used to enforce separate access policies for insiders and outsiders: a *firewall*. By placing a firewall between the organization and the Internet, the organization can define exactly which packets are permitted to travel in each direction between the organization and the Internet. The point is:

> *Users inside an organization usually have more privilege than outsiders. To enforce the distinction, an organization can use a technology such as a firewall that will prevent outsiders from accessing facilities inside the organization.*

Traveling Employees Lose Privilege

Although enforcing a distinction between insiders and outsiders is important, doing so can cause a problem. To understand why, consider an employee who takes a business trip to a distant city. When the employee leaves the organization, the employee crosses the boundary between inside and outside. Effectively, the employee becomes an outsider.

Note that the definitions of inside and outside depend on physical location, not on the computer being used. In particular, even if the computer that an employee takes on the trip is the same laptop computer that was used inside the organization, once the computer connects to an outside network, the computer becomes an outside computer. To summarize:

> *When an employee travels beyond the border of the organization, the employee loses privilege and becomes an outsider; it does not matter which computer the employee uses.*

Telecommuters Do Not Have Privilege

The idea that employees lose privilege when they move beyond their company's boundary is especially important for employees that work from a remote location. Such employees are called *telecommuters*.

To use the Internet, a telecommuter obtains access from a local ISP. Such service works well for general tasks such as browsing web pages or accessing other company's web sites. However, if a telecommuter attempts to access internal networks and services at their company, they will be treated as an outsider and the packets will be blocked. The point is:

A mechanism that denies privilege to all outsiders makes it impossible to telecommute because the employee will be treated as an outsider and the employee's packets will be blocked.

Dedicated Leased Circuits Allow Secure Telecommuting

Telephone companies provide one way to solve the telecommuting problem. Recall that a phone company leases digital circuits and a customer can specify two arbitrary geographic locations when leasing a circuit. Furthermore, recall that the phone company guarantees that the circuit will remain *private* (i.e., only the two designated locations will be able to access the data). We say that a circuit provides a *private network connection*.

To allow an employee to telecommute, lease a digital circuit between the employee's house and the company. Add networking equipment at each end of the circuit that transfers packets in either direction. At the employee's house, the extra equipment connects the circuit to the user's computer; at the company, the equipment connects the circuit to the corporate network. In essence, the circuit "extends" the corporate network to the employee's home — the employee's computer has the same privileges as a computer inside the company. Figure 32.1 illustrates the connections.

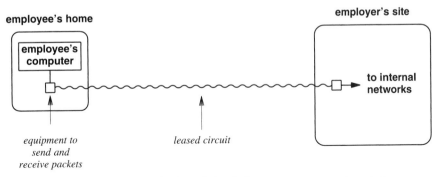

Figure 32.1 Illustration of a leased circuit that connects an employee's home and the company. Such an arrangement permits an employee to telecommute from home and remain secure.

Although a leased circuit provides secure telecommuting, the approach has a significant disadvantage: extremely high cost. Even lower-speed leased circuits cost hundreds of dollars per month. Besides, leased circuits do not solve the problem of providing access for employees who travel; a better solution is needed.

Standard Internet Connections Are Low-Cost

As Chapter 14 describes, DSL and cable modem technologies have allowed carriers and cable companies to offer affordable broadband Internet connections. Such connections provide the high capacity needed for effective telecommuting — applications such as email, file transfer, and remote desktop all work well over a broadband connection.

The availability of broadband connection technologies has also affected travelers. Most hotels now offer affordable Internet service to travelers; in some hotels, Internet access is free.

Can A Technology Combine Advantages?

Unfortunately, broadband access alone does not solve the problem completely. Although broadband technology is inexpensive and provides a high-capacity connection to an ISP, an employee's computer will remain outside the corporate network. To allow an employee to telecommute from home or while traveling, the employee's computer must somehow be given the privileges of an insider. The question arises: can the advantages of a leased circuit be combined with the low cost of broadband access? That is, can a technology be devised that provides full privileges for telecommuters at low cost?

A Virtual Private Network Solves The Problem

Engineers have created a clever and interesting technology that combines low-cost and secure access to allow inexpensive, safe telecommuting. When using the technology, a remote computer is granted full privileges, just as if the computer were present on the company's network. Furthermore, the technology is safe, and can even be used over wireless networks in a public area such as a hotel room. That is, even if others can eavesdrop, they will not be able to understand the transmissions or learn how to gain access.

The networking industry has given the technology a descriptive name: *Virtual Private Network*. The term *private* is used because the technology only allows the sender and receiver to decode and understand packets. The term *virtual* is used because the technology does not require the user to install physical wires or leased circuits. Because the terminology is cumbersome, most professionals prefer the acronym *VPN*. To summarize:

VPN technology solves the problem of providing safe, low-cost telecommuting by allowing a computer to obtain insider privileges over a conventional Internet connection.

How A VPN Works

As one might expect, encryption forms the foundation for VPN technology. To achieve privacy, a VPN encrypts each packet. That is, to ensure that packets remain confidential as they travel in either direction between a company and an employee's computer, each packet is encrypted before transmission and decrypted when it arrives. Thus, although packets pass across the public Internet, other users cannot decrypt the packet and view the contents. Figure 32.2 illustrates the principal components of the VPN.

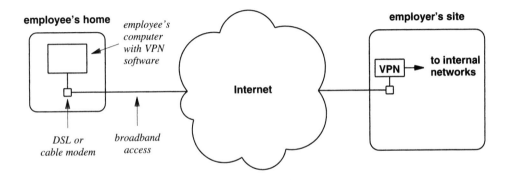

Figure 32.2 Illustration of the facilities needed to permit an employee to telecommute. VPN software runs on the employee's computer and at the corporation.

The Illusion Of A Direct Connection

Although encryption handles the privacy aspect of remote connections, a VPN needs a second technique to handle the "virtual" aspect of remote connections. In essence, VPN software running on an employee's computer must create the illusion that the computer connects directly to the corporate network. All packets (i.e., datagrams) sent from and to the computer must have an IP address that is on the corporate network. To achieve the illusion, VPN software controls the real network connection completely by inserting itself between the Internet and other programs on the computer. Once inserted, VPN software communicates with VPN software at the corporation, obtains an IP address, and gives the new IP address to the operating system. In essence, only the VPN software can use the real Internet connection; all other software on the computer uses an IP address that was obtained from the corporate network. As far as an application program is concerned, the computer appears to connect directly to the corporate network: outgoing and incoming packets contain the corporate address.

If applications running on the computer create packets that appear to belong on the corporate network, how can the packets be sent across the Internet? They cannot be transmitted directly. Instead, the VPN software places each outgoing packet *inside another packet*, and transfers the result across the Internet to the corporation. Once it reaches the corporation, VPN software extracts the inner packet and forwards the inner packet as if it had been generated locally.

To understand what a VPN is doing, imagine that you want to exchange letters with a friend, but want to fool your friend into believing you are in Philadelphia when, in fact, you are in Chicago. To succeed in the ruse, your letters must be postmarked from Philadelphia, and the return address must specify Philadelphia. If you have a relative living in Philadelphia, creating the illusion is straightforward. To send a letter, you create a stamped envelope addressed to your friend with a return address that gives the Philadelphia address of your relative. Once an outgoing letter has been created, place the letter inside a larger envelope and address the outer envelope to your relative in Philadelphia. When the outer envelope arrives, your relative extracts the inner letter and drops it in the mail. Similarly, when your relative receives a reply addressed to you from your friend, your relative places the reply in a large envelope and sends it to you.

Once you have the system set, you can expand the illusion to include arbitrary friends. Interestingly, your relative does not need to know in advance the people to whom you will send letters, nor does your relative need to know who will send you letters. Basically, whenever an envelope arrives from you, your relative opens the envelope and mails all the letters found inside. Similarly, whenever a letter arrives addressed to you, your relative places the letter inside an envelope addressed to you in Chicago and forwards it.

A VPN follows the same approach: it uses the technique of sending a packet inside another packet as a way of fooling receivers into thinking that the employee's computer is located on the corporate network. Figure 32.3 illustrates how a packet appears at various stages as it travels across a VPN.

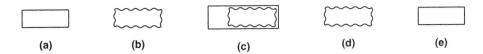

Figure 32.3 A packet at various steps as it travels across a VPN. (a) the original packet, (b) encrypted by the sending VPN, (c) an encrypted packet placed inside another packet for transmission, (d) inner packet removed by the receiving VPN, (e) decrypted to obtain the original packet, which is sent across the corporate network.

Significance Of VPNs

For many Internet users, VPN technology has revolutionized the way they use the Internet. Business travelers can connect to the corporate network and access all services as if they were local. More important, a traveler does not need to worry about whether access networks are secure because a VPN provides privacy and prevents unwanted packets from being processed. Thus, a business traveler who is visiting a customer or even a competitor can use their computer at the remote site without compromising information or losing privilege.

The point is:

A traveler can use VPN technology to connect to the corporate office and obtain full privileges from any location. Because it provides secure access, VPN technology changes the way business travelers use the Internet.

33

Internet Economics And Electronic Commerce

Introduction

This chapter discusses economic aspects of the Internet. It describes basic terminology, and explains how the Internet can be used to conduct business and commercial transactions. It extends the discussion of security in the previous chapters, and considers how encryption technology is used to make transactions safe.

Who Pays For The Internet?

The most fundamental question about Internet economics involves the source of revenue. Who pays for the infrastructure? Of course, individual subscribers pay their ISP for access. The fee depends on the capacity of the link between the subscriber and the ISP. Each customer signs a legal contract that is known as a *Service Level Agreement*, known by the acronym *SLA*. In addition to stating the fee that a customer must pay, an SLA specifies details about the service that will be provided, such as the bandwidth of the physical connection or the amount of data that can be transferred each month. The SLA for a business is more complex than the SLA for a residential customer, and may include a sliding scale of charges that increases if traffic exceeds prestated thresholds. The SLA for a business may also guarantee the response time when problems occur.

What about local (i.e., Tier-3) ISPs? Do they pay fees as well? Yes, a small, Tier-3 ISP is a customer of a larger, Tier-2 ISP, and must pay a fee that depends on the amount of traffic that will be transferred. Similarly, Tier-2 ISPs become customers of Tier-1 ISPs, and must pay a fee for service. Thus, small providers must charge customers enough to cover fees for the next level, and so on.

What about a pair of Tier-1 ISPs? Does one become a customer of another? In general, no. Instead, Tier-1 ISPs treat each other as *peers* (i.e., as equals). Consequently, the contract between them is known as a *peering agreement*. If the same amount of traffic passes in each direction between two peers, they usually split the cost of the connection between them. If during a given month one ISP sends much more traffic than the other, however, the peering agreement specifies how much cash one must pay the other. To summarize:

> *Each residential or business subscriber pays a fee to an ISP for Internet service. Smaller ISPs each pay a larger ISP to accept traffic. At the center of the Internet, Tier-1 ISPs treat each other as peers, and fees are only assessed if traffic is unequal.*

For businesses, Internet service becomes an operating expense similar to other infrastructure expenses. Thus, when a business joins the Internet, the business raises its prices or fees to cover the cost.

E-commerce Is Big Business

The term *electronic commerce* (usually abbreviated *e-commerce*) refers to all commercial transactions conducted over the Internet, including transactions by consumers (e.g., online banking, investing, or bill paying) and business-to-business transactions. Conceptually, e-commerce does not differ from well-known commercial offerings such as banking by phone, ''mail order'' catalogs, or sending a purchase order to a supplier via fax. E-commerce follows the same paradigm used in other business transactions; the difference lies in the details.

To a consumer, the most visible form of e-commerce consists of online ordering. A customer begins with a catalog of possible items, selects an item, arranges a form of payment, and sends in an order. Instead of a physical catalog, e-commerce arranges for catalogs to be visible on the Internet. Instead of sending an order on paper or by telephone, e-commerce arranges for orders to be sent over a computer network. Finally, instead of sending a paper representation of payment such as a check, e-commerce allows one to send payment information electronically.

In the decade after 1993, e-commerce grew from an insignificant novelty to a mainstream business influence. In 1993, few corporations had a web page, and only a handful allowed one to order products or services over the Internet. Ten years later, both large and small businesses had web pages, and most provided users with the opportunity to place an order. In addition, many banks added online access, and online banking and bill paying became widespread. More important, the value of goods and services acquired over the Internet grew dramatically after 1997. For example, according to an article on:

www.thestandard.com/metrics

the 120,000 online retailers using VeriSign authentication took in 8.8 billion dollars between November 25 and December 27 in 2005.

Security Technology Made E-commerce Possible

Retail purchases by individual consumers account for a significant percentage of e-commerce. The most common form of e-commerce transaction consists of a retail purchase from a catalog. An individual begins by using a web browser to search for an item of interest. To enable e-commerce, the company advertising an item for sale provides a way for the user to purchase the item. In most cases, the browser displays a separate frame containing information about purchases, and the user can manipulate a *shopping cart*: one can create a new cart, add an item to a cart, view the contents of a cart along with the current price of each item, or delete an item from a cart. When the user has finished shopping and is ready to purchase the items in the cart, the user selects *purchase*, enters shipping information, a payment method (e.g., a credit card number), and the transaction is complete.

Users realize that their credit card numbers must be kept confidential. If a web browser did not keep such information confidential, no one would purchase items online. As a result, e-commerce did not become feasible until browsers included a mechanism that guarantees confidentiality.

Secure Sockets

How does a browser keep messages private? It uses the encryption technology described in Chapter 31. Whenever a form appears on a web page, a user must enter information that will be sent over the Internet to the server. The browser handles the details. There are two possibilities: automated security or a warning. Automated security requires encryption: if a form specifies secure transfer, the browser automatically encrypts the message before sending it. If the form does not specify secure transfer, the browser issues a warning. To do so, the browser creates a dialog box that appears on the screen. The dialog box explains that the information entered on the form is about to travel across the Internet unsecure, and asks the user to decide whether to proceed†. If

---

†A user who does not care about security can set the security preferences in their browser to avoid the dialog box.

the user approves, the browser sends the unencrypted information. If the user disapproves, the browser does not send the information.

When a browser encrypts information, the process is entirely hidden from a user. The most widely-used technology for automated security is known as the *Secure Socket Layer (SSL)*. With SSL, a browser can encrypt a message so the contents remain private. More important, the entire process is automated; the browser performs the encryption without requiring the user to act. For example, when a URL begins with the prefix *https://* instead of the standard *http*, a browser automatically uses encryption when accessing the page. To determine whether encryption is being used, a user can look at the security icon the browser displays (e.g., a picture of a padlock that is either locked or unlocked).

Public Key Encryption Provides Authenticity

The security technology built into a browser does more than encrypt messages. Before encryption occurs, the browser must obtain the appropriate encryption key (i.e., the public key of the server), and must verify the authenticity of both the server and the key. All steps are automated — no dialog boxes appear, and the user does not need to enter any of the information. Instead, the browser obtains it automatically over the Internet.

Surprisingly, a browser uses public key encryption to verify authenticity, the same technology that is used to keep messages confidential. The point is:

> *Public key encryption is surprisingly general — in addition to guaranteeing that messages remain confidential, it can be used to verify authenticity.*

How can encryption verify authenticity? The answer requires one to understand an important mathematical property of the technology. Recall that any message encrypted with a given user's public key can only be decrypted with the user's private key. Interestingly, the reverse is also true: any message encrypted with a user's private key can only be decrypted with their public key.

Of course, encrypting a message with a user's private key does not keep it confidential because everyone knows the user's public key. However, because the private key is secret, *only the user knows the private key.* Consequently, if you receive a message that has been encrypted with a user's private key, the user must have sent the message. More important, there is a simple and easy way for you to test whether a message was indeed encrypted with a user's private key: try to decrypt it with the user's public key.

If all the keys seem confusing, take heart — public key security is only completely understood after intense study. After all, sophisticated mathematics is involved. In fact, the above discussion has not even begun to explore some of the more complex aspects such as encrypted messages being encrypted again! Simply remember that when you are engaged in online shopping or banking, public key technology allows a browser to verify the authenticity of the web site and ensure the confidentiality of the information you send to the site.

Digital Signatures

One mechanism for authentication is known as a *digital signature* because it allows a receiver to know who sent a given electronic document in the same way that a conventional signature allows a receiver to know who sent a written document. The digital signature is created by encrypting information about the document using the sender's private key. Unfortunately, many people are confused by the terminology. A digital signature is an encrypted message; it is *not* merely a scanned version of a conventional signature. The latter would be a *digitized signature*. The chief difference between a digitized signature and a digital signature is that a digitized signature (i.e., a scanned image) can be duplicated, but a digital signature cannot. We will not go into detail about how a digital signature works, but we can summarize:

> *A digital signature consists of a special form of encrypted message; the encryption technology ensures that a digital signature cannot be forged.*

Certificates Contain Public Keys

We said that anyone can publish their public key. However, before a browser can verify a digital signature, the browser must be absolutely certain it knows the sender's public key. Interestingly, a browser does not ask the user to enter the sender's public key. Instead trusted companies exist that register public keys and communicate them as needed. When a browser needs to obtain or verify a public key, it contacts one of the trusted companies. After the company provides the needed public key, the browser uses the key to verify authenticity of the original message. Of course, the messages sent between a browser and a trusted company must be secure; once again encryption is used to guarantee security.

Although we said that a browser obtains a public key, the technical term for the information that a browser receives from a trusted source is a *digital certificate*. Each certificate contains a public key plus a digital signature from the trusted company to verify that the message is authentic.

A browser usually obtains digital certificates automatically when they are needed without informing the user. In fact, the only way a user can tell that a browser is obtaining a certificate is to watch the area on the screen where a browser displays its current action. Along with items such as *Contacting host*, a user may see the browser display *Obtaining certificate*.

In a few cases, however, a browser may not be able to obtain a certificate from a trusted source. In such cases, the browser asks the user whether to proceed with a certificate obtained from another source. For situations involving financial records (e.g., submitting credit card information), it is not wise to accept certificates from alternative sources.

What Is Digital Money?

Although there are many details we did not cover, it may seem that encryption technology provides everything needed for consumers to conduct e-commerce: privacy to keep messages confidential, authentication of web sites, and the secure communication a browser requires to obtain digital certificates. According to some users, however, another facility is desirable: digital money.

Credit cards are convenient for making large purchases, but they incur overhead because they require a user to enter the number and expiration date. Furthermore, the user must remember the details of the purchase in case there is a question when the bill arrives at the end of the month. Many groups have proposed an alternative known as *digital money* or *digital cash*. The premise is simple: digital cash should be the electronic equivalent of the cash that people carry with them to make small purchases and should have less overhead than credit cards.

Several schemes have been proposed; the easiest to understand views digital cash as a form of *debit card*. A person begins with an electronic visit to the bank to authorize a withdrawal from their bank account and places the money in a *digital wallet* (the equivalent of a debit card). The bank returns an ID for the wallet, which the user stores on their computer. When the person wants to make a purchase on the Web, they specify their digital wallet, and the amount of the purchase is deducted. A user can return to the electronic bank to replenish the amount in their wallet, as needed.

Digital Cash Is Not Widely Available

Behind the scenes, several steps are required to make digital cash operate. Because a bank cannot transfer real money to an electronic wallet, the bank creates an encrypted message that specifies the bank, an account, and an amount. When a business wants to deduct money, the business must obtain authorization from the user who owns the wallet, send the authorization to the bank, and request a transfer of funds. Such transfers are called *micropayments* to reflect the small amount. All the communication involved in setting up a micropayment must be encrypted to keep it confidential, and encryption must be used to ensure that the store, the wallet, and the purchase are authentic.

Because digital money requires extensive use of encryption, engineering the necessary software is difficult. More important, because a viable system requires merchants, banks, and users to agree on software before they can start using the system, building a new digital cash system is costly. Finally, because digital cash is best suited to small purchases, the profit margin is small. As a result, most companies that have tried to create digital cash services have failed, and digital cash is not widely available.

Despite past failures, services are being created. The new services use a variety of approaches to avoid requiring micropayments from banks. Some simply accumulate small charges during the month and make a single monthly charge to the user's credit card. Others pass a monthly charge to the ISP, which adds it to the user's bill. Whether any of these approaches will become popular remains uncertain.

Business And E-commerce

So far we have described e-commerce from a consumer's point of view — shopping from a retail catalog and buying individual items. How does e-commerce affect business? There are two aspects to the answer: external transactions and transactions internal to a single company. When a business makes wholesale purchases, it becomes a customer. Like a consumer, a business can use e-commerce to replace conventional mail, fax, and phone communication. We refer to such items as *business to business communication*, abbreviated *B2B*. As with consumer purchases, B2B transactions use encryption technologies to ensure that transactions remain confidential.

A business can also use electronic communication to handle its internal procedures. For example, most businesses operate on a monthly reporting cycle where each group files a report that summarizes items such as sales, delivery, and stock on hand. Management analyzes the reports and shifts resources appropriately. Electronic communication makes it possible to shorten and automate the reporting process. For example, a company can use wireless network devices to scan inventory and send the results to a centralized server. Companies that have multiple sites use VPN technology to allow arbitrary computers at sites to communicate. A VPN system uses the Internet to provide low-cost connections among sites, and ensures that no third party can decode messages. Thus, a central site in the company can gather reports from multiple sites quickly, and provide mangement with a timely picture of the overall business operation.

The Controversies Over Taxation And Net Neutrality

Whenever money is involved, controversy seems to arise, and the Internet is no exception. Governments are considering the issue of taxation and private service providers are considering how to maximize profits. Government taxes come in two forms: taxes on Internet services and taxes on goods and services purchased over the Internet (known as *sales tax* or *value added tax*). In terms of Internet service: most common carriers are regulated, which means that communication services are subject to tax and the cost is passed on to customers.

A more heated controversy has arisen over the method of charging for Internet service. To understand the issue, observe that when the Internet began, phone companies focused on providing voice service using analog equipment. Consequently, phone companies viewed the leases of phone wires as a secondary source of revenue, and established a system in which the cost of a lease depended on the bandwidth of the circuit — more bandwidth cost more. As government allowed more competition in the telephone industry and the cost of digital technology declined, revenues from voice telephone service declined.

By 2005, common carriers faced a difficult challenge: companies like Skype and Vonage began using the Internet to provide voice telephone service†. To recapture revenues, phone companies and major ISPs proposed a new pricing scheme in which the charge to send or receive a given amount of traffic would depend on the company that was sending or receiving and the type of traffic being sent. For example, a company such as Google, Vonnage, or Skype would pay more for a given amount of traffic than other companies.

The proposal and surrounding discussions worry consumers for three reasons. First, incremental pricing might mean that only large, profitable companies could afford reasonable Internet service; small, speciality web sites might become unusable. Second, an ISP might provide better service to its own business customers, meaning that the service a consumer receives would depend on the ISP to which the consumer connects. Third, a business could merely pass along the increased costs to consumers while carriers and ISPs would receive more money for exactly the same service they provide now. Consumer groups prefer *net neutrality*, a system in which costs depend on the volume of traffic rather than the type of traffic or the destination. The point is:

> *The term* net neutrality *refers to a pricing scheme in which the charge for service depends only on the volume of traffic and not the traffic type or destination. Consumers desire neutrality; carriers and large ISPs desire an alternative that would increase their revenues.*

At the time of this writing, the US government has preserved net neutrality. However, large ISPs continue to lobby for a change.

---

†Chapter 28 explains Voice over IP (VoIP).

34

The Global Digital Library

Introduction

Previous chapters examine services available on the Internet and show how each can be useful. More important, each chapter explains a basic concept, such as hyper-media browsing or automated search, that underlies Internet services.

This chapter concludes the discussion. It explains the digital library concept, and shows how Internet services provide a global, digital library. In addition, the chapter provides perspective about Internet services, explains how each service can use others, and discusses the changes that can be expected.

A Cornucopia Of Services

The text explains many of the basic concepts that provide the foundation for Inter-net services. The concepts include personal communication provided by electronic mail, hypermedia browsing used to access the World Wide Web, automated searching used by search engines, instant messaging, transfer of streaming audio and video, and file transfer. Although the list of example services seems diverse, it does not include all available Internet facilities or services. For example, a *teleconferencing* service permits a group of individuals to hold an online conference in which each participant sees and hears other participants. In fact, so many services exist that an individual would need months of effort to learn about all of them. In summary:

The Internet contains many diverse services. An individual can transfer, browse, or search for information, make purchases, and interact with other users. Internet services handle all forms of digital information, including text, sound, graphic images, real-time audio and video, and multimedia combinations.

New Services Appear Regularly

Although many services exist, the Internet continues to evolve. Programmers and researchers continually devise and implement new services. Some of the most exciting services have existed for less than a decade. One cannot appreciate the Internet without understanding that:

The Internet is still evolving. Internet researchers continue to discover new ways to store, communicate, reference, and access information.

The continual change in available services and facilities has two important consequences. First, continual change means that any printed list of services becomes out-of-date quickly. Second, continual change means that an Internet user always has an opportunity to learn about new facilities.

Flexibility Permits Change

Why has the Internet been able to support such diverse services when other communication systems have not? The answer is simple: the basic technology the Internet uses is more flexible than other technologies.

All the services described in this book communicate using the TCP/IP protocols described in Chapters 12 through 19. TCP/IP allows computers to exchange pictures or sound as easily as electronic mail. In fact, large computers that allow many users to run programs simultaneously usually only have one copy of TCP/IP software that all services use. More important, many of the computers and Internet services that use TCP/IP were invented after TCP/IP; the design is flexible enough to accommodate change. To summarize:

The basic communication technology used in the Internet is extremely flexible. It supports a wide variety of computers and services that had not been invented when the technology was being developed.

A Digital Library

The term *digital library* has been used to characterize a large storehouse of digital information accessible through computers. Like a traditional library, a digital library serves as an archive of knowledge that spans many topics. Like a newsstand, a digital library provides information that changes quickly. Like a telephone or television, a digital library provides access to events as they occur.

Because information can be stored in many forms, a digital library can contain text, sounds, graphics, photographs, videos, and conversations. In addition, a digital library can access information live as it occurs; the information need not be recorded. For example, a digital library can provide access to services that show the changes in a user's face, sample the current weather conditions at a given geographic location, measure current traffic on a highway, or find the current delay at an airport.

Card Catalogs And Search Tools

Although many libraries now use computers, traditional libraries used a file of small cards to record the names of books and periodicals. Known as a *card catalog*, the file contained two sets of cards, one ordered by author and the other ordered by topic.

A library's card catalog served as its primary index mechanism. One could use the card catalog to find books or periodicals without searching the entire library. Furthermore, one could locate an item either from the title or from the name of the author.

A digital library has a much richer and varied set of index and search mechanisms. Computers make it possible to create indexes of documents or to find arbitrary information. Search mechanisms can use basic or advanced matching techniques (e.g., find documents that contain a given word or find documents that contain a complete phrase). The point is:

> *Unlike a traditional library that used a card catalog, a digital library contains many index mechanisms and provides services that use the mechanisms to search for information. As a result, a given piece of information can be located several ways.*

Internet Services Can Be Integrated

The search mechanisms in a digital library can be combined and integrated to form a cross-reference between services. In fact, many of the services discussed in preceding chapters have been integrated, allowing one service to reference information available in another. One of the best examples of integration can be found in browser software.

Designed to display hypermedia documents from the World Wide Web, a browser can also be used to access an FTP site, send email, listen to an audio source, share photographs with friends, or view movies.

Interestingly, integration can improve a service. For example, the original FTP service used a command-line interface that required users to remember and enter specific commands. When accessed from a web browser, however, FTP is viewed entirely through a visual interface. Instead of requiring a user to enter the FTP *dir* command, a browser automatically shows the contents of an FTP directory. Similarly, instead of requiring a user to enter the FTP *get* command, a browser will obtain a copy of a file whenever a user clicks on the file name.

In another example of service integration, some sites provide file access via email. To invoke the service, a user sends an email message to a special address. The email message contains the name of the file the user wishes to retrieve. When the message reaches the special address, a program retrieves the requested file, and sends the results back to the user in a second email message. Such facilities are especially helpful for users who prefer to use email rather than other services. The idea is fundamental:

> *Although each Internet service has been designed independently, services can be combined in interesting ways. A given service can access information available from other services.*

Mr. Dewey, Where Are You?

For centuries, librarians struggled to organize archives of the world's knowledge. Should books be ordered by title, author, or subject? Should a library mix works of fiction and nonfiction, or keep them separate?

Melvil Dewey proposed a solution to the problem of organizing a library. He invented a universal numbering scheme, known as the *Dewey Decimal System*, that allows librarians to organize books by topic. The scheme was successful in standardizing the organization of libraries.

The Internet digital library desperately needs an analogous categorization scheme. Although many tools have been developed, information is still provided in random ways. For example, consider World Wide Web pages. In most organizations, individuals or small groups can decide to establish a web page. Each group can choose the information to include and decide how pages will appear; there is little uniformity. The result is chaos — the order of information and options available on one page do not resemble those on another. After a user learns to navigate the pages at one company, they face a new challenge when they contact another. Similarly, the pages at one university are not organized like those at another. In short,

Because each computer on the Internet that offers a service can organize information however it chooses, there is little uniformity.

Information In The Digital Library

We have focused on the services used to locate and access information in the digital library without considering details of the information itself. One might wonder, "exactly what information is available?" Or one might ask, "where are the locations that contain the most interesting information?" Such questions are similar to asking, "exactly what best-selling novel will I enjoy the most?" or, "which newspaper at the local newsstand contains headlines I will find most interesting?"

The answers to such questions depend on the individual who asks. Furthermore, the questions are extremely difficult to answer when they refer to a digital library because the information is dynamic. For example, some Internet discussions last a few minutes, others last for days, and a few archives persist for years. In a digital library, one must rely on automated search tools to find items of interest. One need only supply key words, phrases, or other descriptions to browsing and searching services to find information.

What Is The Internet?

This book begins with the question, "What is the Internet?" We can summarize the answer in a one-paragraph description:

The Internet is a wildly-successful, rapidly-growing, global, digital library built on a remarkably flexible communication technology. The Internet digital library offers a variety of services used to create, browse, access, search, view, and communicate information on a diverse set of topics ranging from the results of scientific experiments to discussions of recreational activities. Information in the Internet digital library can be recorded in memos, organized into hypermedia documents, or stored in textual documents. In addition, information accessible through the digital library can consist of data, including audio and video, that is gathered, communicated, and delivered instantly without being stored. Furthermore, because the services have been integrated and cross-referenced, a user can move seamlessly from the information on one computer to information on another computer and from one access service to another.

A Personal Note

A few years ago, at a meeting of the network committee at the university where I work, the library staff described how they were enthusiastically installing servers to allow students, faculty, and outsiders to access the library through the Internet. As the meeting began, the librarians discussed access: email, newsgroups, and web pages.

As I listened to the discussion, I suddenly realized that something dramatic was taking place. Librarians were not merely talking about automating the card catalog or providing an index for the local archives. Instead of discussing physical books, they began talking about a future in which all information is stored in digital form, indexed automatically, and transmitted over networks when needed. They anticipated the widespread use of search engines. In short, the librarians were not merely experimenting with ways to access the current library; they were preparing for a digital future in which libraries as we know them will disappear and information will be found on "the Net."

Appendix 1

Glossary Of Internet Terms

Although learning any new terminology can be difficult, learning the Internet terminology can be daunting. The terms used to describe Internet services, network technologies, and specific computer programs make little or no sense to a beginner. Internet terminology combines terms from computer networking, business, government, and commercial products.

This glossary provides a concise definition of terms used throughout the Internet. It focuses on widely-accepted terminology and avoids terms that have been defined by commercial vendors for their products. Although a brief definition cannot provide a complete explanation of a term, readers who stumble across puzzling terminology will find the definitions sufficient to refresh their memory. The Index provides references to pages in the text that provide further explanation.

10Base-T Ethernet

A particular wiring scheme for an Ethernet LAN. *T* abbreviates *twisted pair*, the type of wire used to connect a computer to the network.

A-to-D converter

Abbreviation for *Analog-to-Digital converter*.

ACK

Abbreviation for *acknowledgement*.

acknowledgement

(ACK) A response sent by a receiver to indicate successful reception of information. In a packet-switching network, an acknowledgement is a packet returned when data arrives. Thus, when two computers exchange information, data packets travel in one direction and acknowledgements travel in the opposite direction.

active web page

A web page that consists of a computer program. After being downloaded, an active page can continue to change the display.

address

A numeric value assigned to a computer much like a telephone number is assigned to a home. When a packet of data travels from one computer to another, the packet contains the addresses of the two computers.

ADSL

(Asymmetric Digital Subscriber Line) The specific version of DSL technology used by the phone company to deliver high-speed Internet connectivity to homes and businesses. ADSL and conventional phone calls do not interfere — the phone can be used at the same time data is being sent.

Advanced Research Projects Agency

(ARPA) The U.S. government agency that funded the ARPANET and later, the Internet. At various times, ARPA has been named *DARPA*.

afaik

(as far as i know) An abbreviation used in electronic communication such as email and instant messaging.

American Standard Code for Information Interchange

(ASCII) A character code used on the Internet. ASCII assigns each letter, digit, and punctuation symbol a unique sequence of binary digits. When textual data is transferred across the Internet, it is usually represented in ASCII.

analog

Any representation of information in which the amount of a substance or signal is proportional to the information represented.

Analog-to-Digital converter

(A-to-D converter) An electronic component that converts an analog electrical signal into a sequence of numbers.

anonymous FTP

Use of the special login *anonymous* to obtain access to public files through the FTP service.

applet

The name given to dynamic web pages written using the Java technology. An applet is a computer program that can display smooth animation on a browser's screen.

ARPA

Abbreviation for *Advanced Research Projects Agency*.

ARPANET

An early wide area network funded by ARPA. It served from 1969 through 1989 as the basis for early networking research and as a central backbone network during development of the Internet.

ASCII

Abbreviation for *American Standard Code For Information Interchange*. The representation used for most text.

Asymmetric Digital Subscriber Line

See *ADSL*.

Asynchronous Transfer Mode

(ATM) The name of a particular network technology designed to operate at high speeds. ATM has lost popularity, but is still used in DSL modems

ATM

Abbreviation for *Asynchronous Transfer Mode*.

attachment

An item sent along with an email message using MIME (see *Multi-Purpose Mail Extensions*). Typically, an attachment contains a non-text file, such as an audio clip or a photograph.

audio clip

A (usually short) segment of audio that has been digitized. An audio clip is stored in a file, and can be sent across the Internet in an email message.

audio teleconference

A service that allows a group of users to exchange audio information over the Internet similar to a telephone conference call. Each participant's computer must have a microphone and a speaker (or earphones).

automated search service

Any service that locates information without requiring a user to make decisions or select from menus. Typical automated search services examine complete documents. Examples of automated search services include *Google* and *Yahoo!*.

backbone network

Used to refer to a central network to which many routers connect. In the Internet, backbone networks use Wide Area Network technology. Individual corporations also refer to their central network as a backbone; such backbones may be LANs.

bandwidth

The capacity of a network, usually measured in bits per second. Network systems need higher bandwidth for audio or video than for email or other services. Also see *broadband*.

baud

Literally, the number of times per second the signal can change on a transmission line. Baud rate is most often used as a measure of speed for a dial-up telephone connection.

best-effort delivery

Used to describe computer networks in which congestion can cause the network to discard packets. TCP/IP software can use best-effort delivery networks because the software detects missing packets and retransmits them.

binary

Any number system that uses two values. Computers use binary for all arithmetic.

binary digit

(bit) Either a *0* or *1*. The Internet uses binary digits to represent all information, including audio, video, and text.

binary file

A nontext file such as a digitized photograph or music (see *text file*).

bit

Abbreviation for *binary digit*.

bits per second

(bps) The rate of data transmission which is often used as a measure of the capacity of a network (see *bandwidth*). Modern networks operate at millions of bits per second (Mbps).

bookmark

A facility in a browser used to record the location of a particular page, making it possible to return to the page later. Bookmarks are also known as *favorites*.

bps

Abbreviation for *bits per second*.

broadband

A term used to describe computer networks that operate at high speed. DSL and cable modem technologies are used to provide broadband Internet access to residential and business customers.

broadcast

A packet delivery mechanism that delivers a copy of a given packet to all computers attached to a network. Compare to *unicast* and *multicast*.

browser

A computer program that allows users to view hypermedia documents on the World Wide Web. The Mozilla browser is available from Netscape Communications and the Internet Explorer browser is available from Microsoft Corporation.

browsing

The act of looking through information by repeatedly scanning and selecting. An Internet browsing service presents a page of information. After the user reads the information and selects an item, the service follows the reference and retrieves new information.

btw

An abbreviation for ''by the way'' used in electronic communication, especially in instant messaging.

bulletin board service

A service that permits one person to post a message for others to read. Each bulletin board usually contains discussion of a single topic.

cable modem

A device that allows Internet service to be provided over the same coaxial cable wiring used for cable television. Cable modems do not interfere with normal television reception; both can be used at the same time.

carrier

A steady electrical signal or tone that is used by a modem to encode information for transmission across a communication line or a telephone connection. When a dial-up modem is used, the carrier is the tone one hears if one listens to the telephone.

Cc

(*Carbon copy*) A line used in email headers to specify additional recipients.

Central Processing Unit

(*CPU*) The electronic component in a computer that performs all arithmetic and logical operations.

CGI

See *Common Gateway Interface*

chat room

A service that allows users to join a discussion. When a participant types on the keyboard, all participants in the chat room receive a copy. Compare to *Instant Messaging*.

checksum

A small integer used to detect whether errors occur when transmitting data from one machine to another. Protocol software such as TCP computes a checksum and appends it to a packet when transmitting. Upon reception, the protocol software verifies the contents of the packet by recomputing the checksum and comparing it to the value sent.

chip

An informal term for *integrated circuit*.

client

A program that uses the Internet to contact a remote server. Technically, a separate client program is needed for each Internet service. However, a browser includes many client programs, which means a browser can access many services on the user's behalf.

client-server computing

The interaction between two programs when they communicate across a network. A program at one site sends a request to a program at another site and awaits a response. The requesting program is called a *client*; the program satisfying the request is called the *server*.

Common Gateway Interface

(*CGI*) A technology that uses a computer program to assemble a web page whenever a user requests the page. Pages composed using CGI technology are dynamic; unlike static pages they are not stored on the server's disk before requests arrive.

computer conference

Communication among a set of individuals who each use a computer. Various computer conference services provide text, audio, or video communication. Also see *bulletin board service*.

computer network

A hardware mechanism that computers use to communicate. A network is classified as a Local Area Network or Wide Area Network, depending on the hardware capabilities.

congestion

A problem in computer networks that occurs when too many packets arrive at a point in the network. As on a conventional highway, congestion means higher delays.

connection

Used to describe computer interaction in which two application programs first agree to communicate and then exchange data. TCP software uses a connection style of interaction, which means that most Internet services use connections. Compare to *connectionless*.

connectionless

Used to describe computer interaction in which an application sends data or a request to another application without first agreeing to communicate. The Internet Protocol, IP, uses the connectionless approach.

cookie

A small amount of data (usually a string of less than 50 characters) that is used to identify a World Wide Web user. When a user visits a web site, the server asks their browser to store a cookie so the server can identify the user on the next visit.

CPU

Abbreviation for *Central Processing Unit*

CSNET

(*Computer Science NETwork*) An early network that offered email and Internet connections to Computer Science Departments in colleges and universities. Initially funded by the National Science Foundation (NSF), CSNET later became self-sufficient.

D-to-A converter

Abbreviation for Digital-to-Analog converter.

DARPA

(*Defense Advanced Research Projects Agency*). The alternate name of ARPA.

datagram

Synonym for *IP datagram.*

decryption

The process of decoding a message that has been encrypted to keep it confidential. The receiver decrypts the message after it has traveled across the Internet.

Defense Advanced Research Projects Agency

(*DARPA*) The alternative name of the *Advanced Research Projects Agency.*

demodulation

The process of extracting information from a modulated signal that arrives over a transmission line or telephone connection. Demodulation usually occurs in a device called a modem. Also see *modulation* and *carrier.*

demodulator

The electronic device in a modem that decodes an incoming signal and extracts data. See *modulator.*

destination address

A numeric value in a packet that specifies the computer to which the packet has been sent. The destination address in a packet traveling across the Internet is the IP address of the destination computer.

dial-up access

A technique used to access the Internet using a conventional telephone call. Dial-up is the least expensive type of access and the slowest.

digital

Any technology that uses numbers to represent information. A computer is inherently digital because it represents keystrokes, pictures, text, sounds, and video using numbers.

digital camera

A camera that digitizes an image and stores it in a form suitable for a computer rather than on film.

digital cash

A technology that allows small purchases on the Internet without requiring the customer to fill in credit card information for each purchase. Many companies that have offered digital cash services have been unsuccessful.

digital certificate

A message from a trusted authority that is used during a secure transaction. A digital certificate contains a copy of a public key.

digital library

A large collection of information that has been stored in digital form. A digital library can include documents, images, sounds, books, video, and information gathered from ongoing events (e.g., continuous pictures from a weather satellite).

digital signature

An encrypted message that authenticates the author of a document. A digital signature cannot be forged.

Digital Subscriber Line

See *DSL*.

Digital-to-Analog converter

(*D-to-A converter*) An electronic device that converts a sequence of numbers into an analog electrical signal. A D-to-A-Converter is needed to change the numbers on a compact disc into sounds.

digitized

Information that has been converted into a series of numbers. An image that has been scanned is said to have been digitized.

directory

A collection of files and other directories. Some computer systems use the term *folder*.

distributed computing

A term used to characterize computations that involve more than one computer. In the broadest sense of the term, each Internet service uses distributed computing.

DNS

Abbreviation for *Domain Name System*.

domain name

The name assigned to a computer on the Internet. A single computer's name can contain multiple strings separated by periods (e.g., computer1.company.com). Domain names often end in *.com* (commercial) or *.edu* (educational).

Domain Name System

(*DNS*) The Internet service used to look up a computer's name and find the computer's IP address.

dotted decimal

A notation used to specify an IP address. Dotted decimal is so named because it represents an address as four small, decimal integers separated by periods. Internally, a computer stores each IP address in binary — dotted decimal notation is used to make addresses easier for humans to enter or read.

DSL

(*Digital Subscriber Line*) Any of several technologies used to deliver high-speed Internet access over the same wires used for telephone service. DSL and conventional phone calls do not interfere — the phone can be used at the same time data is being sent. See *ADSL* and *xDSL*.

dynamic content

Any web page that is created by the server at the time a browser requests it. Only pages with dynamic content can provide instantaneous information (e.g., a stock quote).

e-commerce

Abbreviation for *electronic commerce*.

email

Abbreviation for *electronic mail*.

email address

Each user is assigned an electronic mailbox address. To send email, a user must enter the email address of the recipient. On the Internet, email addresses have the form *user@computer*.

email alias

A shorthand for an email address used to allow a user to send electronic mail without remembering or typing a long email address. Most email software permits a user to define many aliases.

electronic bulletin board service

Synonym for *bulletin board service*.

electronic commerce

(e-commerce) A general reference to any business conducted over the Internet. Consumer purchasing is a popular form of electronic commerce.

electronic mail

(email) A service that permits one to send a memo to another person, a group, or a computer program. Electronic mail software also permits one to reply to a memo.

encryption

The process of encoding a message to keep it confidential. A receiver decrypts the message after it has traveled across the Internet.

Ethernet

A popular Local Area Network technology invented at Xerox Corporation. Modern Ethernet technology consists of a small device to which several computers can attach. The connection between a computer and a DSL or cable modem uses Ethernet.

exponential growth

A term mathematicians use to describe the growth of the Internet. The Internet doubled in size approximately each year.

FAQ

(*Frequently Asked Questions*) A document that contains questions and answers regarding a specific topic, technology, or Internet service. Many mailing lists and newsgroups have a FAQ document that helps beginners understand the purpose of the discussion and avoids having basic questions appear repeatedly.

fiber

An informal term for *optical fiber*.

file server

A program running on a computer that provides access to files on that computer. The term is often applied loosely to a computer that runs a file server program.

File Transfer Protocol

(*FTP*) The Internet service used to transfer a copy of a file from one computer to another. FTP is used to download files.

finger

An Internet service used to determine which users are currently logged into a particular computer or to find out more about an individual user. For security reasons, few sites on the Internet currently provide finger service.

firewall

A security mechanism placed between a site and the Internet to protect the site's computers and networks from attack. A small, personal firewall can be used to protect a residential subscriber; firewall software is also available to protect an individual computer.

flame

A slang term used in electronic communication to mean *an emotional or inflammatory note*, often written in response to another message. The word is sometimes used as a verb, meaning *to write an inflammatory message*.

flow control

Control of the rate at which a computer sends data to another computer. On the Internet, TCP software provides flow control, and makes it possible for a fast computer to communicate with a slow computer.

folder

A synonym for *directory*.

forms

A technology used in the World Wide Web that permits a user to interact with a web page. The browser displays a dialog box, into which a user can enter text, as well as buttons the user can select.

frames

A technology used in the World Wide Web that divides a web page into multiple areas (i.e., windows), and allows the contents of each area to change independent of the others. Companies often place an advertisement in one frame, while allowing a user to select the contents of another.

Frequently Asked Questions

See *FAQ*.

FTP

Abbreviation for *File Transfer Protocol*.

FYA

An abbreviation of "For Your Amusement" used in electronic communication.

FYI

An abbreviation of "For Your Information" used in electronic communication.

GIF

(*Graphics Interchange Format*) A format used to represent digitized images. GIF is popular in the World Wide Web. Also see *JPEG*.

gopher

The name of an early Internet browsing service in which all information is organized into a hierarchy of menus. Gopher displays a menu on the screen, and allows a user to select an item. The selection either leads to a file of information or to another menu.

GUI

(*Graphical User Interface*) An interface that presents the user with pictures and icons rather than words. Pronounced "goo-ey".

hacker

Originally used to refer to a programmer of exceptional ability, it now refers to miscreants who break into computers. Companies use security technologies such as firewalls to protect their computers from hackers.

homepage

A page of information accessible through the World Wide Web that is the main page for an individual or a company. A homepage usually includes references to other pages.

hop count

A measure of distance in packet switching networks. If a packet must travel through *N* routers on its trip from its source to its destination, the destination is said to lie *N* hops away from the source.

host

A synonym for a user's computer. Technically, each computer connected to the Internet is classified as a host or a router.

hostname

The name assigned to a computer. See *domain name*.

hot list

The original term used for a list of bookmarks or favorites. Now essentially obsolete.

HTML

(HyperText Markup Language) The computer language used to specify the contents and format of a hypermedia document in the World Wide Web (e.g., a homepage). Users are unlikely to see the HTML form of a page when browsing because browsers interpret HTML and display the results automatically.

HTTP

(HyperText Transfer Protocol) The protocol used to access a World Wide Web document. A user may encounter the string *http* in a *Uniform Resource Locator*.

hub

An electronic device that connects to several computers and serves as the center of a LAN, usually an Ethernet.

hypermedia

An information storage system in which each page of information can contain embedded references to images, sounds, video, and other pages of information. When a user selects an item, the hypermedia system follows the associated reference. See *World Wide Web*.

hypertext

A system for storing pages of textual information that each contain embedded references to other pages of information.

HyperText Markup Language

See *HTML*.

HyperText Transfer Protocol

See *HTTP*.

IAB

Abbreviation for *Internet Architecture Board.*

IETF

Abbreviation for *Internet Engineering Task Force.*

IM

Abbreviation for *Instant Messaging.*

imho

An abbreviation of ''in my humble opinion'' used in electronic communication such as email and instant messaging.

information browsing service

A service that permits a user to browse information by repeatedly scanning and selecting. The service presents a page of information that contains one or more selectable items. After the user reads the information and selects an item, the service follows the reference and retrieves a new page of information.

information superhighway

A term used by the press to refer to the national information infrastructure in the United States. The Internet is the predominant part of the information infrastructure.

infrastructure

A service or facility that is fundamental to a society. Examples include systems for delivering food and water, transportation facilities, and telephones.

Instant Messaging

An Internet service that permits two users to connect and exchange short text messages. Whatever one users types appears on the other's screen and vice-versa. Instant Messaging services have expanded to include computer conferencing (a group of users), audio, and video. Often abbreviated *IM.*

integrated circuit

A small, complex electronic device that contains many transistors. For example, the central processing unit in a computer is usually built on a single integrated circuit. Informally, an integrated circuit is called a *chip.*

International Telecommunication Union

(ITU) An international organization that sets standards for interconnection of telephone equipment. In the past, many organizations responsible for networking in Europe have followed ITU recommendations. (Formerly, the CCITT.)

Internet

The collection of networks and routers that use the TCP/IP protocol suite and function as a single, large network. The Internet reaches government, commercial, and educational organizations around the world.

Internet address

A number used to identify a computer. Each computer attached to the Internet is assigned a unique address. Software uses the address to identify the intended recipient when it sends a message. An Internet address is also called an *IP address*.

Internet Architecture Board

(*IAB*) A group of people who set policy and standards for TCP/IP and the connected Internet.

Internet Engineering Task Force

(*IETF*) A group of people responsible for designing and testing new technologies for TCP/IP and the Internet. The IETF is part of the IAB organization.

Internet Fax

A fax sent across the Internet instead of a conventional telephone connection. A special fax machine is required to use the Internet.

Internet Protocol

See *IP*.

Internet Relay Chat

(*IRC*) A service that allows a group of users to communicate using keyboards. Each group of users creates a channel and sends messages to it. Each active participant on a given channel receives a copy of each message sent to the channel.

Internet Service Provider

See *ISP*.

Internet Society

A non-profit organization established to encourage exploration of the Internet.

internetworking

A term used to refer to planning, building, testing, and using internet systems.

IP

(*Internet Protocol*) Literally, a specification for the format of packets computers use when they communicate across the Internet. In practice, the term usually refers to the IP software that a computer must run to communicate on the Internet.

IP address

A synonym for *Internet address*.

IP datagram

A packet of data sent across the Internet. Each IP datagram contains the address of the computer that sent it, the IP address of the destination computer, and the data being sent.

IPv6

The successor to IPv4, the current version of the Internet Protocol. IPv6 is being developed by the IETF, but industry has resisted changing to the new system for over 10 years.

IRC

Abbreviation for *Internet Relay Chat*.

ISP

(*Internet Service Provider*) A company that offers connections to the Internet. In addition to telephone and cable television companies, many small, private ISPs offer service to smaller areas (e.g., in one town).

ITU

Abbreviation for *International Telecommunication Union*.

Java

A programming language used to create active web pages that was developed by Sun Microsystems, Incorporated. Also see *applet*.

JavaScript

A programming language used to create active web pages that is simpler (and less powerful) than Java.

JPEG

(*Joint Photographic Experts Group*) A format used to represent digitized images. JPEG is popular in the World Wide Web. Also see *GIF*.

Kbps

(*Kilo bits per second*) A measure of the rate of data transmission equal to *1000* bps. Also see *bps*, *Mbps*, *bandwidth*, and *baud*.

key

A string used to encrypt data to keep it secure. One can think of a key as a password. Typical key sizes range from 56 to 256 bits, with more bits providing stronger security.

LAN

Abbreviation for *Local Area Network*.

last mile problem

The problem of providing Internet access to individual residences. See *DSL* and *cable modem*.

Linux

A popular implementation of the UNIX operating system. See *UNIX*.

LISTSERV

(electronic mailing LIST SERVer) A program that maintains lists of electronic mail addresses. A user can request that LISTSERV add their email address to a list or delete their email address.

Local Area Network

(LAN) A computer network technology designed to connect computers across a short distance (e.g., inside a building). Compare to *Wide Area Network (WAN)*.

login

The process of entering an account identifier and password to obtain access to a computer.

long-haul network

A synonym for *Wide Area Network*.

mail alias

A synonym for *email alias*.

mailbox

A storage area, usually on disk, that holds incoming email messages until a user reads the mail. Each mailbox has a unique address; a user must have a mailbox to receive electronic mail.

mailbox address

A synonym for *email address*.

mailing list

An electronic mail address that includes a list of recipients. Mailing lists have become popular as a way to disseminate information.

Mbps

(Millions of bits per second) A measure of the rate of data transmission equal to one million bps. Also see *bps*, *Kbps*, *bandwidth*, and *baud*.

menu

A list of items from which a user can select. Some Internet services permit a user to browse information by following a sequence of menus.

micropayment

A small monetary transfer that results when someone purchases an item with digital cash.

MIME

Abbreviation for *Multipurpose Internet Mail Extensions.*

modem

(modulator — demodulator) A device used to transmit digital data a long distance across an analog transmission path. The path can consist of a long wire or a connection through the dial-up telephone system. Modems are used in pairs — one modem attaches to each end of the connection. The modem contains a modulator (used to send data) and a demodulator (used to receive data).

moderated

A mailing list or network news discussion group in which each submission must be sent to a person who checks and edits the contents before forwarding the submission to the recipients.

modulation

The technique a modem uses to encode digital data in an electrical signal for transmission across a wire. Modulation can also be used over telephone connections. Also see *demodulation* and *carrier.*

modulator

The electronic device in a modem that encodes data for transmission. See *demodulator.*

MP3

A format used to encode audio. MP3 is most popular for recording music.

MUD

(Multi-User Dungeon) The name of an Internet game.

multicast

The technique used to send copies of a packet to a selected set of other computers. Internet audio and video services use multicast delivery to send a packet from a single source to many computers on the Internet, or to allow a group of users to interact in an audio or video teleconference. Compare to *unicast* and *broadcast.*

multimedia

A term describing any facility that can display text, graphics, images, video, and sounds. A computer needs special hardware to handle multimedia output.

Multipurpose Internet Mail Extensions

(MIME) Standard Internet email messages can contain only ASCII text. MIME extensions allow an email message to contain a non-ASCII file such as a video image or a sound. Email interfaces often use the term *attachment* to refer to a non-text file sent using MIME.

navigating the Internet

A phrase used by the press that means, "using Internet services to browse information."

Netiquette

A list of suggestions for how to behave when using the Internet. Many are common sense.

netnews

Abbreviation for *network news*.

Netscape

A company that sells Internet products. Netscape is most well-known for its web browsers, such as Mozilla, which are available free of charge.

network news

The name of an Internet bulletin board service.

network of networks

A phrase used to describe the Internet; the characterization is appropriate because the Internet consists of many physical networks interconnected by routers.

network printer

A printer that attaches directly to a network where it can be accessed by any computer on the network. A network printer contains a small microprocessor that handles communication details.

network provider

See *ISP*.

news article

A message that appears on a bulletin board in the network news service. Each news article has the same form as an electronic mail memo.

newsgroup

A single bulletin board in the network news service. A single user can subscribe to multiple newsgroups; each newsgroup contains articles related to one topic.

NFS

(*Network File System*) A service that allows cooperating computers to access each other's file systems as if they were local. The key difference between NFS and FTP is that NFS accesses pieces of a file as needed without copying the entire file.

NSF

(*National Science Foundation*) A U.S. government agency that has funded the development of a WAN for the Internet and helped scientists connect to the Internet. NSF has also funded individual researchers working in the network area as well as large projects spanning multiple institutions.

NSFNET

(*National Science Foundation NETwork*) Loosely used to describe the Wide Area Network that formed the backbone of the Internet in the United States in the mid-1990s.

open system

A non-proprietary technology or system; any vendor can use the specifications of an open system to build products and services. The Internet and its technologies are *open*.

optical fiber

A thin, flexible glass fiber used to transmit information using pulses of light. A fiber can span longer distances than an electrical cable. Often abbreviated *fiber*.

packet

Used to describe the unit of data sent across a packet switching network. An Internet packet is called an *IP datagram*.

packet switching

A technique used on computer networks that requires a computer to divide a message into small packets of data before sending them. Like most computer networks, the Internet uses packet switching.

password

The secret code a user enters to gain access to a timesharing system or to obtain authorization for a service. Usually, a computer does not display a password while the user enters it.

peer-to-peer networking

Any network system in which all computers are equal. That is, a program running on one computer can contact a program running on another computer. The Internet is a peer-to-peer technology.

personalized search results

Results from a search engine that are personalized to the user who makes the request. Personalization depends on a history of searches and web accesses.

PGP

(Pretty Good Privacy) An encryption mechanism used to keep email confidential.

ping

(Packet InterNet Groper) The name of a program used with TCP/IP internets to test whether a specific computer can be reached. Ping sends the computer a packet and waits for a reply. The term is often used like a verb as in, "please ping computer *hobbes* to see if it is alive."

plugin

A technology in which a browser can dynamically load additional software that allows the browser to interpret new or alternative data formats. Plugins are required before a browser can play the recorded audio that is found on a web page.

point-and-click interface

A style of interacting with a computer that uses a mouse instead of a keyboard. The user moves the mouse to position the cursor, and presses a button on the mouse to select the item under the cursor.

POP

Abbreviation for *Post Office Protocol.*

Post Office Protocol

(POP) A protocol used to access a mailbox and download email. POP is often used by ISPs that offer dial-up access.

Post, Telegraph, and Telephone

(PTT) In European countries, the government organization that controls data networking.

postmaster

By convention, an email alias for the person who manages the electronic mail software on a given computer. One can address a request to *postmaster@site* to ask questions about the site or the rules for joining or leaving a mailing list.

Pretty Good Privacy

See *PGP*.

private email

Electronic mail that has been encrypted so that only the sender and receiver can interpret it. Usually, email messages are sent across the Internet with no encryption, which means that a wiretapper who intercepts an email message can read the contents.

private key

One of two keys issued to a user for security. A user must keep their private key secret. See *public key*.

protocol

The rules two or more computers must follow to exchange messages. A protocol describes both the format of messages that can be sent as well as the way a computer should respond to each message.

PTT

Abbreviation for *Post, Telegraph, and Telephone*.

public files

Files that are available to any Internet user. Typically, public files are downloaded using the FTP service.

public key

One of two keys issued to a user for security. A user tells everyone their public key. See *private key*.

public key encryption

A security system in which each user is issued two keys, one of which must be secret and the other can be distributed. See *private key* and *public key*.

public mailing list

An electronic mailing list to which anyone can add themselves, delete themselves, or send a memo. A memo sent to a public mailing list can reach many people.

RealAudio

A popular technology used to send audio across the Internet; many radio stations use it to transmit their programs. A browser needs a plugin to receive and play sounds that are encoded using RealAudio.

remote desktop

A system that allows a user at one computer to connect their display, keyboard, and mouse to a remote computer. See *remote login*.

remote login

A service that allows a user on one computer to connect their keyboard and character-oriented display to a remote computer and run programs. See *TELNET* and *remote desktop*.

Request For Comments

(RFC) The name of a series of notes that contain the TCP/IP protocol standards as well as related documents. RFCs are available on the Internet.

RFC

Abbreviation for *Request For Comments*.

route

In general, a route is the path that network traffic takes from its source to its destination. In a TCP/IP internet, each IP datagram follows a path through a sequence of networks and routers.

router

A special purpose, dedicated device that attaches to two or more networks and routes IP datagrams from one to the other. Each router forwards a datagram to another router until the datagram can be delivered to its final destination.

search engine

A term applied to automated search services. Technically, the term refers to computer programs that such services use to respond to a user's request.

search key

A string of characters that a user provides to a search service. The service searches for documents that contain the string.

search tool

Any program that permits a user to find the location of information. In particular, automated search tools operate without requiring the user to interact during the search.

Secure Multipurpose Internet Mail Extensions

See *SMIME*.

Secure Socket Layer

See *SSL*.

server

A program that offers a service. Many computers on the Internet run servers to offer services. A user invokes a client program on their computer; the client contacts a server.

shopping cart

A mechanism used on the World Wide Web to allow someone to select multiple items from an online catalog before they make a purchase.

smiley

A sequence of characters, usually found in an email message, that indicates humorous intent. The three-character sequence :-) is especially popular because it resembles a smiling face turned sideways.

SMIME

(Secure Multipurpose Internet Mail Extensions) A security mechanism used with email to keep messages confidential.

source address

The address of the computer sending data. Each packet contains the address of the source computer as well as the address of the destination computer.

spam

Unwanted email, often an advertisement, sent in bulk to many recipients.

spider

A computer program used by search engine companies to probe the Web and compile an index of contents.

SSL

(Secure Socket Layer) A mechanism invented by Netscape, Inc. to provide secure communication between a browser and a server.

stack

A term that refers to all the TCP/IP software on a computer. The term arises from the way software is organized internally.

surfing the Internet

A slang phrase used by the press that means, ''using Internet services to browse information.''

talk

An early instant messaging service available on the Unix operating system.

TCP

Abbreviation for *Transmission Control Protocol.*

TCP/IP

Literally, the name of protocols that specify how computers communicate on the Internet. Informally, the name refers to the software that implements the protocols. All computers that use the Internet need TCP/IP software.

TCP/IP Internet Protocol Suite

The official name of TCP/IP.

TELNET

The Internet remote login service. TELNET allows a user at one site to interact with a remote timesharing system at another site as if the user's terminal connected directly to the remote machine.

text file

Any file that consists of textual characters separated into lines. Text files on the Internet use the ASCII character encoding. A non-text file is often called a *binary file*.

textual interface

A style of interacting with a computer that uses a keyboard. A user enters keystrokes to which the computer responds. Compare to *point-and-click interface* and *GUI*.

timesharing computer

A computer system that permits multiple users to run programs at the same time. Most large computers are designed as timesharing systems.

traceroute

A program that permits a user to find the path a packet will take as it crosses the Internet to a specific destination. *Traceroute* prints one line for each router along the path.

Transmission Control Protocol

(TCP) One of the two major TCP/IP protocols. TCP handles the difficult task of ensuring that all data arrives at the destination in the correct order. The term often refers to software that implements the TCP standard.

traveling the information superhighway

A phrase used by the press that means, "using Internet services to browse information."

Trojan horse

A security attack in which someone inside a company is tricked into running a computer program that sends information from the person's computer to an outsider.

unicast

The usual technique for sending a packet through the Internet from a single source to a single destination. Compare to *broadcast* and *multicast*.

Uniform Resource Locator

(URL) A short character string used by browsers to identify a particular page of information on the World Wide Web. Given a Uniform Resource Locator, a browser can fetch and display the page quickly.

UNIX

A particular computer operating system developed at AT&T Bell Laboratories and popular on Web servers. See *Linux*.

unsecure

A computer or a network in which information is not protected against being read, copied, or changed.

URL

Abbreviation for *Uniform Resource Locator*.

UUCP

(Unix to Unix Copy Program) Software developed in the mid 1970s that allows one computer to copy files to or from another over a (usually dial-up) connection. UUCP was used in the original version of USENET.

video teleconference service

A service that allows a group of users to exchange video information over the Internet. Most video teleconferences include an audio teleconference facility. Each participant's computer must have a camera, microphone, and speaker (or earphones).

virtual network

Although the Internet consists of many physical networks interconnected by routers, communication software makes the Internet appear to be a single, large network. The term *virtual network* is used to refer to the appearance of a single, seamless network system.

Virtual Private Network

See *VPN*.

VPN

(Virtual Private Network) A technology that allows an employee to telecommute. A VPN establishes secure communication between the employee's computer and the employer's network, and provides access to services as if the employee were local.

WAN

Abbreviation for *Wide Area Network*.

Web

See *World Wide Web*.

web authoring tool

A tool used to create web pages. Usually, a web authoring tool has a GUI interface.

web browser

See *browser*.

web page

A single page of information available on the World Wide Web. A user views one page at a time.

web server

A program that runs continuously at a particular web site and responds to requests from browsers. Each request specifies a particular page that the server returns.

web site

Conceptually, a set of web pages owned by a single company or individual. Each web site is implemented by a computer attached to the Internet that runs a web server; the server provides pages from the site to browsers when requested. Most companies have their own web site, and often choose a name of the form www.*company.com* for the computer on which the server is located.

webcasting

A service in which continuous audio (and possibly video) is sent to many users at the same time. Each user accesses the service with a web browser.

whiteboard service

A service that permits a group of users to establish a session that enables all of them to see and modify the same display. The display can begin blank or can start with a document. Whenever a participant modifies the display by adding text or graphics, all other users see the changes immediately. A whiteboard service is usually combined with an audio teleconference service.

whois

An Internet service that looks up information about a user in a database. Many organizations have disabled the *whois* service because giving out information about users leads to email or spam.

Wide Area Network

(WAN) Any network technology that can span long geographic distances. Compare to *Local Area Network (LAN)*. Also called long-haul networks, WANs usually cost more than LANs.

Wi-Fi

A marketing term used for a set of wireless network technologies that provide Local Area Network service (in a building). Many laptop computers come equipped with Wi-Fi interface hardware.

window

A rectangular area on a screen devoted to one particular application program. Windows can overlap, and a user can move windows on top of other windows. When a computer uses Internet services, a window can connect to a remote computer.

wireless network

A network that uses radio waves to transmit in place of wires. Many wireless technologies exist; some are used within a single building and others cover a wide area like the cellular phone system.

World Wide Web

(WWW) An Internet service that organizes information using hypermedia. Each document can contain embedded references to images, audio, video, or other documents. A user browses for information by following references.

WWW

Abbreviation for *World Wide Web*.

X Window system

A particular window system used on the Internet that permits each window to connect to a remote computer.

xDSL

A term used to denote all of the DSL services, of which ADSL is the most popular.

Index

X